Ryan Green

RANSLATING
PARTITION

OUR RECENT RELEASES

Short Fiction

Inspector Matadeen on the Moon
  By Harishankar Parsai
  Trans C M Naim
Seven Sixes are Forty Three
  By Kiran Nagarkar
  Trans ShubhaSlee
Selected Fiction: Hindi Short Stories
  Trans & Ed Sara Rai
Waterness
  By Na Muthuswamy
  Trans by Lakshmi Holmström
Downfall by Degrees
  By Abdullah Hussein
  Trans by Mohammad Umar Memon
The Resthouse
  By Ahmad Nadeem Qasimi
  Trans by Faruq Hassan
Katha Prize Stories 12
  Ed Geeta Dharmarajan
Best of the Nineties: Katha Prize Stories 11
  Ed Geeta Dharmarajan
The End of Human History
  By Hasan Manzar
  Trans by Mohammad Umar Memon

Non-Ficton

Links in the Chain
  By Mahadevi Varma
  Trans by Neera Kuckreja Sohoni
Travel Writing and the Empire
  Ed Sachidananda Mohanty

ALT (Approaches to Literatures in Translation)

Ismat: Her Life, Her Times
  Eds Sukrita Paul Kumar &
  Sadique
Translating Partition
  Eds Ravikant & Tarun K Saint
Translating Caste
  Ed Tapan Basu
Translating Desire
  Ed Brinda Bose
Vijay Tendulkar

Trailblazers

Ambai: Two Novellas and a Story
  Trans by C T Indra,
  Prema Seetharam & Uma Narayanan
Paul Zacharia: Two Novellas
  Trans by Gita Krishnankutty
Ashokamitran: Water
  Trans by Lakshmi Holmström
Bhupen Khakhar: Selected Works
  Trans by Bina Srinivasan,
  Ganesh Devy & Naushil Mehta,
Indira Goswami: Pages Stained with Blood
  Trans by Pradip Acharya

Katha Classics

Pudumaippittan
  Ed Lakshmi Holmström
Basheer Ed Vanajam Ravindran
Mauni Ed Lakshmi Holmström
Raja Rao Ed Makarand Paranjape
A Madhaviah: Padmavati
  Trans by Meenakshi Tyagarajan

Katha Novels

Singarevva and the Palace
  By Chandrasekhar Kambar
  Trans by Laxmi Chandrashekar
Listen Girl!
  By Krishna Sobti
  Trans by Shivanath

YuvaKatha

Lukose's Church
Night of the Third Crescent
Bhiku's Diary
The Verdict
The Dragonfly

FORTHCOMING

Mountain of the Moon
  By Bibhutibhushan Bandopadhyay
  Trans by Santanu Sinha Chaudhuri
Short Shorts Long Shots
  By Uday Prakash
  Trans Robert A Hueckstedt &
  Amit Tripurareni

TRANSLATING PARTITION

Stories by
Attia Hosain, Bhisham Sahni,
Joginder Paul, Kamleshwar,
Sa'adat Hasan Manto,
Surendra Prakash

Essays ● Criticism

Edited by
Ravikant & Tarun K Saint

ॐ

First published by Katha in 2001

The collection as a whole © 2001 Katha.
The individual contributions
© 2001 the respective authors.

KATHA
A3 Sarvodaya Enclave
Sri Aurobindo Marg,
New Delhi 110 017
Phone: 2652 4350, 2652 4511
Fax: 2651 4373
E-mail: academic@katha.org
Internet address: http://www.katha.org

KATHA is a registered nonprofit society
devoted to enhancing the pleasures of reading.
KATHA VILASAM is its story research and resource centre.

Studies in Culture and Translation
SCT Committee: Krishna Sobti, Malashri Lal, K Satchidanandan,
Sukrita Paul Kumar and Geeta Dharmarajan
Assistant Directors, Marketing: Tanmoy Roy Chowdhury and Amrita Akhil
Book and Cover Design: Geeta Dharmarajan
Line Drawings: Vikram Nayak

Katha books are distributed by
KATHAMELA
distributors of quality books
A3 Sarvodaya Enclave, Sri Aurobindo Marg, New Delhi 110 017

Typeset in 11.5 on 14.5pt Lapidary333 BT by Suresh Sharma at Katha
Printed at Pauls Press, New Delhi

ISBN 81-87649-04-6
3 5 7 9 10 8 6 4

CONTENTS

Acknowledgements   vii

Toba Tek Singh by Gulzar   viii

       Transcription in Hindi by Anisur Rahman   ix

       English translation by Anisur Rahman   x

Introduction by Ravikant and Tarun K Saint   xi

Stories

The Dog of Tetwal by Sa'adat Hasan Manto   1

       Translated by Ravikant and Tarun K Saint

How Many Pakistans? by Kamleshwar   11

       Translated by Stuti Khanna

Pali by Bhisham Sahni   29

       Translated by the author

Dream Images by Surendra Prakash   53

       Translated by M Asaduddin

Toba Tek Singh by Sa'adat Hasan Manto   63

       Translated by M Asaduddin

Phoenix Fled by Attia Hosain   73

Thirst of Rivers by Joginder Paul   79

       Translated by Atanu Bhattacharya

Pandit Manto's First Letter to Pandit Nehru by Sa'adat Hasan Manto   87

       Translated by M Asaduddin

Critical Commentaries

"The Dog of Tetwal" in Context: The Nation and its Victims   94

       by Ravikant and Tarun K Saint

"How Many Pakistans?": An Overview by Stuti Khanna   104

"Pali" and Communalism Today by Anuradha Marwah Roy   112

Against Forgetting: Memory as Metaphor in "Dream Images"   120

       by M Asaduddin

Partition Overview

Partition and the Urdu Short Story by Naiyer Masud   130
        Translated by Deeba Zafir
Partition Narratives: Some Observations by Arjun Mahey   135
Partition: Strategies of Oblivion, Ways of Remembering by Ravikant   159
The *Vartman* and Pakistan: The "Daily" Reality of Partition   175
        by Saumya Gupta
The Woman Protagonist in Partition Literature by Bodh Prakash   194

Timeline   211
Select Annotated Bibliography   220
List of Select Fiction   227
User's guide to notes and bibliographic reference   230
Biographical Notes   231
Index   235

ACKNOWLEDGEMENTS

Our contributors have gone out of their way to make this collective endeavour a pleasant journey. Our heartfelt thanks to them. The editors also wish to acknowledge the inputs and suggestions received from the following: Anil Sethi, Ashis Nandy, Awadhendra Sharan, Malashri Lal, Meenakshi Verma, Shahid Amin, Sukrita Paul Kumar, Tapan Kumar Basu.

We are grateful for assistance with the Urdu version of "Tetwal ka Kutta" to S A R Geelani and Shahid Tasleem.

Without the contributions of the Katha team this volume would not have been possible: Chandana Dutta, Swaati Sahi, and others have been unremitting in their efforts.

Participants of the Simla Workshop organized by Katha in March '98 gave valuable comments. The interventions of Krishna Sobti helped us rethink the Introduction.

We thank Brinda Bose and Geeta Dharmarajan for conceptualizing the title of the volume.

Geeta and Sukrita have been a constant source of support and encouragement as the book took shape. Without their guidance this project would not have reached completion.

ٹوبہ ٹیک سنگھ

مجھے واگا پہ ٹوبہ ٹیک سنگھ والے بشن سے جاکر ملنا ہے
سنا ہے وہ ابھی تک سوجے پیروں پر کھڑا ہے
جس جگہ منٹو نے چھوڑا تھا
ابھی تک بڑبڑاتا ہے: ''اوپڑ دی گڑ گڑ دی مونگ دی دال دی لالٹین۔۔۔''

پتہ لینا ہے اس پاگل کا
او اونچی ڈال پر چڑھ کر جو کہتا تھا:
''خدا ہے وہ۔۔۔
اس کو فیصلہ کرنا ہے کس کا گاؤں کس کے حصے میں جائے گا!''

وہ کب اترے گا اپنی ڈال سے
اس کو بتانا ہے:
ابھی کچھ اور بھی دل ہیں
کہ جن کو بانٹنے کا، کاٹنے کا کام جاری ہے۔۔۔
وہ بٹوارہ تو پہلا تھا
ابھی کچھ اور بٹوارے ہیں۔۔۔ باقی ہیں!

مجھے واگا پہ ٹوبہ ٹیک سنگھ والے بشن سے ملنا ہے
خبر دینی ہے اس کے دوست افضل کو
وہ لہنا سنگھ، وہ دھاوا سنگھ، وہ بھین امرت
وہ سارے قتل ہوکر اس طرف آئے تھے۔
ان کی گردنیں سامان ہی میں لٹ گئیں پیچھے!

ذبح کردے وہ ''بھوری'' اب کوئی لینے نہ آئے گا
وہ لڑکی کی ایک انگلی جو بڑی ہوئی تھی، ہر بارہ مہینوں میں
وہ اب ہر ایک برس ایک پوٹا۔ پوٹا گھٹتی رہتی ہے!
بتانا ہے سب پاگل ابھی پہنچے نہیں اپنے ٹھکانوں پر
بہت سے اُس طرف ہیں
اور بہت سے اِس طرف بھی ہیں

مجھے واگا پہ ٹوبہ ٹیک سنگھ والا بشن اکثر یہی کہہ کر بلاتا ہے
''اوپڑ دی گڑ گڑ دی مونگ دی دال دی لالٹین دی ہندوستان تے پاکستان دی ذرے پھٹے منہ!''

گلزار

टोबा टेक सिंह

मुझे वागा पे टोबा टेक सिंह वाले बिशन से जाके मिलना है!

सुना है वह अभी तक सूजे पैरों पर खड़ा है
जिस जगह मंटो ने छोड़ा था
अभी तक बड़बड़ाता है, ''ओपड़ दी गुड़गुड़ दी मूंग दी दाल दी लालटेन ...''

पता लेना है उस पागल का
ऊँची डाल पर चढ़कर जो कहता थाः
''खुदा है वह —
उसको फ़ैसला करना है किसका गाँव किस हिस्से में जाएगा!''

वो कब उतरेगा अपनी डाल से
उसको बताना हैः
अभी कुछ और भी दिल हैं
कि जिनको बांटने का, काटने का काम जारी है —
वो बंटवारा तो पहला था
अभी कुछ और बंटवारे हैं — बाक़ी हैं!

मुझे वागा में टोबा टेक सिंह वाले बिशन से मिलना है
ख़बर देनी है उसके दोस्त अफ़ज़ल को
वह लहना सिंह, बधावा सिंह, वह भीन अमृत,
वो सारे क़त्ल होकर इस तरफ़ आये थे —
उनकी गरदनें सामान ही में लुट गईं पीछे —!

ज़बह करदे वो ''भूरी,'' अब कोई लेने न आएगा
वो लड़की एक उंगली जो बड़ी होती थी, हर बारह महीनों में
वो अब हर एक बरस एक पोटा-पोटा घटती रहती है!

बताना है कि सब पागल अभी पहुंचे नहीं अपने ठिकानों पर
बहुत से उस तरफ़ हैं —
और बहुत से इस तरफ़ भी हैं

मुझे वागा पे टोबा टेक सिंह वाला बिशन अक्सर यही कहकर बुलाता है
''ओपड़ दी गुड़गुड़ दी मूंग दी दाल दी लालटेन दी हिंदुस्तान ते पाकिस्तान दी दुर फिटे मुंह!''

गुलज़ार

Devnagari transliteration from Urdu by Anisur Rahman & Ravikant

Toba Tek Singh

I've to go and meet Toba Tek Singh's Bishan at Wagah!

I'm told he still stands on his swollen feet
Where Manto had left him,
He still mutters:
Opad di gud gud di moong di dal di laltain

I've to locate that mad fellow
Who used to speak up from a branch high above:
"He's god —
He alone has to decide — whose village to whose side."

When will he move down that branch —
He is to be told:
"There are some more — left still
Who are being divided, made into pieces —
There are some more partitions to be done
That partition was only the first one."

I've to go and meet Toba Tek Singh's Bishan at Wagah,
His friend Afzal has to be informed —
Lahna Singh, Wadhwa Singh, Bheen Amrit
Had arrived here butchered —
Their heads were looted with the luggage on the way behind.

Slay that "Bhuri," none will come to claim her now.
That girl who grew one finger every twelve months,
Now shortens one phalanx each year.

It's to be told that all the mad ones haven't yet reached their
destinations —
There are many on that side
And many on this.

Toba Tek Singh's Bishan beckons me often to say:
*"Opad di gud gud di moong di dal di laltain di Hindustan te Pakistan di dur
fitey munh."*

Gulzar

Translated from the Urdu by Anisur Rahman

INTRODUCTION

RAVIKANT AND TARUN K SAINT

The best of the literature[1] that emerged in the wake of the Partition bears the imprint of the struggle to grapple with pain and suffering on a scale that was unprecedented in South Asia. This collection brings together some of the writings that have stood the test of time, moving beyond simply attempting to record what was incomprehensible. In the present anthology we include writings in Urdu and Hindi, thus restricting our focus to the North and North-Western part of India, the region which witnessed the worst of the carnage unleashed during this time. As some of our contributors argue, what has come to be known as Partition Literature became a repository of localized truths, sought to be evaded and minimized by the dominant discourse on the Partition.[2] These narratives offer insights into the nature of individual experience, and break the silence in the collective sphere.

It is perhaps relevant to recall the events leading up to the Partition. While points of departure in the accounts of the Partition are varied, and in most cases preoccupied with causation, we can outline some major events which in turn were the culmination of certain processes earlier set into motion in the second half of the nineteenth century.[3]

The imperative governing British administrators and academics alike, to demarcate "Hindus" and "Muslims" as two essentially different communities, was given tangible form in the census operations, the community-centred reform agendas and the politics of language (identifying languages with religious communities). This hardened religious identities and brought them into the public sphere, manifested in the form of communalism.[4] While attempts were made to forge a secular consensus, especially after a spate of riots in the 1920s, by 1940 it was evident that this had not been achieved. In that year, the Lahore Resolution of the Muslim League articulated the demand for a separate Muslim nation premised on the two-nation theory, according to which Muslims represented one qaum or nation in contradistinction to Hindus. However, it was only in 1946 that the proposal for a Pakistani state with two wings was formally put forward. Prior to this, the Pakistan demand may have been a mere bargaining counter for Jinnah. It now became visible as a reality to come. The failure of the Cripps Mission in 1942, the intransigence of the Congress leadership, especially when faced with the propensity of the British to treat the Muslim League as representative of Muslim interests, the electoral success of the Muslim League in 1946, and the political upsurge across the country culminated in the speeding up of the process leading up to the Partition.[5]

Political groupings like the Unionist Party in the Punjab and the Krishak Praja Party in Bengal, which did not rely on religion, lost their political base in the 1940s, setting the stage for polarization between the Muslim League and the Congress, amongst whom negotiations became increasingly acrimonious.[6] It is ironical that the Muslim League won its demand for Pakistan without having launched any extensive mass movement, or acquiring a mass base similar to the Congress. Perhaps on account of sheer exhaustion, after prolonged wrangling and the pressure from the British to conclude negotiations towards the transfer of power, to Gandhi's utter dismay, the decision to partition the country was taken by the principal players – the British Labour Government led by Attlee, the Indian National Congress and the Muslim League.[7] The cartographer Cyril Radcliffe, a man without any understanding of the composite culture of India, was assigned to draw the lines that would eventually become the national boundaries.[8]

As Sumit Sarkar points out, the Indian scene was transformed after mid-August 1946.[9] Jinnah's Direct Action Day spilled over into communal rioting across Northern India from Bengal to Bombay, and further north into the Punjab. Rumours about the eventual fate of those to be left behind as minorities in the newly formed states spread, and large scale migrations began. Rape, arson, kidnapping, plunder and murder became commonplace in Punjab from March 1947 onwards. Systematic killings were perpetrated, and evacuations became necessary for survival. Trains loaded with dead bodies began to pull into stations on both sides of the border, precipitating further atrocities in the name of revenge. Facts bear out the scale of the calamity – at least one million died and more than ten million refugees were displaced.[10] Perhaps ten times the official figure of twelve thousand five hundred women (in 1948) may have been abducted during the Partition.[11]

The conjuncture which brought about this terrible cataclysm was constituted, in the first instance, by the passivity of the British Government, and the complete breakdown of law and order. The administrative vacuum which ensued, allowed unscrupulous, greedy and power-hungry elements to rush in to grab the spoils; latent economic tensions relating to property relations thus came to the surface.[12] A variety of submerged and conscious political motivations came into play, resulting in the victimization of the weakest and most vulnerable. Stereotypes fed into communal violence, wherein the body became the privileged site for subjecting the other to indiscriminate violation and disfigurement. Signs and markers of personal identity such as circumcision and the Sikh turban became crucial determinants of one's being, while women's bodies were often mutilated beyond recognition. The widespread rioting only abated after Gandhiji's assassination in January 1948.[13]

The promise of freedom, the new dawn that Independence was supposed to usher in, was thus not to be realized. The disillusionment that followed was captured by a number of writers on both sides of the border. Such writings lament the loss of a world, though not only in the form of romanticized nostalgia. Partition was irrevocably etched on the minds of a people as a watershed, which brutally severed them from their own past. Indeed, Intizar Husain, the famous Pakistani writer, regards the Partition as an experience that was crucial in shaping the writer in him. For him, the Partition represented the loss of the Taj Mahal and neem trees, so as he puts it, "I started writing mournful stories about my separation from neem trees."[14]

The initial response of many was one of sheer disbelief. Several Partition stories register this sense of shock and bewilderment. Sa'adat Hasan Manto's story "Gurmukh Singh ki Vasiyat" portrays the beginnings of the riots.[15] The protagonist of the story, Mian Abdul Hai, in fact sets a deadline, the forthcoming Id, for the return of peace. This was not to be. This was a riot different from all others so far, unusual in its scale, magnitude and longevity.

Elsewhere, Manto deploys irony to demonstrate the suddenness with which the symbols of a new nation were inscribed on the body of the city.[16] The signboards of the shops across the bazaar were rewritten, the old names giving way to new ones, starting with "Pakistan," "Jinnah," "Qaid-e-Azam," et cetera. There is a sense of an over-enthusiastic attempt to write history anew at Pakistan's "moment of arrival." What gives Manto's irony its edge is the disjunction posed between the familiar and the unfamiliar, for the geographical spaces remained the same.

However, this was not the case for the displaced refugees. The pictures of long kafilas of peoples, their belongings and their bullock carts moving from one place to another, have, in the world of images, become a metaphor for the longest human migration in history. Fiction uses vehicular metaphors to communicate this sense of dislocation, the train being the most prominent one. Krishan Chander assigns the narrator's role to the Peshawar Express, traversing the blood and gore of the vast terrain of the North-Western region.[17] Khushwant Singh's novel *Train to Pakistan*,[18] and Bhisham Sahni's story "We Have Arrived in Amritsar"[19] use the train as a site to articulate the fragility of life, and the uncertainty of being able to reach one's destination. In Sahni's story, the Hindu weakling shifts from being in a state of terror in a Muslim majority area to a state of revengeful and homicidal arrogance in the Hindu majority area.

Passing from one warring territory to another, the train carried not just dead bodies, but horrific tales and rumours as well. Thus, the motif of the train acquires the status of a reporter, travelling far and wide to report on violence. The compartment, or the train's internal space, is where passengers face each other with an enhanced sense of insecurity and distrust. Lack of water, food, and basic hygiene, as well as the hustle-bustle of platform life are the indicators of the misery of refugee existence – a life in flux.

Those sitting in the train compartment in Amrit Rai's story "Kichar"[20] are not uprooted refugees, but well-heeled members of society, ensconced in their middle class comforts. They talk about "national" (Hindu-Muslim) and "international" (India-Pakistan) issues with the same nonchalance as they talk about the hike in the monthly charges for food at Nirula's. The murders in East Punjab are reduced to statistics in their conversation, and pride is taken in the fact that Partition has brought to the fore the militancy of the Hindus, who are no more the punching bags of the "eternally aggressive Muslims," since the ratio of killings is now 3:2! And the tales of violation of women are nothing more than pornography written in epic proportions. Indeed, the women have disappeared, but such tales remained in circulation. Rai's story thus records with anguish the patriarchal snobbery and vicariousness underlying the narration of abduction, rape and other forms of violation to women.

This story reminds us that the initial outpouring of writing was often uneven in quality (the world was writing the text, as it were). In his survey of stories written in the immediate aftermath of 1947, Alok Rai terms this unreflective portrayal of blood, gore and barbarism, a "pornography of violence."[21] Images of dismemberment and mutilation proliferated as if in a sensorium. Veena Das, on the other hand, reminds us that this was a time which produced a condition of dumbness, as language itself was brutalized.[22] Both Rai and Das cite Manto as the writer who was able to negotiate the perils of writing about the unspeakable at the level of aesthetics and language. Manto's initial response was to write bitterly ironic pieces which he aptly termed *Siyah Hashiye*, examples of anecdotal black humour. Stories such as "Thanda Gosht" and "Khol Do"[23] prompted the new government of Pakistan to prosecute him for obscenity. The stories also elicited the ire of progressives who denounced Manto's alleged obsession with sex. On the contrary, Veena Das's sensitive and nuanced reading of "Khol Do" demonstrates Manto's elegance of style, restraint and economy of expression. In the story, Sakina, the traumatized victim, subjected to repeated rape, perhaps by men masquerading as do-gooders, exemplifies this condition of dumbness.

Manto is certainly the most important of the first generation of writers. His ability to empathize with the marginalized, the downtrodden and the outcast, and to evoke moral outrage at the atrocities committed, is unique.[24] "Toba Tek Singh" is a triumph of ambivalence and a great story because it proclaims the in-betweenness of its protagonist and his triumph over those who want to fix his identity. The madman's death takes place in no-man's land, where the writ of neither nation prevails. Indeed, the term "madness" itself has a privileged status in the discourse on Partition. Analogies of madness appear in abundance and with frightening frequency. The Nationalist leaders were often heard saying, "Our people have gone mad."[25] Gandhi appealed to the people not to "meet madness with madness."[26] The newspaper editors said so, and so did ordinary men and women. Even now, the Partition is seen by some as a period of insanity.

At one level, the metaphor of madness could be used as conventional shorthand to communicate a sense of incomprehension. At another deeper level, it could denote a refusal to understand. It was a comfortable way out, for having consigned the irrational to the domain of madness, the speaker/writer could preserve the domain of the rational for himself/herself. This strategy achieved a double purpose. The Partition could be dismissed as an aberration, and the responsibility of owning up to its ugly reality, denied. By contrast, it is interesting to note the subversive way in which the motif of madness is deployed in the story. In Toba Tek Singh's fatal defiance and his mad satyagraha, the wide ranging consensus about the Partition as an outbreak of collective madness is turned upside down. Manto's searching critique unsettles conventional rationality and its basis for comfort, as well as the consequent and facile exculpation of blame for the Partition.

The instrumental rationality at work in the process of Nation-state formation, with its scissor-and-paste logic, is thus laid bare. Likewise, in Bhisham Sahni's *Tamas*,[27] the reader encounters Jarnail, a Gandhian nationalist, whose enthusiasm for the cause borders on obsession. His entire personality seems to have merged with the tricolour which he invariably carries on his body, yet his military uniform, unkempt hair and beard, incoherent speech and movement differentiate him from the nationalist brigade. With the spread of riots and consequent communal tension, leaders of various hues are depicted appealing to the administration to restore normalcy, or organizing meetings for communal harmony, while Jarnail is the lone crusader on the street, delivering in his own inchoate and frenetic ways Gandhi's message for peace. He meets the same tragic end as Bishan Singh, or for that matter Gandhi.

The trope of madness, inverted or elevated, recurs in other literary productions on Hindu-Muslim relations. In Rahi Masoom Raza's *Topi Shukla*,[28] Balbhadra Narayan or Topi Shukla (a Hindu who sought to learn Urdu and be friends with Muslims) commits suicide in the oppressive confines of the orthodoxy dominated Aligarh Muslim University. Raza's novel delivers a severe indictment of a world that could not tolerate Topi's mad ambivalence. During his lifetime, Topi could not belong either to Hindustan or to Pakistan, to Hindus or to Muslims, to sanity or to insanity, and his death consummates a rejection of all these binaries.

Similarly, Abdullah Hussein's protagonist, Naim, refuses to speak at the end of his novel, *Udas Naslein*,[29] as he finds himself part of the endless procession of refugees en route to Pakistan, and is mistaken for a half-wit. In an existential gesture, he leaves behind him the comfortable and mannered lifestyle of the Muslim elite, for the hazards of the road. His death at the hands of a thug is an absurd event, mirroring the irrationality and absurdity that surrounds him. Yet his whimsical action of joining the fleeing masses in solidarity, rather than travelling by air with his family, lends his end a certain aura of tragic dignity.

The instrumentalist outlook of the two Nation-states culminated in war immediately after the Partition, further widening the gulf which years of propaganda leading up to the grotesque dance of death had created. "Tetwal ka Kutta" and "Aakhri Salute"[30] are searching indictments of the divisions that found expression in war. These stories are Manto's most direct treatment of the experience of conflict, besides the stories which deal with the worst violence of the Partition. Manto's prescience has been borne out, even as reverberations of the Partition continued to echo through the years, resulting in several wars, the Kargil conflict and the current nuclear showdown. We include "Pandit Manto's letter to Pandit Nehru" as a further illustration of Manto's ironic vision, and his ambivalent response to the question of national allegiance.

It was inevitable that Manto's shadow should loom large on the corpus of Partition Literature. However, subsequent writers fashioned their own response to Partition in the context of the concerns and pressures of their specific time. For Manto, the Partition was primarily a lived reality which became a metaphor for human depravity. Through the use of nostalgia, later writers sought to recover the time before the Partition, or sought to explore the aftermath of refugee life, the experience of exile, of being unable to return to one's roots. The experience of dislocation and the struggle to rebuild lives became the new focus, while the Partition receded into the background as the primordial cataclysm. Others sought explanations for the continuing communal strife which seemed to indicate that the saga of the Partition had not ended. The Partition became a metaphor for the post-Independence communal divide. As one collection put it, "Partition Jari Hai."[31] In an ironical tribute to Manto, Bhisham Sahni titles his anthology of stories on communalism *Kitne Toba Tek Singh*.[32]

Nostalgia is a distinct strain in many of the later writings. However, this nostalgia is often tempered by a keen awareness that pre-Partition society too had its tensions. A contrast is sought to be established, nevertheless, between the composite culture of yore and the breakdown of trust in the present. In Rahi Masoom Raza's *Adha Gaon*,[33] harmonious village life becomes a topos, a symbolic domain against which to measure the later fragmentation and loss. Nostalgia is here subsumed into the wider political processes that deprived common people of agency. The suffering of the people of Gangauli is again a result of a decision that is not of their making. Their bewilderment and anguish are intensified, as part of the community depart for Pakistan, leaving behind a vacuum. The remaining few Muslims deal with the new power equations emergent in post-Independence India. Raza gives a thick description of a community's splintered existence, and joins issue with groups that cast aspersions on the loyalty of Muslims who chose to stay in India.

This thematic of an irretrievably lost way of life – time past which can never become time future – recurs in the short stories as well. In Mohan Rakesh's "Malbe ka Malik,"[34] the protagonist Abdul Ghani carries with him broken remnants of memory as he revisits his home in Amritsar. His home, now in ruins, is in the possession of the thug who killed his family members, but whom he unknowingly treats as a confidant now. In Agyeya's story "Getting Even,"[35] a Sikh refugee travels between Delhi and Aligarh by train, seeking to safeguard the honour of women after his own wife had been violated – an almost Gandhian way of getting even. He is initially regarded as a threat by the single Muslim woman in his compartment, until he firmly reproves the Hindu who joins them. The Hindu magnifies his own sense of grievance by emphasizing violence against Hindu women. For the Sikh, it is the honour of women that is all important.

The Mohajirs in Joginder Paul's novella *Khwabrau*[36] carry a bit of Lucknow with themselves, and seek to reconstruct it in Karachi by renaming streets and preserving the Lakhnavi tahzib. Diwane Maulvi Sahab, the protagonist, is an eccentric who believes that he has never left Lucknow at all. And in Attia Hosain's story "Phoenix Fled," an old woman is unable to conceive of any mode of existence other than the one she has been used to. Her relatives depart one by one, and she is finally left alone with her memories which become a bulwark, even as rioters loom at her door. The doll's house, which she seeks to protect, becomes the symbol of the fragility of the world she once knew. The restrained narration which stops short of describing the violence to come, emphasizes her vulnerability.

Nostalgia, thus, emerges as an ambivalent motif in Partition writing. It can veer towards the romanticization of the pre-Partition experience, which appears, as if clad in translucent hues. The occasional lapse into sentimentalism may be discerned, as in the case of "Pali," where Bhisham Sahni relies on the image of domestic bliss which is disrupted abruptly with the advent of the Partition. Even so, in his writings, Sahni also offers an analysis of the economic and political motivations that underpin historical change. The combination of realism and melodrama in *Tamas*[37] effectively counters the ideology of communalism premised on a sharply demarcated "us" and "them." There is no gainsaying Sahni's attempt to counterpose communal amity to the hostility generated during the riots. In "Pali," the manoeuverings of the religious leaders who seek to convert Pali is exposed for what it is – a perversion of the true ends of religiosity. In such writings then, nostalgia serves to illustrate the irrevocable break with traditional values that the Partition brought about. The vision of coexistence which Sahni invokes is significant as a reservoir of potentialities that could be tapped to arrive at alternative modes of being, outside the sectarian and exclusivist framework sought to be imposed.

Long kafilas of refugees marched across the plains of Punjab and Bengal, and those who survived the journey found themselves in refugee camps. Begum Anees Kidwai's "Azadi ki Chhaon Mein"[38] gives a moving account of the hardships they encountered. Her experience of working with riot victims and refugees is the basis for this memoir which explores the complex problem of rehabilitation. Agyeya's "Asylum"[39] and Ashfaq Ahmed's "Gadariya"[40] depict the existential predicament of those who sought to flee or were left behind in the turmoil. Rajinder Singh Bedi's "Lajwanti"[41] and Jamila Hashmi's "Banished"[42] give voice to the anguish of the abducted woman in different ways. In this volume, we include Joginder Paul's little-known story, "Dariyaon Pyas." Bebe, the main character, lives in the past, and has been unable to recognize the fact that she has actually been displaced from her ancestral haveli. Her old house keys become a symbol of her continued attachment to precious memories that sustain her, even as her son and family neglect her, assuming her to be mad. Indeed, within many Partition affected families, a disruptive, disintegrative process did erode the traditional value of caring.

Joginder Paul brings out sensitively, the loneliness and isolation of the old woman who oscillates between the past and the present, denying the reality of the Partition. The story resonates with many contemporary accounts of neglected old people, traumatized by what they had to undergo, and not given adequate support by the younger family members who faced the pressure of building life anew. The old woman's rambling utterances and recollections convey the poignancy of her situation. Bebe is unable to unlock the doors of the ancestral haveli, even in her imagination, however many keys she tries. Time itself forecloses this possibility. Paul's bleak vision thus searches deep into the fractured sense of family and community that characterized the way of life of the refugees, with all its despair, mistrust and cynicism.

Contrary to the optimism of the leaders who decided in favour of the Partition, communal riots became a recurrent feature in each decade after Independence. Communal ideologies still exercised their hold on the collective imagination, leading to an unprecedented ghettoization of culture. In their attempt to build bridges and recover a sense of the plurality of possible selves available to the members of each community, writers often glanced back at the Partition as a watershed, a defining moment. There came into being a body of literature emphasizing that the lessons of the Partition have not been learnt, and that the nightmare could still be upon us. Communal riots flared up with disturbing regularity, resurrecting the trauma of the Partition in Bhiwandi, Surat, Meerut, Maliana, Bhagalpur and a host of other places. Further, the virtual ban on any explicit reference to Partition violence discouraged attempts to make connections between the past events and the present. The controversies surrounding the release of M S Sathyu's *Garam Hawa* (1973) and the telecast of Govind Nihalani's *Tamas* (1988) bear out this fact. Paradoxically, writers were thus forced to look for indirect ways of representing the contemporary predicament. Subtle allusions and references to the Partition as a metaphor thus became a way out.

Badiuzzaman's story "Antim Iccha"[43] takes a fresh look at the situation of Muslims who chose to migrate to Pakistan, but who in exile were not entirely able to sever their roots. Despite having shared initially the fiery idealism of the Muslim League movement that causes him to recite verses of the later Iqbal in praise of Pakistan, Kamal Bhai, the central character, suffers terribly in Lahore from homesickness, and is haunted by images of his homeland. This precipitates his early death in Pakistan. The narrator, the brother who has stayed behind in Gaya, is witness to this change of attitude, and realizes the fallacy underlying the ideology of those like Kamal Bhai who left behind their all. The utopian promise upon which the Pakistan Movement was based is shown to be brittle and hollow at the core. Thus Badiuzzaman achieves a complex reflection on the situation of families divided by ideology at the time of the Partition, and gives us an insight into the reasons for many Muslims staying on. The Partition here becomes a metaphor for fissures in the community that can never be joined. Exile is a condition that damages the spirit, draining away the content of social and ritual life. The void that remains in its place, it is suggested, may never be filled. Neither sloganeering nor communal/nationalist rhetoric can make up for this loss. It is true, of course, that for many migrants, the question of choice did not arise.

A classic tale on the subject of exile in the wake of renewed communal violence, Kamleshwar's "How Many Pakistans?" touches upon a subject generally considered taboo – the relationship between a Muslim girl and a Hindu boy. The vivisection of the subcontinent becomes a metaphor for the separation of the lovers in the wake of communal tension. The narrator's unrequited love signals an incompleteness at the level of the self which echoes in the refrain – "How Many Pakistans?" Contrary to Alok Rai's critical view of the use of somewhat melodramatic images of violence,[44] in our reading, Kamleshwar skillfully interweaves evocation of psychic disfigurement with images of physical mutilation in the wake of communal violence. Though the depiction may seem to verge on the excessive, the violence is subsumed within the symbolic economy of the story. The image of Pakistan as a limb cut off from the whole body, and the memory of Banno the lover (sundered from the self), coalesce in the imagination of the narrator, causing pain akin to that of a phantom limb. The narrator cannot shirk responsibility even for events for which he may not be directly responsible. Whether it is communal tension in his hometown, the Bhiwandi riots when his grandfather's arm is cut off and Banno's child is killed, or the curious turn of events that brings him face to face with Banno in a whorehouse – there can be no evasion of accountability. Nor indeed can there be absolution for those who have trodden the dark paths of the soul – neither for Banno, nor for the narrator. The metaphor of Partition (How Many Pakistans?) emerges again and again, like a tear in the fabric of time, destabilizing the narrator's hold on the present.

Surendra Prakash's story "Dream Images," on the other hand, plumbs the psychic debris generated by the experience of migration. The dream-like return to a homeland that has been transformed beyond recognition, where memory seems to play tricks upon oneself, is brilliantly rendered. The narrator's longing to rejoin his friends and the places of his youth triggers this dream voyage, almost surrealistic in tone. The abrupt separation from the children at the end of the story may remind us of Aijaz Ahmad's perceptive observation that an entire generation of Hindu migrants were unable to transmit their cultural heritage, as encoded in the nuances of the Urdu language, to their descendants.[45] This hiatus and erasure of emotional associations and registers is symbolically represented in the disappearance of the children from the dream passage. The children cannot share the sensibility of the parents, as it were, since Urdu for them became an alien language – the language of the enemy. The story hints at this colossal rupture and loss, as a result of the politics of language and identity that long preceded the Partition. This vivid moment in Prakash's story condenses a historical experience not immediately manifest, but which had its repercussions at the level of the political unconscious. Urdu, for most of the subsequent generations, became the other language, disconnected from the self.

Trends in recent Partition research represent a shift away from the parleys and betrayals in the domain of High Politics, towards an emphasis on the subalterns as both victims and perpetrators of violence, the sociology and motivation for widespread rioting, the resulting psychological trauma, and most importantly, the feminist concern with recovering lost stories of sexually violated and abducted women during the Partition.

New archives of survivors' memories are being created to supplement the available sources such as autobiographies and biographies, poetry and fictional accounts. In fact, the magnitude of the task before scholars working on the Partition is comparable in some respects to that of researching the Holocaust. It would require immense collective and individual efforts to come to terms with the event and its fallout.

The essays included in this volume amplify our understanding of the issues at stake in contemporary debates on the Partition in the social sciences and literary criticism. The contributions range across fiction in Urdu and Hindi, social history of the print media, the feminist concern about representation, the historiography of the Partition, modes of remembrance and forgetting. Naiyer Masud, the well-known writer, provides a fresh perspective as regards the body of Urdu writing on the Partition. His categorization brings into focus the differences and commonalities that inhere in the expression of succeeding generations. His essay concludes with a personal selection of some of the great Partition stories.

Certain journalistic discourses in Hindi are taken up for analysis by Saumya Gupta who focuses on the print culture of Kanpur in the 1930s and 1940s. She examines the narrative strategies at work in the newspaper *Vartman* as it commented upon events, both local and national. The structuring of the communal imagination becomes visible as the *Vartman* veers towards the right-wing Hindu position in the 1940s. Bodh Prakash's essay takes into account recent feminist interventions about the effects of the Partition on women's consciousness and subjectivity, and seeks to unravel the threads of this complex history with reference to some well-known stories and novels. Drawing on historiography and literature, Arjun Mahey analyses the narrative tropes informing various writings on the Partition. "Toba Tek Singh," characterized by him as a fable, marks a radical break with conventional narrativizations of the Partition. In a similar vein, Ravikant's essay touches upon aspects of historiography, while juxtaposing the official nationalist discourse with fragments from popular memory.

Besides these essays, this volume includes stories from Urdu, Hindi and English, as well as analyses of four stories, incorporating a discussion of each story and a note on the translations. While some of these stories have appeared elsewhere, we have also chosen some little-known stories as well as new translations of older stories from different decades. We have striven for accuracy in terms of translation, as well as a degree of readability, so that the stories remain relevant to contemporary readers. Wherever necessary, a gloss has been provided to explain obscure cultural nuances. In the case of "Pali" the author himself has translated the piece. An analysis by a creative writer and critic brings out the problems associated with an author's attempt to translate his own work.

The translators, M Asaduddin ("Dream Images"), Stuti Khanna ("How Many Pakistans?"), and we, the editors, ("The Dog of Tetwal") attempt a close reading of chosen stories to emphasize the difficulty of conveying certain culture specific references in the target language. The multiple layers of the texts become visible in terms of language, culture and historical context. Additional readings exemplify the diversity of literary responses to the Partition. As a counter-point, Attia Hosain's story, written in English, is also reproduced here to give a feel of the response to the Partition by writers working in English.

Through the analyses of the stories, we seek to move the discussion of Partition Literature towards the concrete and the specific. Previous anthologies, though covering a good deal of ground, have not paid sufficient attention to interpretation, in most cases collating the various writings, and sometimes creating restrictive typologies. For instance, Alok Bhalla classifies certain stories as "communally charged." According to him, such stories deny "the claim to holiness of religions" and present members of the community as victims of another. In Bhalla's view, communal prejudice can be discerned in stories like Krishna Sobti's "Meri Maa Kahan..." and Ahmad Nadeem Qasimi's "Parmeshar Singh." In his terms, the former story presents Pathans as mindless killers, thus furthering the communal stereotype, while Qasimi portrays an innocent child as the embodiment of Islam, in contrast to murderous Sikhs (and the half-wit Parmeshar Singh).[46]

In our view, the attribution of a communal charge may be too easily arrived at. What indeed are the criteria used to assess such stories? Is stereotypification a sufficient criterion? We need to be alert to the use of irony and parody as modes of undermining stereotypes in literary discourse. Both the stories in question are undoubtedly implicated in the ideological cross currents of the time, and yet convey to an extent, the pain and confusion that resulted from communal clashes.

It became apparent to us as we read further, that a certain kind of writing (such as the novels of Guru Dutt[47]) trivializes the Partition experience by looking for scapegoats and reproducing cliches about the other community. The heroes and villains, so familiar in the dominant discourse dealing with High Politics, are reproduced here ad nauseam. This tendency to attribute blame to certain leaders or a community is often an attempt to achieve a cessation of guilt. Such escapist writing may be deemed to be the worst by-product of the collective imagination's attempt to negotiate the Partition trauma. Even the efficacy of this writing as propaganda is open to question, though, since it often remains caught up in predictable and banal rhetoric. A banal literature can never enable a genuine coming to terms with the past. Indeed, evil itself may be reduced to something too easily assimilated and conveniently distanced.

The early writings, with their outpouring of descriptions of blood and gore, bear this out. By way of contrast, in Manto's often visceral treatment, it is as if there is a seeming disembowelment of reality. The horrors of a time in which a profusion of reports on violence saturate the senses of the readers, are registered in his story "Khuda ki Kasam."[48] The pathos and occasional futility of the exercise of rehabilitation are laid bare through the use of irony and reversal, as the abducted Muslim woman refuses to recognize her own mother. For, it is true that many women did find a new life after being abducted. Such savagely honest renderings of negativity initiate a process of valuation – though not necessarily in strictly moral terms.

Such counter-narratives which focus on the local situation, rather than the national narrative of recovery of "honour" embodied in the abducted women, may be opposed to the conventional ways of narrativizing the Partition experience. As we have seen, each subsequent generation reinvented the metaphor of the Partition in its own way. Perhaps the most significant aspect of this reinvention has been the attempt to devise ways to contend with renewed communal upsurges. The untold stories of the Partition era are thus excavated, creating linkages with the reality unfolding before us today. The traps of excessive idealism and nostalgia, and regressive assertion of nationalist identity become visible for what they are in the stories of Intizar Husain, Surendra Prakash and Kamleshwar. Deterministic accounts of the past are demystified in these narratives as exercises in wish-fulfilment and false Utopianism.

Partition Literature thus emerges as a category that encompasses a range of attitudes and voices.[49] The thematic focus, as we have seen, shifts from the large-scale killings and abductions to the retrieval of memory and the experience of exile. Subsequently, the emphasis on communalism as a problem that refuses to disappear, (especially in the context of deteriorating Indo-Pak relations), leads to a different mode of recuperation of historical memory.

Kamleshwar's most recent novel, also titled *Kitne Pakistan?* (trans. *How Many Pakistans?*)[50] extends the metaphor of the Partition in space and time. In his novel, a writer holds court and summons figures from history, (including Hitler and Mussolini) to answer the charges framed against them for practising the politics of hatred and blood. Partition becomes a metaphor for a civilizational crisis, manifesting itself in the cases of Bosnia, Kosovo, the Babri Masjid demolition, the Pokhran blasts and Kargil. While the characters are dissimilar from those in the story, centred around the core story of the Partition, the anguish of displaced refugees is the thread that binds together the disparate narratives in the novel.

It is thus evident that the Partition continues to reverberate in the literary imagination, generating narratives of considerable complexity. The imaginative cartography of Partition literature continues to contest and resist the logic that led to the imposition of man-made boundaries half a century ago, mapping out effects in the realms of the spirit and emotion, as well as in the body politic. It thus constitutes an alternative domain of collective memory.

Notes

1   Important compilations of Partition stories translated into English include S Cowasjee and K S Duggal, eds., *Orphans of the Storm: Stories on the Partition of India* (New Delhi: UBS, 1995); Alok Bhalla, ed., *Stories about the Partition of India*, 3 vols. (New Delhi: Indus, 1994); Mushirul Hasan ed., *India Partitioned: The Other Face of Freedom*, 2 vols. (New Delhi: Roli Books, 1997); M U Memon, ed. and trans., *An Epic Unwritten* (New Delhi: Penguin, 1998).

2   The dominant discourse includes the official accounts produced by the state machinery, as well as much of the history writing which was confined till recently to the domain of High Politics. For a historiographic analysis, see Gyanendra Pandey "The Prose of Otherness" in D Arnold and D Hardiman, eds., *Subaltern Studies*, vol. 8 (New Delhi: Oxford UP, 1994) 188-221. Also, for a comparison of the Partition "genocide" with the Nazi holocaust, see Ashis Nandy, "The Invisible Holocaust and

the Journey as an Exodus: The Poisoned Village and the Stranger City" in *Postcolonial Studies*, 2. 3 (1999): 305-29.

3   See for example, Gyanendra Pandey, *Construction of Communalism in Colonial North India* (New Delhi: Oxford UP, 1990). For an excellent new work on the growth of communalism in Punjab, see A Sethi, "The Creation of Religious Identities in the Punjab, *circa* 1850-1920" Ph D diss. U of Cambridge, 1998.

4   Sudipta Kaviraj, "The Imaginary Institution of India" in Partha Chatterjee and Gyanendra Pandey, eds., *Subaltern Studies*, vol. 7 (New Delhi: Oxford UP, 1997) 1-39; K W Jones, *Socio-religious Reform Movements in British India*, vol 3/1 (Cambridge: Cambridge UP, 1989); Vasudha Dalmia, *The Nationalization of Hindu Traditions: Bharatendu Harischandra and Nineteenth-Century Banaras* (New Delhi: Oxford UP, 1997), esp. ch 4. For a discussion of the role of the Muslim intelligentsia of the Aligarh School, see "Introduction," in Mushirul Hasan, *India Partitioned: The Other Face of Freedom*, vol. 1 (New Delhi: Roli Books, 1997).

5   On the events leading up to the Partition, and for a general history, see Sumit Sarkar, *Modern India: 1885-1947* (New Delhi: Macmillan, 1983). Also P French, *Liberty or Death: India's Journey to Independence and Division* (New Delhi: HarperCollins, 1998).

6   For a discussion of the decline in the influence of the Unionist Party in the Punjab, see I A Talbot, "The Growth of the Muslim League in the Punjab, 1937-46" in M Hasan, ed., *India's Partition: Process, Strategy and Mobilization* (New Delhi: Oxford UP, 1993) 233-57.

7   For a personal account of this phase, see R Zakaria, *Price of Partition: Recollections and Reflections* (Mumbai: Bharatiya Vidya Bhawan, 1998).

8   W H Auden wrote a bitingly satirical poem on the role played by Radcliffe. Quoted in K N Datta, "Interpreting Partition" in A Singh, ed., *The Partition in Retrospect* (New Delhi: Anamika, 2000).

9   S Sarkar, *Modern India: 1885-1947* (New Delhi: Macmillan, 1983) 432-38.

10   The accuracy of figures is somewhat difficult to ascertain. Muslims, however, died in greater numbers. See Mushirul Hasan, "Imaginary Homelands" in *Outlook*, a special issue on the Partition, 28 May, 1997, and P French, *Liberty or Death: India's Journey to Independence and Division* (New Delhi: HarperCollins, 1998) 347-49.

11   The actual number of women recovered in both countries till December 1949 was 12,552 for India and 6,272 for Pakistan. See Ritu Menon, and Kamla Bhasin, *Borders and Boundaries: Women in India's Partition* (New Delhi: Kali for Women, 1998).

12   For a novelistic treatment of the situation in Uttar Pradesh, see Attia Hosain, *Sunlight on a Broken Column* (New Delhi: Penguin, 1992). A devastating indictment of the new power structures that were set into place after the Partition can be found in Qurratulain Hyder, "Housing Society," trans., S S Gilbert, in *A Season of Betrayals*, ed. C M Naim (New Delhi: Kali for Women, 1999).

13   See Veena Das, *Critical Events: An Anthropological Perspective on Contemporary India* (New Delhi: Oxford UP, 1995), esp. ch 4. Also, G Pandey, *Memory, History and the Question of Violence: Reflections on the Reconstruction of Partition* (Calcutta: Centre for Studies in Social Sciences, 1999).

14   See Intizar Husain, "Taj Mahal aur Neem ka Ped," *Hans*, January 1992.

15 See, Sa'adat Hasan Manto, "Gurmukh Singh ki Vasiyat" in Balraj Menra and Sharad Dutt, eds., *Sa'adat Hasan Manto: Dastavez*, vol. 2 (New Delhi: Rajkamal, 1993) 243-48, trans. as "The Assignment" in S H Manto, *Kingdom's End and Other Stories*, trans., K Hasan (New Delhi: Penguin, 1987)113-19.

16 S H Manto, "Savere Jo Kal Aankh Meri Khuli" in Menra and Dutt, eds., *Sa'adat Hasan Manto: Dastavez*, vol. 4 (New Delhi: Rajkamal, 1993) 304-9.

17 K Chander, "Peshawar Express," trans., K S Duggal from Urdu in S Cowasjee and K S Duggal, *Orphans of the Storm: Stories on the Partition of India* (New Delhi: UBS, 1995) 79-88.

18 Khushwant Singh, *Train to Pakistan* (New Delhi: Ravi Dayal, 1996).

19 Bhisham Sahni, "Amritsar Aa Gaya Hai," trans. by the author as "We have Arrived in Amritsar" in M Hasan, *India Partitioned: The Other Face of Freedom,* vol. 1 (New Delhi: Roli Books, 1997) 114-27.

20 Amrit Rai, "Kichar" (1949) in *Kasbe ka Ek Din* (Allahabad: Hans Prakashan, 1995) 48-57.

21 The series of examples Rai offers inadvertently includes an allusion to Kamleshwar's "Kitne Pakistan," published much later, in 1966-67. Alok Rai, "The Trauma of Independence: Some Aspects of Progressive Hindi Literature, 1945-47," *Journal of Arts and Ideas*, 6 (1984): 31.

22 Veena Das, Review of Alok Bhalla's *Stories about the Partition of India* in *Seminar* 420 (1994). Also, V Das, and A Nandy, "Violence, Victimhood and the Language of Silence," in *Contributions to Indian Sociology*, 19.1 (New Delhi: Sage, 1985) 177-95.

23 "Siyah Hashiye" in S H Manto, *Sa'adat Hasan Manto: Dastavez*, vol. 2 (New Delhi: Rajkamal, 1993) 275-315, trans. as "Black Margins" in M Hasan, *India Partitioned: The Other Face of Freedom*, vol. 1 (New Delhi: Roli Books, 1997) 88-102. "Thanda Gosht" in *Manto: Dastavez*, vol. 2, pp 268-75, trans., A Bhalla, as "Cold Meat" in *Stories about the Partition of India*, vol. 1 (New Delhi: Indus, 1994) 91-97. "Khol Do" in *Manto: Dastavez*, vol. 2, pp 199-203, trans., A Bhalla as "Open It" in *Stories about the Partition of India*, vol. 2, pp 69-73.

24 As Aijaz Ahmad points out, Manto's naturalism is in turn indebted to Emile Zola and Guy de Maupassant, whom he read in his youth. A Ahmad, "In the Mirror of Urdu" in *Lineages of the Present: Political Essays* (New Delhi: Tulika, 1996) 193.

25 L Collins and D Lapierre, *Freedom at Midnight* (New Delhi: Vikas, 1983) 284.

26 Quoted by Alok Bhalla in the "Introduction," *Stories about the Partition of India*, vol. 1 (New Delhi: Indus, 1994) xxxiii.

27 Bhisham Sahni, *Tamas* (Delhi: Rajkamal, 1980).

28 Rahi Masoom Raza, *Topi Shukla* (Delhi: Rajkamal, 1977).

29 Abdullah Hussein, *The Weary Generations* (New Delhi: HarperCollins, 1999). Written originally in 1963 and trans. by the author from the Urdu, *Udas Naslein*.

30 S H Manto, *Sa'adat Hasan Manto: Dastavez*, vol. 2, pp. 234-42, trans. as "The Last Salute" in S H Manto, *Kingdom's End and Other Stories*, trans. K Hasan (New Delhi: Penguin, 1987) 25-35.

31 See "Partition Jari Hai," in the special issue of *Samkaleen Dastavez*, 3 (1991).

32 Bhisham Sahni, *Kitne Toba Tek Singh* (New Delhi: People's Publishing House, 1987).

33 Rahi Masoom Raza, *Adha Gaon* (New Delhi: Akshar Prakashan, 1966).

34 Mohan Rakesh, "His Heap of Rubble" trans. from the Hindi "Malbe ka Malik" by Harish Trivedi in M Hasan, *India Partitioned: The Other Face of Freedom*, vol. 2 (New Delhi: Roli Books, 1997) 238-49.

35 S H V Agyeya, "Getting Even" trans. from the Hindi "Badla" in *India Partitioned: The Other Face of Freedom*, vol. 1 (New Delhi: Roli Books, 1997).

36 Joginder Paul, *Sleepwalkers*, 1990, trans. from the Urdu, *Khwabrau* by Sunil Trivedi and Sukrita Paul Kumar (New Delhi: Katha, 1998).

37 Bhisham Sahni, *Tamas* (New Delhi: Rajkamal, 1980).

38 Begum Anees Kidwai, *Azadi ki Chhaon Mein* (New Delhi: National Book Trust, 1990).

39 S H V Agyeya, "Asylum," trans. from the Hindi by Jai Ratan in M Hasan, *India Partitioned: The Other Face of Freedom*, vol. 1 (New Delhi: Roli Books, 1997) 169-78.

40 Ashfaq Ahmad, "The Shepherd," trans. from the Urdu "Gadariya" by M U Memon in *An Epic Unwritten* (New Delhi: Penguin, 1998) 30-87.

41 Rajinder Singh Bedi, "Lajwanti," trans. from the Urdu by M U Memon in *An Epic Unwritten* (New Delhi: Penguin, 1998) 14-30.

42 Jamila Hashmi, "Banished," trans. from the Urdu by M U Memon in *An Epic Unwritten* (New Delhi: Penguin, 1998) 87-106.

43 Badiuzzaman, "Antim Iccha" in his collection of stories *Chautha Brahman* (Delhi: Praveen Prakashan, 1991) 118-29. A translation into English by the editors appears in the forthcoming volume *Bruised Memories: Communal Violence and the Writer*.

44 Alok Rai, "The Trauma of Independence: Some Aspects of Progressive Hindi Literature, 1945-47," *Journal of Arts and Ideas*, 6 (1984): 31.

45 Aijaz Ahmad, "In the Mirror of Urdu," *Lineages of the Present: Political Essays* (New Delhi: Tulika, 1996) 215. The gradual marginalisation of Urdu in Northern India was reflected in the decline of the number of people declaring Urdu as their mother tongue in the censuses undertaken after Independence. Ahmad notes that fewer Hindu and Sikh names appear in the Urdu literary periodicals.

46 Alok Bhalla, "Introduction" to *Stories about the Partition of India*, vol.1 (New Delhi: Indus, 1994) xv; K S Sobti, "Meri Maa Kahan ..." trans. from the Hindi by K S Duggal in S Cowasjee, and K S Duggal, eds., *When the British Left: Stories on the Partitioning of India* (New Delhi: Arnold Heinnemann, 1987). Ahmad Nadeem Qasimi, "Parmeshar Singh" in M U Memon, ed. and trans., *An Epic Unwritten* (New Delhi: Penguin, 1998) 127-53.

47 Guru Dutt, *Pratinidhi Rachnayein* (New Delhi: Bharatiya Sahitya Sadan, 1988-91).

48 S H Manto, "Khuda ki Kasam" in *Sa'adat Hasan Manto: Dastavez*, vol 2. (New Delhi: Rajkamal, 1993) 203-8, trans. from the Urdu by Khalid Hasan as "Xuda ki Qasam" in S Cowasjee and K S Duggal, eds., *Orphans of the Storm: Stories on the Partition of India* (New Delhi: UBS, 1995) 165-70.

49 For a discussion of the relationship between literary modernism in the Hindi and Urdu contexts, and the impact of the Partition, see S P Kumar, *The New Story* (New Delhi: IIAS, 1990), esp. ch 2, pp. 19-34. A recent collection of essays on Partition Literatures in different Indian languages has been compiled by S R Chakravarty, and M Hussain, *Partititon of India: Literary Responses* (New Delhi: Har Anand, 1998).

50 See Kamleshwar, *Kitne Pakistan* (New Delhi: Rajpal, 2000).

Sa'adat Hasan Manto
THE DOG OF TETWAL

TRANSLATED BY RAVIKANT AND TARUN K SAINT

COMMENTARY ON PAGE 94

The two sides had not budged from their positions for several days now. Occasional bursts of firing – about ten or twelve rounds in a day – were to be heard, but never the sound of human shrieks.

The weather was pleasant; the wind wafted across, spreading the scent of wild flowers. Oblivious to the battle on the peaks and slopes, nature was immersed in its necessary work – the birds chirped as before, the flowers continued to bloom, and lazy honeybearing bees sleepily sipped nectar in the old, time honoured way.

Each time a shot echoed in the hills, the chirping birds would cry out in alarm and fly up, as though someone had struck a wrong note on an instrument, and shocked their hearing.

September-end was meeting the beginning of October in roseate hue. It seemed that winter and summer were negotiating peace with one another. Thin light clouds like fluffed-up cotton sailed in the blue sky, as if out on an excursion in their white shikaras.

For several days now, the soldiers on both sides of the mountain posts had been restless, as no decisive action was taking place. Lying in their positions, they would get bored, and then attempt to recite sh'ers to one another. If no one listened, they would hum to themselves. They remained lying down on their stomachs or backs on the rocky ground, and when the order came, let off a round or two.

The two sides were entrenched in rather safe positions. The high velocity bullets crashed against the shields of stone and fell to the ground. The two mountains on which the forces were ranged were of about the same height. Between them was a green valley – a rivulet wriggling like a fat snake on its chest.

There was no danger of air raids. Neither side possessed artillery. Therefore fires would be lit without fear or danger, and smoke from fires on both sides would rise and mingle in the air. At night, it was absolutely quiet. The soldiers on both sides could hear bursts of laughter from the other. Once in a while, entering into this spirit, a soldier would begin to sing, and his voice would awaken the silence of the night. The echoes would then reverberate, and it would seem that the mountains were repeating what they had just heard.

One round of tea had just been taken. The pine coals in the stone chulhas had grown cold. The sky was clear. There was a chill in the air. The wind had ceased to carry the scent of flowers, as though they had shut up their vial of perfume for the night. However, the sweat of the pines, their resin, left an odour in the air which was not wholly unpleasant.

Everybody slept wrapped in their blankets, but in such a way, that in a single movement they could arise, ready for battle.

Jamadar Harnam Singh was on guard. When his Rascope watch showed that it was two o'clock, he woke Ganda Singh and told him to take station. He wanted to sleep, but when he lay down he found sleep a distant proposition, as distant as the stars in the sky. Jamadar Harnam Singh lay on his back, and gazing up at the stars, began to hum:

> *Bring me a pair of shoes, studded with stars*
> *Studded with stars*
> *O Harnam Singh*
> *O Yaara*
> *Even if you have to sell your buffalo.*

Harnam Singh saw star-studded shoes scattered all over the sky, all a-twinkle.

> *I will bring you shoes, studded with stars*
> *Studded with stars O Harnam Kaur*
> *O Lady, even if I have to sell my buffalo.*

He smiled as the song came to an end, and realizing that he would not be able to sleep, he rose and woke up everybody else. The thought of his beloved had made him restless. He wished for some nonsensical chatter that would recreate the mood of the beloved in the song.

They did begin to talk, but in a desultory fashion. Banta Singh, the youngest, and the one with the best voice, went and sat on one side. The rest, though yawning all the while, kept gossiping about trivial but entertaining matters. After a while, suddenly, Banta Singh began singing "Heer" in a melancholic voice.

Heer said, the jogi lied, no one placates a hurt
lover. I have found no one; grown weary, looking
for the one who calls back the departed lover.
A falcon has lost the kunj to the crow — see, does it
remain silent or weep?
Happy talk and stories to entertain the world are
not for the suffering one.

After a pause he began singing Ranjha's reply to Heer's words:

The falcon that lost the kunj to the crow has,
thank god, been annihilated.
His condition is like the fakir who gave away his
all, and was left with nothing.
Be contented, feel the pain less and God will be
your witness.
Renouncing the world and donning the garb of
sorrow, Saiyed Waris has become Waris Shah.

Just as abruptly as Banta Singh had begun to sing, he fell silent. It appeared as if the soil-tinted mountains too had taken on the mantle of grief.

After a while, Jamadar Harnam Singh let out a mighty oath at an imaginary object, then lay down. Suddenly, in the melancholy stillness of the last quarter of the night, the barking of a dog began to resound. Everyone was startled. The sound did not come from too far off. Jamadar Harnam Singh sat up and said, "From where has this barking one come?"

The dog barked again. Now the sound was much closer. After a few moments there was a rustling in the bushes.

Banta Singh rose and moved towards the bushes. When he returned, he had with him a stray dog, its tail wagging.

He smiled, "Jamadar sahab, when I asked him, he said, I am Chapad Jhunjhun."

Everyone laughed. Jamadar Harnam Singh addressed the dog affectionately, "Come here, Chapad Jhunjhun."

The dog approached Harnam Singh, wagging its tail. It began sniffing

4

the stones on the ground, in the belief that some food had been thrown there.

Jamadar Harnam Singh reached into his bag, took out a biscuit and threw it in his direction. The dog sniffed at the biscuit and opened its mouth. But Harnam Singh leapt at it and picked it up, "Wait ... He could be a Pakistani."

Everybody laughed at this. Banta Singh came forward, stroked the dog on its back, and said to Jamadar Harnam Singh, "No, Jamadar sahab, Chapad Jhunjhun is a Hindustani."

Jamadar Harnam Singh laughed, and looking at the dog, said, "Oye, show me the identification!"

The dog wagged its tail.

Harnam Singh laughed heartily, "This is no identification ... All dogs wag their tails."

Banta Singh caught the dog's trembling tail. "The poor thing is a refugee!"

Jamadar Harnam Singh threw down the biscuit, and the dog immediately pounced on it.

Digging up the ground with the heel of his boot, one of the soldiers said, "Now, even dogs will have to be either Hindustani or Pakistani!"

The Jamadar took out another biscuit from his bag and threw it towards the dog, "Like the Pakistanis, Pakistani dogs too will be shot."

"Hindustan Zindabad!" Another soldier loudly raised the slogan.

The dog which had just begun to move forward to pick up the biscuit, suddenly grew frightened and backed off with its tail between its legs.

Harnam Singh laughed, "Why do you fear our slogan, Chapad Jhunjhun ... Eat ... Here, take another biscuit!" And so saying he took another biscuit out and threw it.

The soldiers talked on and soon it was morning.

In the blink of an eye, just as when one presses a button and the electricity generates light, the sun's rays flooded the mountainous region of Tetwal.

The battle had been raging in that area for some time. Dozens of lives of soldiers would be lost for each mountain, and even then the hold of either side was tenuous. If they held the range today, tomorrow their

5

enemies did; the following day they captured it back, and the day after that, their enemies did so.

Jamadar Harnam Singh picked up his binoculars and surveyed the surrounding area – smoke was rising from the mountain in front. This meant that a fire was being stoked there too, tea was being readied, and the thought of breakfast was on the mind; undoubtedly, the other side too could see smoke rising from their camp.

At breakfast, each soldier gave a little to the dog, which it ate with gusto. Everyone was taking a keen interest in the dog, as if they wanted to make it a friend. Its arrival had brought with it an element of cheerfulness. From time to time, each one would affectionately address it as Chapad Jhunjhun and cuddle it.

On the other side, in the Pakistani camp, Subedar Himmat Khan was twirling his impressive moustaches – which had many a story in its past – and was carefully studying the map of Tetwal. With him sat the wireless operator, who was taking orders from the Platoon Commander for Subedar Himmat Khan. At some distance, Bashir, leaning against a rock, was holding his gun and softly humming:

> Where did you spend the night,
> my love. Where did you spend ...

As Bashir swung into the mood and raised his pitch, he heard Subedar Himmat Khan's stern admonition, "Oye, where were you last night?"

When Bashir's inquiring gaze shifted towards Himmat Khan, he saw him looking elsewhere, "Tell me, oye ... !"

Bashir turned to see what Himmat was looking at.

The same stray dog, which, a few days earlier, had come to their camp like an uninvited guest and stayed on, was back, sitting a little distance away.

Bashir smiled, and turning to the dog, began,

> Where did you spend the night,
> my love. Where did you...

The dog began wagging its tail vigorously, sweeping the rocky ground around him.

Subedar Himmat Khan picked up a pebble and threw it at the dog, "Saala knows nothing except how to wag his tail."

All of a sudden Bashir looked carefully at the dog. "What's this around his neck?" He started walking towards the dog, but even before he reached it, another soldier took off the rope tied around its neck. A piece of cardboard with something written on it was strung to it. Subedar Himmat Khan took the piece of cardboard and asked the soldiers, "Does any one of you know how to read this?"

Bashir came forward and picked up the cardboard piece and said, "Yes I can read a bit." With great difficulty he spelled out "Cha-p-Chapad-Jhun-Jhun ... Chapad Jhunjhun ... What's this?"

Subedar Himmat Khan twirled his legendary long moustaches vigorously, "It must be some word, some ..." Then he asked, "Bashir, is there anything else written there ...?"

Bashir, immersed in deciphering the writing, replied, "Yes, there is. This is a Hindustani dog."

Subedar Himmat Khan began thinking aloud, "What does this mean? What was it you read? ... Chapad ...?"

Bashir then answered, "Chapad Jhunjhun!"

One soldier spoke as if with great knowledge, "Whatever the matter is, it lies here."

Subedar Himmat Khan thought this appropriate. "Yes, it does seem so!"

Bashir read the text inscribed on the cardboard once more, "Chapad Jhunjhun. This is a Hindustani dog."

Subedar Himmat Khan took up the wireless set and placing the headphones firmly over his ears, personally spoke to the Platoon Commander about the dog – how it had first come to them and stayed for several days, and how one night, it disappeared from their midst. Now that it had returned, there was a rope tied around its neck with a cardboard piece strung on it, on which was written ... and this message he repeated three or four times to the Platoon Commander, "Chapad Jhunjhun. This is a Hindustani dog." But they too could not come to any conclusion.

Bashir sat on one side with the dog, speaking lovingly and harshly by turns, and asked it where it had disappeared for the night, who had tied the rope and the cardboard around its neck. But, he did not get the answer he desired. When questioned, the dog would just wag its tail in answer. Finally, in anger, Bashir caught it and gave it a violent shake. The dog whined in pain.

Having spoken on the wireless set, Subedar Himmat Khan contemplated the map of Tetwal for some time. He then rose in a decisive manner. Tearing off the top of a cigarette packet, he handed it over to Bashir, "Here, Bashir, scribble on this in the same creepy-crawly Gurmukhi, as they have."

Bashir took the piece of the cigarette packet and asked, "What should I write, Subedar Sahab?"

Subedar Himmat Khan twirled his moustaches and reflected, "Write ... just write." He took out a pencil from his pocket. Giving it to Bashir, he asked, "What should we write?"

Bashir passed the pencil tip between his lips and began thinking. Suddenly, in a contemplative, questioning tone he asked "Sapar Sunsun ...?" Then, satisfied, said in a determined way, "Okay, the answer to Chapad Jhunjhun can only be Sapar Sunsun. They will remember their mothers, these Sikhras!" Bashir put the pencil to the top of the cigarette pack, "Sapar Sunsun."

"One hundred per cent ... write Sa-pa-r-Sunsun!" Subedar Khan laughed loudly. "And write further ... This is a Pakistani dog!"

Subedar Himmat Khan took the cardboard piece from Bashir's hand, made a hole in it with the pencil, and after stringing the rope through it, moved towards the dog, "Take this to your offspring!"

All the soldiers laughed at this.

Subedar Himmat Khan tied the rope around the dog's neck. The dog kept wagging its tail all the while. The Subedar then gave it something to eat, and in a didactic manner, said, "Look friend, don't commit treachery ... Remember, the punishment for a traitor is death."

The dog kept wagging its tail ... After it had eaten its fill, Subedar Himmat Khan picked up the rope and led it towards the sole trail on the hill and said, "Go, deliver our letter to our enemies ... But make sure you come back. This is the command of your officer, understand?"

The dog, still wagging its tail, began walking ever so slowly, along the trail that took a winding route into the lap of the mountains.

Subedar Himmat Khan took up his gun, and fired once into the air.

The shot and its echo were heard on the other side, at the Hindustani camp, but they could not fathom its meaning.

For some reason, Jamadar Harnam Singh had been grumpy that day, and the sound of the shot made him even more irritable. He gave the order to fire. Consequently, for the next half hour a futile rain of bullets poured from either side. Eventually sated of the diversion, Jamadar Harnam Singh called a halt to the firing and began combing his beard with greater ferocity. Having done that, he methodically bundled his hair into the net and asked Banta Singh, "Oye, Banta Singh, tell me, where has Chapad Jhunjhun gone? The ghee didn't go down well with the dog."

Banta Singh missed the implication of the idiom and said, "But we didn't feed him any ghee."

Jamadar Harnam Singh laughed boisterously, "Oye, ill-read lout, there is no use talking to you."

Meanwhile, the soldier on watch, who was scanning the horizon with his binoculars, suddenly shouted, "There, he's coming..."

Everybody looked up.

Jamadar Harnam Singh asked, "What was the name again?"

The soldier on duty said, "Chapad Jhunjhun ... Who else!"

"Chapad Jhunjhun?" Jamadar Harnam Singh got up. "What is he doing?"

The soldier answered, "He's coming."

Jamadar Harnam Singh took the binoculars from the soldier and began looking around. "He's coming our way. The rope is tied around his neck ... but he's coming from there ... the enemy camp ..." He let out a great oath at the dog's mother, raised the gun, aimed and fired.

The shot was off its mark. The bullet hit a short distance away from the dog, causing the stones to fly up, and buried itself in the ground. The dog, fearful, stopped.

On the other side, Subedar Himmat Khan saw through the binoculars that the dog was standing on the path. Another shot and the dog started running the opposite way. It ran, with its tail between its legs, towards

Subedar Himmat Khan's camp.

Himmat Khan called out loudly, "The brave are never afraid ... Go back!" And he fired a shot to scare the dog.

The dog stopped again.

From the other side, Jamadar Harnam Singh fired his gun. The bullet whizzed by, past the dog's ear.

The dog jumped and flapped its ears violently.

From his position, Subedar Himmat Khan fired his second shot that buried itself near the front paws of the dog.

Frightened out of its wits, it ran about – sometimes in one direction, sometimes the other.

Its fear gave both Subedar Himmat Khan and Jamadar Harnam Singh, in their respective places, a great deal of pleasure and they began guffawing.

When the dog began running in his direction, Jamadar Harnam Singh, in a state of great fury, uttered a terrible oath, took careful aim and fired.

The bullet struck the dog in the leg and its cry pierced the sky.

The dog changed its direction and limping, began running towards Subedar Himmat Khan's camp.

Now the shot came from this side – just to scare it. While firing Himmat Khan shouted, "The brave pay no attention to wounds. Put your life on the line ... go back ..."

Terrified, the dog turned the other way – one of its legs had become useless. It had just about managed to drag itself a few steps in the other direction on three legs, when Jamadar Harnam Singh aimed and fired. The dog fell dead on the spot.

Subedar Himmat Khan expressed regret, "Tch tch ... the poor thing became a martyr!"

Jamadar Harnam Singh took the warm barrel of the gun in his hand and said, "He died a dog's death."

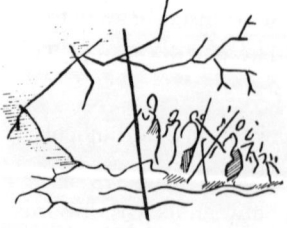

"Tetwal ka Kutta" was first published in Urdu during Manto's lifetime. The translators have relied on the Devnagari version, published in *Sa'adat Hasan Manto: Dastavez*, vol. 2, eds. Balraj Menra and Sharad Dutt (Delhi: Rajkamal, 1993), rpt. 1998, while consulting the original as well.

COMMENTARY ON PAGE 104

Kamleshwar

HOW MANY PAKISTANS?

TRANSLATED BY STUTI KHANNA

Such a long journey. And yet I don't understand why this Pakistan confronts me at every turn. Saleema! I never did anything to hurt you ... then why did you do this to yourself? You laugh ... but I know, this laugh of yours conceals arrows dipped in poison. These are not mehandi flowers, Saleema, which release their fragrance only when the wind blows.

The wind! Makes me laugh to think of it. Remember how you said there was something in the air ... that it had gone to my head?

Of course you remember. Women never forget anything, only pretend to. Life would become difficult otherwise. To think of you as a woman or even Saleema, feels so odd. I want to call you Banno. Banno of the mehandi flowers. I remember those sighs, Banno, the smell of your breath mingling with the fragrance of mehandi flowers. You'd bring the flowers close to my nose and blow on them, making their fragrance waft up, and say, "Their scent rises only when the wind blows."

Well, it was the wind that got to me. That something in the air, Banno. But now I hesitate to call you Banno – I don't know if even *you* can bear to hear this name now. Does this name have any significance, anymore?

That night, I wanted to go back, up the stairs, to ask you, to make you remember ... But was there anything you didn't remember?

God knows how many Pakistans were made! With the making of one Pakistan, somehow, somewhere, everything got tangled up. Nothing could ever be resolved.

That night was like the other one. Was it the peepal in the backyard that spoke, or was it Badru miyan – "Kadir miyan! Saala Pakistan has been formed ... Bhaiyon, a brand new Pakistan has been formed ..."

What a terrible night that was – that moonlit night, you lying in the courtyard below, Banno, milk-bathed in moonlight, the peepal rustling in the backyard and Badru miyan's voice coming as if from the nether world – "Kadir miyan, saala Pakistan has been formed ..."

Friend! This long journey has three points of rest – first, the fragrance of Banno's mehandi flowers which got to me. Second, that moonlit night when I saw Banno naked for the first time. And third, Banno standing in the doorway, her hand on the doorframe, asking, "Anyone else?"

Yes, there was, there was someone else! ... Someone ...

Banno, why did you laugh after one trembling, blind moment? When had I harmed you? Who were you taking revenge on? Me? Munir? Or Pakistan? Who were you shaming – me, yourself, Munir, or ...

This Pakistan comes between us again and again. For us – for you and me – it is not just the name of a country, it is a painful reality. It is that thing or cause that separates us further, that comes between our conversations like a gulf of silence. It renders shallow the depth of one's feelings for your family members, for people of the same religion. And then their pain does not seem as painful to one, as it really is, nor their happiness hold the same for one as it really should. Somewhere, something is diminished. It is this deadening of feeling that is called Pakistan – just as there are mehandi flowers, but no breeze, or no one to blow on them to spread their fragrance. Like flowers without colour, or with colour but no fragrance, or with fragrance but no breeze. This stagnant wind of feeling is what Pakistan is.

Listen, if it wasn't so, why would I have had to leave Chunar and become a dervish? Chunar – the land of mehandi flowers. Near the boundary walls of the mission school ... from where we'd walk to the peepal on the Ganga's bank, and sit sucking imli on the broken wall of King Bharathari's fort.

I distinctly remember that evening, when compounder Zamin Ali had come to Dada and said, "It isn't anything much, but people won't listen. Please send Mangal away for a few days. If he stays here, the reference to Banno will come up again and again. Their marriage is not possible, but a riot certainly is."

You cannot imagine what I went through. Leave Chunar! But, I left it behind. The nights in Chunar ... the water of the Ganga, the boats going towards Kashi, the deserted walls of Bharathari's ruined fort, the one-roomed toll office at the riverside, the roof on which I would sit and look out for Banno. The dry, cracked drains through which Banno always tried to wend her way to the riverside, but never managed. Waiting ... waiting ...

We never realized when we began to be seen as grown-ups, when our innocent meetings became the cause of such major events.

We never imagined this would lead to tension in the basti. How and

13

why did this happen, Banno? But how would you know? We never even spoke after that.

The three landmarks came and went – we never managed to stop and talk. Not even when the scent of mehandi flowers got to me, not when I saw you naked that moonlit night, and not when, with your hand on the doorframe you asked, "Anyone else?"

Mehandi flowers.

Chunar! My home, your home! A brick lane passed in front of my house, leading to the town bazaars. Winding along the banks of the Ganga, it reached the big gateway of Bharathari Maharaj's fort.

Where the lane turned towards the fort there was a toll office. Taxes were levied on the goods brought in by the boats, and unloaded at the Ganga ghat. Fish, crabs, turtles were brought; mangoes too, in the right season. The munshi at the toll office went about his work, muttering the name of Ram to himself all day, and collecting grain in lieu of tax. He poured holy water on the Shiva idol under the peepal tree at least ten times a day, and tutored some boys on the rooftop.

Near the toll office was an elbow turn. On the left, a brick road went towards the fort. The road coming in from the left that joined it was unpaved. Running water had made gullies for itself in that lane, drains almost, the water slowly drying up on the sandy riverbank. Many small lanes went parallel to the gullies – lanes crisscrossed by water channels. These were Banno's lanes.

Where Banno's lanes came to an end, a paved road began, which went up to the mission school – a reconverted English bungalow. Here one found the mehandi bushes, and the maidan, overgrown with thorn-apple bushes.

These dhatura bushes had caused me much grief. When tension arose in the basti about me and Banno, she somehow managed to come to the toll office one day, and said, "If Maulvi sahab and his supporters create a ruckus, Mangal, I'll take dhatura and sleep – forever! Don't leave the town and go. If you go, don't forget – Gangaji is right here."

We couldn't talk for long. She had to go. I couldn't even tell her about the commotion in my house, about how Dadaji was being threatened daily by unknown men in the bazaar. Everyone feared I would be murdered someday, that the Muslims would break into the house in the middle of the night.

Pakistan had been formed, Banno, and your Abba was still writing the *Bharatharinama*.

> *Earlier penance made me king,*
> *From king I would be fakir now.*
> *Hearts would meet at the time of death.*
> *My used clothes, my words, I give up here.*
> *Destroy my empire and wander about a hermit.*

People said the Drillmaster had lost his mind to be writing the *Bharatharinama*. He is only a low caste convert, he does not have true Turk blood in him. It was then that we learnt that only the Iranians and the Turks were "true" Muslims — not the ones from here. Everyone had isolated the Drillmaster from their midst, and yet everyone wanted to interfere in Banno's affair. As though they were the supreme guardians of morality.

You don't know, Banno, but I do. Drillmaster sahab did not say anything, except to go along with whatever Maulvi sahab and the others thought best. He was unable to think for himself. One day, he came secretly to meet Dadaji, and wept bitterly in front of him. After that day, he never dared to show anyone his work on the *Bharatharinama*. That he was still writing it, I learnt only when — because of my family's anxiety and my own confusion and indecision — I was leaving town. Bidding me a silent farewell, Munshiji had slipped a piece of paper into my clammy palm.

That was a fearful night. Kaal hovered over the basti. Everyone was terror stricken. Anything could happen. Any moment chants of "Yaa Ali" could rise, and bloodshed ensue. The Ganga, as if in sympathy, had been turbulent all day. The peepal at its bank was also restless. There was a strong wind whistling through the fort. Dada, along with some Hindus — yes, Banno, I have to say it, with some Hindus — had gone with me to the railway station, so that I could go somewhere else, somewhere far away, and live. At first it was proposed that I go to Jaunpur where Mama lived. But then, somehow, it was decided that I should go to Bombay and stay with my mausa who worked in the railway workshop at Kurla, and find a job there.

15

What a night that was, Banno. And such a humiliating exit. A thousand hammers were pounding inside my head. One part of me wanted to go back, pick up an axe, and charge those "Mussalmans" of yours. To win you in a bloody fight, and if not, to kill you and seek a watery grave in the Ganga.

But somewhere I was also afraid, and couldn't forget that after all, Drillmaster sahab hadn't said anything. He hadn't even put up an opposition — except to say nothing. He only wanted to write the *Bharatharinama*. It seems to me now that if he hadn't been writing the *Bharatharinama*, there might not have been so much opposition ...

The town seemed lifeless, dead. Dada had been told to get me out of there by the next morning. Consultations went on till midnight. Only the night's last train, the parcel train to Mughalsarai, was yet to go.

Yes, some Hindus escorted me to the railway station. We didn't even go through the bazaar, but took the deserted lane that passed the fort. Munshiji, lantern in hand, had walked with us till the beginning of the paved road, and it was there that he had slipped that piece of paper into my sweating palm. There was no light there, and everyone clustered together at the station. The train left at two thirty in the night. Dadaji was worried sick. Everyone was scared and humiliated, and therefore, perhaps, bloodthirsty. It looked like riots would break out as soon as I was safely out of the way. Now it was these Hindus, who would attack on their way back. In the waning night they would butcher the sleeping Muslims. It is so agonizing for a Hindu to be a Hindu, Banno. When this happens, something precious lessens in value ...

It was a painful parting. There was a nip in the night air, and the stone floor of the station was cold. Before us, the Vindhya Hills and their pine trees stood silent, motionless.

What can I tell you ... Who would've imagined, someday I'd be homeless? A man humiliated in his hometown cannot be at peace anywhere. I thought of the lanes that Banno would try to take, to come to me. I would sit for hours at the toll office, waiting. Finally, defeated, afraid, I would walk those lanes. Mehandi flowers scattered on the ground marked the point till where Banno had managed to come. She had not been able to come further. Someone must have spotted her, questioned her, stopped her.

To tell you the truth – from that very day a Pakistan had pierced my heart like a sword. People's names seemed changed, incomplete. The wind seemed to have stopped blowing in the basti. Banno seemed surrounded, trapped. Shame, fear, anger, tears, blood, exhaustion, madness, love – were boiling, seething inside me. After all this, it didn't really matter, whether or not I got Banno. What had to happen, had already happened.

Sitting in the parcel train, I read that piece of paper. You, Banno, had the same things to say as Master sahab. And I also got to know that Master sahab was continuing his work on the *Bharatharinama*.

> *Why become a dervish leaving troops, army, cavalry.*
> *Why live in the wild forests, leaving nargis filled*
> *gardens.*
> *Why wear saffron robes, leaving brocade and silk.*
> *Why wander from door to door leaving Kamrup,*
> *Dhaka, Bengal.*
> *Why become a madman. Forget all kingly splendour.*

Yes, madness is the word. Brocades and crimson flowers – we had everything. Were neem, aakh, mehandi and dhatura flowers any less than the nargis, Banno? But what could we have done with that Pakistan?

The train ran on, and I silently became a dervish, a wanderer. After that, I never even felt the desire to return home.

I knew that Chunar was becoming stifling for Master sahab too. I knew nothing about Banno's existence. Only felt sometimes that she must have drowned herself in the Ganga. She is, she must be, somewhere, with someone – laughing, crying, grumbling, happy. Warming someone's bed at night. Giving affection and receiving beatings. Having to put up with rape. Asking blessings for her husband like a dutiful wife, applying mehandi. Wiping her children's bottoms. Happy, regretful. Must have forgotten everything. And what she didn't manage to forget – that stilled time must have become her Pakistan. To torture her …

Anyway, Banno … What happened had to happen. I came to Allahabad from Mughalsarai, and from there to Bombay. Mausa got me a job at the railway workshop in Kurla. After some time I went to Poona – to a limb factory in a hospital, where wooden arms and legs were made. I knew no one could live any more in that place called Chunar — not my family, not your family. But I did not know that Dada would come so far and bring so many families with him.

In fact, to tell the truth, what was there in Chunar now? Whenever a Pakistan is formed, it leaves man sundered in two. Crops are destroyed, the roads shrink, and the sky is shredded into pieces. Clouds dry up and the winds are still, imprisoned.

Years later, Dada's letter informed me that some households, along with families of weavers and carpenters, had set out from Chunar in search of the old crops, roads, sky, clouds and wind, and had reached Bhiwandi. What it did not tell me was that Banno's family had also come. What would the Drillmaster come for? Dada's coming here was understandable. He was a trader in cotton cloth. They had come to Bhiwandi with eight families of Muslim weavers, and two families of Hindu carpenters. God knows what problems they had had to face in the beginning.

I got to know of you, Banno, only when Dada came to Poona to see me. He mentioned very casually that the Drillmaster sahab's family had also come. He had got a position in a school in Bhiwandi, and that he had also got Banno married. His son-in-law stayed nearby and worked at the loom. A fine silk weaver.

The deliberate, forced quality of Dada's casualness was not lost on me.

But I was not told, Banno, that Dada and you lived in the same house in the Waje mohalla, he upstairs and all of you on the ground floor. The other families were in Bengalpura and Nai Basti. Perhaps Master sahab had done this to be able to forget his former regrets. I badly wanted to go and see you, but if you really ask me, I was upset. Somehow, hearing about your presence here, being married only made me feel worse. And then Dadaji had hinted indirectly that it would be best if I didn't come to Bhiwandi — out of respect for Master sahab. He knew that Master sahab had not done anything, and he did not want to shame or upset him by my presence. Such a strange situation — couldn't I have a place in that house? You and I could have been together at least, if not one.

So many painful thoughts inside me — what if all this buried anger erupted some day? What if the pulsating Pakistan within me erupted? If

I stopped your husband from sleeping with you? If I managed to evict him from Bhiwandi, the way I had been evicted once? If some night, I lost control and burst into your room?

I know both Dada and Master sahab were trying to assure each other of their innocence. But what assurance did I get? What had they lost? The loss was entirely mine. Since then I had been roaming around with a mask on my face, gloves on my hands, and a dagger at my waist.

But Banno, the riots broke out in Bhiwandi as well. Not because of me and you – because of that same diminished feeling. I was struck dumb when I heard. God knows what had happened this time! Five years ago, I might have been the cause, but this time I wasn't even there. I hadn't even been to the place, only because I knew I would see you and start a riot.

But what a state you were in when I *did* see you.

The night was moonlit and Banno was naked

When I reached Bhiwandi, it had been almost a fortnight since the riots. Black mounds here and there greeted the eye. Some houses, then a charred maidan, then a cluster of houses, beyond it another black maidan. Ashes flying in the wind, no more smell of fire and cinders. Ash has a peculiar smell of its own – the smell of burnt alkali, a pungent smell that sears through the nostrils and penetrates deep inside.

Listen, you too must have experienced this smell of ash – is there anyone in this country who hasn't? It was evening when I alighted at the S T bus stand. There was no evidence of the terror that rises at the sight of patrols. Some policemen were chatting in front of a wall plastered with film posters. The buses were mostly empty. All were standing silently. Forget about buses going to Sangamner, Alibagh, Bhirwada or Sinnar, there was not one going even to Shirdi.

Under the tin shed of the bus stand there were a few more policemen. They had set up a makeshift household there, like wandering gypsies. If their rifles hadn't been lying in a corner like a pile of sugarcane, no one would have known they were policemen.

Both roads were empty. At the dak bungalow where the collector was staying, a few people could be seen. There were no taxis going even to Thane or Kalyan.

Maybe you knew how it was to pass through a riot torn street. I didn't. A strange kind of silence, or a dull beat. Deserted roads, and an almost tangible emptiness. People look but don't see you. And if they do, they look closely, but without any sense of human bonding. Why does this happen? Why do feelings die like this? Or is it faith that gets shattered so completely? Why did the Hindus do this ... Can any human being live in the midst of this silence?

Even in that small township, it was difficult to ask people for the way to Waje mohalla. Somehow, I managed to reach there and locate the house, but it was steeped in silence.

I knew Banno, Drillmaster sahab, your husband Munir – everyone would be there, my family members too. But the upper storey was lost in darkness. If it hadn't been a moonlit night, I would have panicked.

Really, for a moment I felt that if I hadn't left Chunar, the same would have happened there. Then, Banno, I thought of you. How would I face you? My blood, raging till now, went cold. As though I had entered those very lanes in Chunar ... Gone back in time.

The door to the house was open. I slowly stepped inside, into something like a courtyard. A couple of earthen pots stood in a corner. Beside them, two dark shadows. Both women. One of them was naked from the waist upwards. The other, squatting beside her, was continually stroking her from neck to waist, massaging her naked breasts. I had no idea what she was doing. But I could see a woman's naked back. What those women were doing sitting there, I couldn't understand. I came out, bewildered.

Suddenly Drillmaster sahab came into view. He took a minute to recognize me. But there was no welcome. He was at a loss as to how to deal with me. What day, what year, was he to begin his conversation from, with what relationship? Before he could say anything, I saved the situation. I asked him about Dadaji as I would ask a stranger.

"He left for Chunar the day before yesterday," Master sahab said.

"The day before ..." What could I say?

"Yes, he wouldn't stay. Many people went back," he said.

And I immediately understood, that despite everything, Dadaji could still return to Chunar but not Master sahab. Master sahab's leaving

Chunar did not mean the same as Dadaji's leaving it, or mine. Only a few people had issued my exile. His was a decree issued by fate. It is not easy to return from such an exile.

My family was no longer there, and I didn't know what to say. A riot-stricken town – where would I find refuge? Master sahab's putting me up at his house was not possible. Banno was there. And yet things had not reached the point where he could shut his door on me, leaving me standing outside like a stranger.

"Have they taken all their things?" I asked further.

"No, most of the stuff is here," he said.

"Have they locked up?"

"Yes, but I have a spare key." He hesitantly offered me help.

"I only need to spend the night – I'm leaving tomorrow evening, anyway." I elaborated unnecessarily, since this was no help. Where could I have stayed in a strange town?

He went inside and returned a moment later, carrying a candle and a key, and began walking up the stairs. Opening the door, he handed me the lock, and asked, "Have you eaten?"

"Yes," I said, and went inside.

"If you need anything just say it ..." he said, and went downstairs. The poet of the *Bharatharinama* knew how to be subtle. Say it! Not ask ...

Banno, what a strange night it was. You didn't even know that I was upstairs. Who knows whether Master sahab mentioned it or not? He could have said anything. If the police hadn't come early next morning, you would probably never have known who the wandering shadow on the terrace was.

A resounding silence, a stillness all around.

A moonlit night. A windless night. I had pulled my cot out on the terrace to get some air, or perhaps to get a glimpse of Banno. I lay down for a while, tossing and turning. Waiting expectantly for some sound, some sign, from you. But then my heart sank. No matter how hot, a woman has to lie beside her man.

The peepal in the backyard stood bathed in moonlight. I had positioned my cot in such a way that I could view the courtyard below – but what a dreadful view it was.

21

Two cots lay in the courtyard – Ammi on one, and Banno on the other. It was so strange to see Banno lying ...

The moonlight streamed down on Banno, who, with her blouse open, dhoti pushed down to the waist, was lying naked. Her exposed breasts throbbed like water balloons, and she writhed slowly like a dying fish.

"Hai Allah ..." This was Banno's voice.

"Sleep, sleep," Ammi said.

"They are bursting," Banno said, and pressed her breasts so hard as if to squeeze them dry.

Ammi sat up. "Let me massage them." Saying this, she began to rub Banno's full breasts. Thin jets of milk squirted from Banno's breasts while she moaned and writhed on her cot. Broken streams of milk, like a bottle of perfume with a blocked nozzle. Then suddenly some drops would fall, glistening in the moonlight. A few droplets entered the creases of her stomach and sparkled like mercury. The milk in her navel shone like a large pearl.

Ammi would keep soaking up the milk with the corner of her odhni, and squeeze it out, from time to time, in the drain beside them. A thin snake of watery milk would crawl some distance in the muddy drain and then disappear.

Oh Banno! What was this I had seen? I stood petrified with terror. My body was bathed in perspiration. Writhing, cries of pain, and two swollen breasts suspended in the sky. Some fear, some confusion, some repentance at having seen something terribly wrong ...

I paced the terrace till late at night. It was only when everything was quiet below, and I saw Banno lying down fully covered, that I could lie down. What kind of scene was this? All across the sky there hung breasts dripping with milk ...

I had just dozed off when there was a clatter in the backyard. Someone was crying and sniffling and saying, "Kadir miyan. Saala Pakistan has been formed. Bhaiyon, a brand new Pakistan has been formed ..."

The crying stopped. A little while later the same voice said, "Kadir miyan, now this is where we'll bind the ihram and say the talbia. Our Haj is complete, understand, Kadir miyan!"

If it wasn't for the peepal in the backyard, I might have tried to run away from that voice coming from the netherworld. Pictures flashed before my eyes – the sky dripping blood, corpses running helter-skelter in the dark. Fountains of blood erupting from amputated bodies standing in the bazaar. People dancing naked in the midst of flames ...

If the peepal hadn't rustled, I would have been petrified with fear. The rustling of the leaves sounded like the clerk typing on his typewriter in the hospital office .... This was the only familiar sound. Everything else was new, frightening, of another world.

In the morning my head was heavy. My eyes were burning and my limbs were numb. But I had to get up because the Police had come. Master sahab came to wake me up. He seemed scared. He said, "The Police is asking for you ...."

"Why?"

"All outsiders are under surveillance. They asked us, "Who came at night, where did he come from, why did he come?"

I began to burn with anger. Tell me, when I was made to leave my home in the dead of the night, had anyone come to ask who was going, where was he going, why was he going?

Understanding, or trying to understand, not the whole man, but only an incidental part of him is what Pakistan is, Banno. When the Police woke me up that morning and took me to the Police Station, I understood that you and I – both of us – are trapped in this Pakistan together ... But what a painful togetherness.

I was subjected to a long cross-examination at the Police Station. Why had I come here? What could I tell them? Why does a man go somewhere? The Police would have given me no end of trouble, if Master sahab hadn't come there himself. He was the one who gave them all the details. At that point, his being a Muslim proved useful. A Muslim vouching for a Hindu's innocence was solid evidence. But I wondered, was Master sahab not repeating the mistake he had made when he began working on the *Bharatharinama*?

Answering questions in the Police Station was simple as well as tricky. Finally, we got out of there, walked across and sat on a pile of logs. Master sahab wanted me to regain my composure – I was looking deathly pale.

Two or three other people were sitting nearby. They too had probably

23

come for someone's bail or inquiry. They had long faces and sad expressions. There was fear in the Maulana's eyes. He was saying to the others, "The prophet says that the trumpet will be blown thrice. At the first sound, people will panic. At the second sound, everyone will die. And at the third, the dead will rise and assemble before God ... This will come to pass. This is the first sound of the trumpet ..."

"Are you still writing the *Bharatharinama?*" I asked.

"Yes ...

> *My soul is wandering, let us rest here tonight.*
> *Talk through the night, and dawn will come*
> *sooner ...*

Master sahab was looking at the tiny yellow flowers growing on the grass, lining the deserted terraces as he recited these lines. Doves would jump out of the dense grass like tiny fishes. Plucking the yellow flowers from the grass stems with their beaks, they would fly away. If the flowers fell from their beaks, they would come back to pluck more – their popping up from between the dense grass, their plucking of the yellow flowers, and their flying back – the flowers circled as they fell from the air and they returned from the sky to pluck more ...

Master sahab was watching all this in silence. At last I spoke – "Last night ..."

"Yes, that was Badru – he's lost his mind. He had forty looms – they were all set ablaze. Now he keeps sitting under the peepal in the backyard. Cries all night, shouts out abuses ..." Master sahab said.

"Something at home ..." I said hesitantly. Master sahab, sage-like, understood me perfectly, and said, "Yes, Banno is not well. She delivered a child three days before the riots broke out. She was at Dr Sarang's maternity home. The rioters set that on fire too. With the doorways blocked, the women were asked to jump off the second floor to save their lives. The children were thrown down too. There were nine women. Two died. Five infants died – Banno's child among them. People were being killed all around. The next morning, we somehow brought Banno home. Now the milk in her breasts gives her pain."

We both fell silent. The birds were plucking the yellow flowers and flying around. Looking for an excuse to get up, I said, "I think I'll leave for Poona this afternoon."

"If possible, go to Chunar. See your Dada," Master sahab said.

"Why, has anything happened to him?"

"Yes, his arm was cut off. The rioters came to the house. If it weren't for him, we probably wouldn't have survived. The attack was directed at us. He came down to intervene. He was attacked. His left arm was cut off – it fell to the ground. And yet his courage – he picked up his own severed limb and continued fighting, a torrent of blood flowing from him. The severed arm became his weapon – the rioters threw bombs and ran away. Shreds of his blown up arm lay scattered around him. When we went to him, he had lost consciousness. One hand still clenched the other's severed wrist. A thousand thanks to the Almighty. We took him to the Thane hospital. He returned after eight days. The very next day, he left for Chunar."

"How was his arm?" I asked, stunned.

"All right. He could walk around. He assured us he would get the wound dressed regularly at Chunar hospital. Yaa Khuda, have mercy. It'll help if you went and saw him," Master sahab said, and shaded his eyes with his palms.

I felt like I was losing my grip on reality. What was this world I was living in? Who were these people around me? These few people who looked like human beings – were they for real or part of a sinister dream? Only broken, torn men seemed real now. People with complete, whole bodies, struck terror in the heart.

I came back and lay down in my room. Master sahab went inside. Then, voices floated up from downstairs. Everyone was there – Ammi, Master sahab, Banno's husband Munir, and Banno. Munir was saying, "I don't understand this obstinate resolve to stay here."

"You won't understand." The voice was Banno's. "We will first get back our child from this very soil where we lost it. Then we can go anywhere – wherever you say."

I peeped below. Munir's thin wiry frame was shaking with anger. He screamed – "Take your child from here then, from whomever you like."

I stood shocked. Was this ... Was this a reference to me? But I was probably wrong. Banno retaliated with – "How can I expect a child from you? You, who have wasted yourself, selling blood for drink."

Tadaak! Munir must have hit Banno. A minor commotion arose.

Banno went on with her diatribe, "Don't I know? Whenever he goes to Bombay, he sells his blood. Then lies trembling on the bed all night."

What was this I was hearing, Banno? Another Pakistan was howling within you too. Aren't all of us writhing under the burdens of our own individual Pakistans? Partial, incomplete, cut into pieces.

It was so dark that night – the night I left Bhiwandi in the same manner that I had once left Chunar. A taxi was going to Thane from the bus stand. I took a seat. Till we were clear of the township, charred maidans could be seen intermittently. The strong acrid smell of ash penetrated deep into me. The swollen breasts stayed suspended in the sky. Fountains of blood kept spouting from the headless bodies in the bazaar.

Thane! From Thane, a bus to Bombay. From Bombay a train to Poona, where I lay burning with fever for many days.

I wanted to forget everything, Banno, wanted to curl up within myself. How unsightly is this journey called life, where a man, cut into pieces, bloody all over, has to keep going on.

And in this lonely journey if one hears a voice saying, "Anyone else?" – nobody can begin to understand what one can go through. Not even you, Banno.

"Anyone else?"

Four or five months had passed. Dadaji had sent a letter saying he had returned to Bhiwandi. The Sindhis and Marwaris, with their larger shares in the market did not leave much scope for other traders. Some looms had to be shut down as well. The loss of an arm had destabilized the balance of his body. He had even jokingly mentioned that people were beginning to call him "Tonta."

The only other piece of information he gave was that Munir had gone to Bombay and had taken Banno with him. God knows whether they had stayed on in Bombay or gone over to Pakistan. Master Sahab had gone partially insane – he did his drill in the house and kept writing his tome in school.

If I hadn't come to Bombay that day, I would not have met you, Banno! And how painful that meeting was. Later, I kept wishing it had been me instead of him. You, on your part, must've thought that this is all I do. To be honest, Banno, I have been doing all this, but not with you. Perhaps, because of you.

That friend was not from Poona. He was from Bombay. His name is Kedar. He'd stayed for a while with me in Poona, and we had become friends. I was going to Bhiwandi, and had stopped at Bombay on the way. Then I felt restless – what would I do in Bhiwandi? Why was I going?

You had nothing to do with that evening, Banno. Kedar and I wanted to spend that evening together. We'd been drinking at a club in Colaba, after which we strolled towards Handloom House.

A lane next to it – I will recognize it if I go there, but can't remember it now. Kedar and I entered it. A little way on, I think, we turned to the right. We crossed a shack, selling cigarettes. Cars were parked all around. It seemed like a Bohra Muslim locality. Very peaceful and clean.

The building had a lift. The staircase was clean too. We used the stairs. I was panting with the exertion of climbing five floors. The fragrance of cooking wafted out from open windows. The sixth floor was deserted. The flat at which Kedar stopped and pressed the doorbell, did not seem as clean as the others.

The door opened to reveal a Sindhi panting like a hippo. He took us to a sort of waiting room, lined with cheap sofas. The Sindhi was still breathing heavily. It seemed that if he talked too much, he would lose his breath and never get it back.

I was troubled. I went and stood at the open window for some fresh air. Dirty rooftops, as far as the eyes could see. Of all shapes and sizes. Kedar told the man that I would sit there and wait. The wheezing Sindhi brought a bottle of coke for me, and took Kedar to his table. There he began showing Kedar a bundled up black burqa. I couldn't catch what he was saying.

After this, they both disappeared somewhere. After a minute or two I heard Kedar laugh.

Kedar didn't return to where I was sitting, but the Sindhi did. Panting heavily as before, he said, "Beer ..." The rest of the sentence was swallowed up by his wheezing – "Would you like to drink?"

"Okay ..." I said, and he breathlessly asked the servant to get one. He didn't drink himself. I sat there, drinking on my own.

"You ..." He was panting as before. "Bombay ..." He meant, "Don't you live in ...?"

"No, I stay in Poona," I said.

"Business ...?" the panting continued.

"No, some personal work. I'm going to Bhiwandi."

After that he sat there panting till Kedar came and stood before us. Seeing him, the Sindhi got up in confusion. I too was feeling confused. I drained my glass and walked towards Kedar. The three of us came out to the big central hall. Kedar was just paying for my beer, when a side door opened. I saw a woman's hand give Kedar his comb and keys. Seeing me there next to the panting Sindhi, a voice asked, "Anyone else?"

I turned to look – hand on the doorframe, in a blouse and petticoat, you stood there, Banno! Asking – "Anyone else ..."

Yes! Someone – there was someone else.

After a blind, trembling moment, you recognized me, and a twisted smile came to your lips. A smile steeped in poison. Or was it a smile of absolute rejection? Or was it just a smile – I don't know.

Who were you taking revenge on, Banno – me, yourself, Munir, or Pakistan?

I descended the stairs with Kedar behind me. I had a sudden impulse to climb back up the stairs and ask you, Banno! Was this inevitable? Was it fated to be like this for me?

Now, from which other place can I flee? Where can I run to escape from Pakistan? Is there any place where there is no Pakistan? Where I can become whole again, and live with all my emotions and desires intact?

Banno! Every place is a Pakistan that wounds you and me, defeats us. It still hasn't stopped beating and humiliating us.

"Kitne Pakistan" was originally written in Hindi in the 1966-67 period. Later it appeared in the collection *Kohra* (Delhi: Rajpal, 1994).

Bhisham Sahni
PALI

TRANSLATED BY THE AUTHOR

COMMENTARY ON PAGE 112

Life goes on and on. Its ends never meet. Neither in the mundane world of realities, nor in fiction. We drag on drearily in the hope that some day these ends may meet. And sometimes we have the illusion that the ends have really joined.

Manohar Lal and his wife had also once lived under a similar illusion. They believed that a great calamity had at last passed over their heads. That the knots that had formed in their lives had been untied. But knots of life never get fully resolved even in stories, much less in one's life. No sooner is one knot untied than another knot forms in its place. The story thus never comes to an end.

One end of Manohar Lal and his family's life was left behind in a small town distantly situated across the border of Pakistan, a country newly carved out at the time of the Partition. With their meagre belongings, the little that they could carry, Manohar Lal and his family had also joined the caravan of the countless uprooted people heading for India. The dust raised by their feet hung like a haze in the atmosphere. Like a big river forming into many channels on its onward sweep towards the sea, this vast concourse of unfortunate humanity also proceeded towards the boundary line demarcating the two countries.

Manohar Lal, his wife and two children – a little girl in her mother's arms, and Pali, a boy of four, holding his father's finger – trudged along, carrying their bundles on their heads, their weary eyes searching their way through the haze, their ears pricked for any stray remark that might guide them on to the correct path. They were anxious to know the lay of the land and, more than that, what was in store for them.

On the last day, the refugee camp had started emptying out. Carrying their belongings on their heads, the refugees left the camp and proceeded towards the convoy of lorries, ranged one after the other along the road, which would carry them to the border. Holding his son's finger and carrying a heavy bundle on his head, Manohar Lal went towards the lorries, his wife, Kaushalya, following close on his heels, her baby daughter nestled in her arms. Like her husband, she also carried a big bundle on her head. The refugees were frantically throwing their things into the lorries and storming their way into the vehicles, some of them wriggling in through the windows. Manohal Lal was struggling to push his way towards the entrance, when he suddenly realized that his son, Pali, was not holding his finger. Kaushalya had already managed to enter the lorry. Manohar Lal showed no alarm, thinking that the child must be somewhere around. The sensation of the child's grip still lingered on his hand. Everybody was madly pushing forward from behind. There was a babble of sounds, and the crowd got more and more frantic with the passing of every moment. The camp managers shouted at the top of their voices, urging the passengers to hurry up and get into the lorries. They had to cross the border before nightfall.

When Manohar Lal failed to find Pali around, he really got anxious. He rushed back crying, "Pali! Pali!" but failed to get any response. Getting alarmed, he raised his voice. His son's name, Pali, rang in the air above the pervading din. Then he started running frantically alongside the lorries. The lorries had started leaving one by one. The lorry in which his wife was standing with her suckling child was jam-packed, and its horn was blowing insistently, warning the people that it was ready to start. Manohar Lal's throat had gone dry, shouting "Pali! Pali!" His legs shook and his head reeled. Such was the irony of the situation for this homeless man – he was shouting for his son on a road crowded with people, and yet he appeared to be shouting in a desert.

He was still searching for Pali, when the lorry started moving. His wife's anxious eyes were fixed on her husband in the crowd and, to her horror, he suddenly disappeared from her view. Alarmed, she started wailing. Her locks of hair tumbled over her face, blinding her for a moment, and her child nearly slipped from her arms. She breathed heavily, her chest working like bellows.

"Stop! Stop! Hai, stop the lorry!"

But nobody listened to her. All of them had their own worries to contend with. They were all shouting and crying. Hers was not the only family being driven from its home. There were many of those whose only half luggage had ! n hoisted onto the lorry, while the other half lay scattered on the road. An old woman, apparently a grandmother, was having difficulty in climbing into the moving lorry. She was pushed from all sides, and struggled to keep her foot on the footboard. As the lorry moved forward, Kaushalya's eyes went wide with horror. In a daze, she

31

searched for only one image in the crowd – her husband. Then she burst out crying, her plight like that of a bird whose nest was being destroyed before its very eyes.

She heard someone shouting, "Stop the lorry! Stop the lorry!" Other voices joined the cry. The lorry slowed down.

Kaushalya had thrown out one of her bundles, and was going to hand down her wailing child to a man standing on the road, when she saw Manohar Lal running up. But their son was not with him. God only knew which whirlpool had sucked in poor Pali!

Manohar Lal heard some voices being directed towards his wife, "The child must be somewhere here." The people gestured to Manohar Lal to come nearer. "Get in, get in!" they advised him. "He must have got on to some other lorry." There were other voices, loaded with venom and irritation, "Will the lorry keep waiting for your child? If you want to search for your child, you'd better get down from the lorry." The people had suddenly become callous. If they had not seen Manohar Lal running up, perhaps Kaushalya would have got down from the lorry, wailing, and they would have thrown out her luggage after her. They were right. They must get across the border before nightfall. So many lives were at stake. Surely, the lorry could not keep waiting for one child.

The refugees' hearts had dried of all sentiments. The same Pali had once got lost, and the whole mohalla had gone out in search of him. And here someone kept crying repeatedly, "Get down, you! If you want to search for your child get down, and let us proceed!"

The husband and wife could not decide whether to get down from the lorry or proceed in it. Having failed to find any trace of Pali, Manohar Lal and Kaushalya kept looking out on the road. Slowly, the town was left behind, and the noise abated. Only Kaushalya kept wailing. The trees, the fields full of greenery, swept past their gaze. Pali, lost somewhere in the crowded small town, receded from his parents. Kaushalya's wailing gradually changed into a whimper. The mental anguish of the passengers expressed itself in the moans of the insane, and then changed into heart-rending cries before petering out into an anguished silence. The lorries moved on, lurching from side to side. Slowly, the morning haze cleared up. Looking up at the vast expanse of the impassive sky where one or two stars were still winking at him, Manohar Lal tried to console his wife. "We may yet find him," he said. "He can't get lost like this. Some kindly soul must have taken charge of him and pushed him into some other lorry." He looked at Kaushalya's abstracted gaze and, seeing the grief on her face, he said in utter desperation, "What can we do if we don't find him? God had been benign enough to spare a child for us. We must be thankful to him for that. You know Lekhraj's three children were killed before his very eyes. It's God's will. We must resign ourselves to it."

Kaushalya's empty eyes were still glued on to the road. There was nothing strange about losing a child under these circumstances. There was no sense in creating so much hubbub over it. As time passed, the uprooted passengers fell to talking with one another. The women also followed their men's example. Here and there, they could also hear the sound of laughter.

The evening shadows lengthened as they neared the border. The convoy stopped for a short while at one point. Manohar Lal promptly got down from his lorry and ran past the lined up lorries, shouting, "Pali! Pali!" He peeped into all the lorries through their windows, but he got no response from any lorry. His voice seemed to be echoing back from the wilderness. He could not find Pali anywhere.

On reaching the border, the refugees were transferred to other lorries which were parked there to receive them. The lorries raced through the darkness towards Amritsar. The sky, studded with myriads of stars, looked so mysterious! Overwhelmed by the immensity of the situation, the refugees had become very quiet, and some of them had started dozing to the rhythmic jolts of the lorries. There were others who just sat there, staring at nothing. Manohar Lal's wife had again started crying. Her incoherent loudness made people think that she was going mad. Then her crying would change into moans, and the onlookers would feel reassured that she was not mad yet. She must indeed be missing her child very much. At last, she rested her head against Manohar Lal's shoulder and fell asleep. Manohar Lal silently resolved that if he failed to find Pali, he would go back to his old town in Pakistan and, following up certain clues, try to locate and bring him back home.

The convoy tore through the darkness on its way to Amritsar.

Everyone was too absorbed in themselves to think of what lay in store for him. Perhaps their minds had stopped thinking. Fate had thrown a black curtain across their eyes, so that they could discern no ray of hope through it. There were only the joltings of the lorries and weariness. Their eyes had become glazed and their throats were parched, and above them were myriads of twinkling stars which seemed to mock at them.

That night, after crying for hours when Pali fell asleep at last, his head resting against Zenab's bosom, his sobs slowly dissolved in a sea of affection. A woman's bosom is the greatest shield against man's afflictions, and the greatest source of love and affection. Zenab had, so to say, caught the child firmly within her citadel of love. For the first time in her life, Zenab was overwhelmed by a sense of joy, which only a woman bereft of a child can experience. A tiny, delicate body was clinging to her, as if the child was specially made to fit into the contours of her body.

Her heart swelled up with maternal feeling. "Why don't you speak?" she asked the child.

Shakur, who had been lying in the courtyard in a cot adjacent to Zenab's, kept gazing at the sky sprinkled with millions of stars. It reminded him of Zenab's deep blue chunri in which she had first come to his house as a bride. Her chunri had glittered like stars. As he looked at her glowing face from behind her chunri, Shakur had felt as if the sun had descended into his courtyard.

Shakur made a living by selling chinaware. Carrying a big basket loaded with cups, saucers, plates and pots on his head, he would go from lane to lane and from street to street hawking his wares, waving a thin cane stick over his basket. He had been doing it for years together. That late afternoon, as the evening came down upon the small town, he had chanced upon a small boy who had been thrown to one side by the ebb and tide of the crowd. He was standing at the corner of the lane crying, "Pitaji! Pitaji!"

Shakur stopped on seeing the small boy. Then he sat down by the boy's side, uttering soothing words to him. He wiped the child's tears with the end of his kurta, and the child stopped crying. "Come, I'll take you to your father," Shakur had said. "But where's your father?" Holding the child's hand, Shakur had taken him to the place from where the convoy of lorries had departed carrying the refugees. The lorries had left long ago, and even the dust raised by them had long since settled down. The refugee camp was lying deserted. In the darkness of the night, when Shakur climbed the steps to his house, Pali was fast asleep, his head resting against Shakur's shoulder.

Shakur was a god fearing man, timidly taking every step in life. When rioting started in the town, he kept himself aloof from the trouble makers. When the grain market was set on fire and there were stray cases of stabbing in the streets, Shakur had remarked, "It is God's anger visiting us." He would repeat this remark every time there was a violent occurrence.

"Why are you silent?" Shakur asked his wife.

"What's there to say?" Zenab said in a lazy voice, which trailed into silence. She was enjoying the feel of the child's small body. She felt for a moment, as if all the obstructions had crumbled away from her path, and her body was getting lighter. But she did not want to tell her husband that she had come upon a precious boon. Even the touch of that small unknown child as he clung to her, had sent a thrill through her body.

"All the Hindus and Sikhs left their houses," Shakur said. "They have gone for good. The camp has emptied. Now nobody would dare venture this way."

Zenab gave no reply. The child mumbled in his sleep, heaved a deep sigh and, resting his head upon Zenab's bosom, fell asleep again.

Zenab looked up at the sky. It was looking so resplendent, as if auguring her good fortune. As if echoing Shakur's thoughts, she said, "Leave him at the place from where you picked him up, lest some unfortunate curse should befall us."

"Why should any curse befall us? We are giving the child shelter," Shakur mumbled. "If we deliver him to the Police Station, they can't restore him to his parents."

They were trying to read each other's mind.

"What's his name?" Zenab asked, rubbing her cheek against the child's cheek.

"How do I know? When I asked him he said Pali. Pali."

35

"These Hindus have such queer names. What a funny name! Pali! If I had a son I would have named him Altaf."

They lay silent for a long time, lost in their own thoughts. If nobody came to claim the child, he would become hers. A child prancing about in the courtyard! She hoped nobody would turn up to enquire. The tailor, Mahmud, had kept a Hindu woman in his house and no one had bothered to investigate. Mir Zaman had ransacked the Hindu tailoring shop next to his, and had kept the stolen things in his shop for all to see. Nobody had taken him to task for it. And as for her, she was only giving refuge to a child – a lost child whom her husband had picked up on finding him crying in the street. What was wrong with it? But Shakur's mind was sometimes filled with fear.

On waking up the next morning, when the child found himself among strangers, he again started crying and repeating, "Pitaji, Pitaji!" Zenab put a bowl of milk against his lips, and kept fondling his head and caressing his back. But little Pali would not stop crying and broke into hiccups. Zenab's eyes went to the door, lest someone should hear the child crying and force his way into her house. Yes, the child was there all right and, all said and done, it was a stolen child. What if someone got wind of it? She must keep the child hidden from prying eyes for some days.

Pali stopped crying at last. Now he sat in a corner, maintaining a grim silence and emptily staring this way and that. He kept sighing, and Zenab sometimes felt that with the coming of the child, she had herself become rootless.

Shakur had thought that within a day or two, after becoming familiar with his environment, the child would start feeling at home. But he still had his misgivings. One never knew. His parents may be knocking about in search of their child, and may track him down to this house. There were still a large number of refugees who had yet to migrate. He feared the police may come to know about the lost child, and they may create serious trouble for him.

The first two days were nothing short of an ordeal. On the third day, the child became a little communicative. He saw a white cat sitting on the wall of the courtyard and beamed at it. The cat jumped down and sat on the floor. The child ran towards it, crying, "A cat! A cat!" Zenab felt so happy.

There was a knock on the door. It sounded loud and ominous. Zenab and Shakur looked towards the door in alarm, their hearts pounding hard.

"They have come," Zenab said apprehensively. "The people to whom the child belongs!" Fear streaked across her eyes.

"Could be the people from the Police Station!" Shakur said, his fear mounting, moment by moment.

Another powerful blow. It was like a heavy lathi crashing against the door. "Open the door!" A voice invaded the house from across the door.

As Shakur proceeded to open the door, Zenab hurriedly moved into the inner room with the child.

It was neither the police havildar on the other side of the door, nor the child's parents. It was the bearded maulvi of the neighbouring mosque standing there, holding a thick lathi. There were two men standing behind him, both armed with lathis.

"Is there a kafir's child in here?" the maulvi barked, stepping into the courtyard. "Who has brought him here?" The two men wielding lathis had also followed the maulvi into the courtyard.

"Are you hiding some other kafir also in your house?"

Shakur ran in and hurriedly returned, carrying a murha.

"I swear by the Holy Quran, we are not hiding any kafir in our house," Shakur said. "We have only given shelter to an orphan boy."

"Where's that orphan?"

"Ji, he's sleeping inside."

The maulvi cast a suspicious look at Shakur, and then tapped the floor sharply with his lathi.

"Produce him before me! I want to see him."

Zenab came out carrying Pali in her arms.

"So you are giving refuge to a kafir child?"

"I've adopted the child, Maulvi sahab. It's no sin to adopt a child," Zenab said in a firm, steady voice.

"Have you had him circumcised? Has he read the kalma?"

New life surged back into Zenab. The maulvi had not come to snatch away the child from her. He had come only to make him a Mussalman. Zenab stood silent before the maulvi.

37

"Why don't you speak? You give a kafir's polluted child a place in your lap. You give him your breast to suckle. Do you want to nurture a snake?"

The maulvi's argument had driven Zenab against the wall. No, she couldn't refute his argument. Why hadn't she thought of it before? But she had found nothing polluted about the boy, nor did he look like the young one of a serpent. She was going to speak when the maulvi banged his lathi on the ground and said, "Bring this kafir's son to the holy mosque. Early tomorrow morning. Or you must be prepared to face serious consequences!"

The maulvi dramatically took a full turn and walked off towards the door. As soon as the maulvi had gone, Zenab tossed her head happily and smiled. All that the maulvi wanted was that the boy should say the kalma and be circumcised. Why wait till tomorrow? She was prepared to do it right now. What was there to fear? He had not threatened to take away the child from her. He had not even hinted at it.

The circumcision was performed the very next morning. Little Pali got terrified at the sight of the razor and clung to Zenab's legs.

The circumcision done, the maulvi petted and consoled little Pali, ignoring the fact that all the time the child had kept uttering "Pitaji! Pitaji!" in great agony. The maulvi did not mind it at all. He just smiled indulgently. The neighbours came and felicitated Shakur and Zenab.

The maulvi gave the boy the gift of a red Rumi cap with a black tassel, and himself placed it on the boy's head. Zenab gave him a brand new white muslin kurta to wear, and helped him to put it on then and there. The maulvi then lifted the boy and placed him in Zenab's arms.

"Take him!" the maulvi said happily. "He's your own child, not a kafir's. He belongs to the whole community."

The child was renamed Altaf – from Pali to Altaf. Carrying Altaf in her arms, Zenab went around distributing sweets in the mohalla.

Gradually, the child took to his new ways. Within a year, little Pali, now crockery seller Shakur Ahmed's son, Altaf Husain, became a familiar figure in the area. Now, he played in his courtyard hawking chinaware, aping his father's drawnout lusty cry. He would collect all the utensils from the kitchen and put them in a basket, which he carried on his head and trotted round the courtyard announcing like his father, the articles he had to offer for sale.

When the month of Ramzan came, he would plant himself in the middle of his courtyard and proclaim to the beat of an empty tin canister, "Get up, you pious Muslims! Wake up from your sleep! Keep your holy fast!"

Shakur and Zenab lost no time in putting Altaf in the school attached to the local mosque where, sitting on the brick platform outside the mosque, he memorized the Quran along with other boys, swaying his head rhythmically in consonance with the lines from the holy book.

Zenab and Shakur's lives started revolving on a new orbit with Altaf as its focal point. They wove their dreams around Altaf. One day Shakur would stop going around, hawking his wares from door to door. Instead, he would set up a regular shop where father and son would sit together, conducting sales. They would not be at the mercy of others. They would be their own masters and sleep peacefully with not a care in the world. Zenab eagerly looked forward to the day when Altaf's bride would set foot in her house, wearing ceremonial anklets.

Two years passed happily in this manner. One day, the chinaware seller had gone on his rounds and little Altaf was at school. Only Zenab was at home. Sitting behind the tarpaulin curtain, she was grinding wheat.

There was a knock at the door. "My man is not at home," she replied from where she was sitting. "Come in the evening."

After a pause, a voice said, "There's a court summons in Shakur Ahmed's name. He has been asked to report himself at the Police Station."

Zenab stopped grinding the wheat. Adjusting her palla over her head, she came and stood behind the tarpaulin curtain. A tremor of fear ran through her spine. "What's the matter, ji?" she asked.

"Send him to the Police Station tomorrow morning. It's urgent."

"What for, ji?" Zenab asked in a tremulous voice.

"They have come from Hindustan to claim the child. There is a letter to that effect."

Zenab again shook from head to foot.

"Send him to the Police Station tomorrow morning," the man repeated. "Don't forget."

Zenab heard the man's retreating steps from behind the curtain.

There are some wounds which heal with the passage of time, leaving a mark on the mind. But there are certain griefs which slowly eat into the heart like termites, completely ravaging the body. There is nothing a man can do about it. When Kaushalya reached India with her husband, her lap was bereft of a child.

That day if the convoy of lorries had safely reached the border and Manohar Lal had gone across it with his wife and child, they would have forgotten about Pali's separation from them as time passed. But, unfortunately, it did not happen like that. They had just crossed the city limits when something untoward happened. The convoy was passing along the road when a mob suddenly emerged from the fields flanking the road, raising war cries. Rushing up, they blocked the road. They wore masks, brandished swords and spears and shouted filthy abuses. Most of the lorries had already passed, but the last three could not escape the attention of the marauders. Those in the lorries heard the same heart chilling sounds of the brandishing of swords and spears which Manohar Lal and Kaushalya had heard back in the town from where they were escaping. Kaushalya did not even know when she felt a heavy jolt and fell down. She only heard Manohar Lal's voice, "Here, give me the child." Then that sound also faded out as she got another powerful push from behind, which sent her crashing to the floor of the lorry. When she regained her senses, all round her in the darkness, she heard whistles blowing to the accompaniment of groans behind her. She felt something clammy on the floor under her hand. It could have been water, it could as well have been blood. The lorry suddenly started and, as she looked out, she felt as if the stars were also moving with the lorry. Her throat was parched, and she felt desperately in need of water. Then the stars started revolving, and she passed out.

Even on reaching Delhi, Manohar Lal could not get over the feeling that he was still lying crushed under a heap of dead bodies. He feared that if he could not extricate himself from under this heap, he would die under the weight of these dead bodies. While slogging on the roads of Delhi along with his wife, bemoaning the loss of the children, he realized that if he did not turn his back on the calamities of the past, he would perish on these very roads of Delhi. He hired a push cart and set up shop on it in one of the bazaars of Delhi. When he returned home, late at night, tired and weary, and found his wife moaning as if she was on the verge of insanity, his courage would desert him. What if she really went mad? How would he take care of her with so many other problems on hand? The small spark of life that was still left in him would also be extinguished.

Taking her hand in his own, Manohar Lal assured Kaushalya it was not too late for them to have another child. But at the mention of children her condition would worsen. She would start trembling, and sometimes she wailed in such a heart-rending manner that even Manohar Lal got jittery.

The government had set up big establishments to trace abducted women and lost children, and retrieve stolen goods. Government officials made frequent trips to Pakistan in this connection. Manohar Lal took time off his work to visit these government offices and meet influential people in order to seek their help in tracing his child. But he was just a nobody, and no one took much notice of him. Month after month passed, but he found no lead. It was not easy to trace a lost child in a town, swarming with people. When he had begun the job, he had hoped that he had only to visit the town and identify the particular spot where Pali had got separated from him. He may find Pali at the entrance of some lane, eagerly looking out for his father. He would immediately pick up the child in his arms, and on returning to Delhi, put him in Kaushalya's lap.

What vain hopes! Things were just the reverse of what he had thought. Much less pick up a thread out of a tangled mass and go where it led him, he didn't even know where the thread was and where to start. For two full years Manohar Lal's case kept hanging in the air. Then he was allowed to accompany rescue parties consisting of government officials and social workers that visited Pakistan from time to time. Manohar Lal would pick up his small tin trunk and join them. But each time he returned, plucking his hair in despair.

After another two years, he at last got a definite clue to his son's whereabouts. He learnt that the boy was living in his erstwhile home town with one Shakur Ahmed who owned a chinaware shop. This time Manohar Lal was quite sanguine that his trip would not prove abortive.

41

The first time the police havildar came with the summons for Shakur, Zenab felt greatly upset, her condition being like that of a fish that has been thrown out of water. Her dreams were crumbling before her very eyes.

When Shakur came in the evening, his face turned pale on hearing the news. The news soon went round the mohalla, and many sympathizers dropped in to console Shakur. The maulvi also came tapping his lathi on the ground.

"You need have no fears," the maulvi said. "How dare they touch the child? Now that he has accepted Islam, we won't let him fall in the hands of kafirs."

Maulvi sahab's words revived Zenab's drooping spirits. He was right. Now he was not the same child who had slept in Zenab's arms on the first night of his arrival in her house. If someone had come to claim him at that time, she wouldn't have stood in his way. But now things were different.

The elders of the town went into a huddle, and it was decided that Maulvi sahab would himself deal with the police. Maulvi sahab had an ingenious device up his sleeve. The police havildar would be tutored to report that he had not found Shakur at home, and hence the summons could not be served on him. If the havildar persisted in making the calls, Shakur and his wife would go away from the town for a few months and stay somewhere else with the child.

"The havildar be damned!" Maulvi sahab said. "I know how to cut him down to size!" He went away tapping his lathi and feeling very important.

A strange game of hide-and-seek started thereafter. The high-ups in the governments make agreements, but it is the petty government functionaries who execute these agreements. The orders would come from above to produce the boy before the authorities. Walking straight in line with his nose, a police constable from the Police Station would come to the right house. He would bang on the door, make threatening noises, pocket a rupee, write on the summons papers that he had found the house locked, and that on enquiry he had learnt that the inmates had gone away and there was no knowing when they would return.

This was not a question of a small bribe, nor one of returning an adopted child. The matter was taking on a religious slant. By not sending away the child they were doing a service to religion – something which was considered to be a pious act.

Months passed and merged into years.

On one occasion, the entire rescue party descended upon Shakur Ahmed's house, but found it locked. They had got news in advance, and the family had disappeared before the arrival of the party. Shakur Ahmed, it transpired, had gone to Shekhupura to meet his brother, and they had no information as to when he would return. As the party reached Shekhupura, it learnt that Shakur Ahmed had left the place only a day earlier with his wife and child for Lyallpur. "Yes, there was a child with them. But we do not know the man's address. He didn't leave any address behind before going away."

In this game of hide-and-seek, three years passed. Manohar Lal's face had started turning dark. His cheeks became deeply lined, and his hair showed streaks of gray. All the time the dust of despair kept blowing before his eyes. He could not even distinguish between a truth and a lie. Life was mauling Manohar Lal with the same ferocity with which a hawk tears a bird apart with its beak.

Whether it was the result of Manohar Lal's determination or the effect of Kaushalya's sighs, after seven years Manohar Lal found himself sitting in Shakur Ahmed's courtyard. He had gone there with a government rescue party and a woman representative of a social service organization. From the Pakistani side there were two police officers and a magistrate to conduct the proceedings. The meeting had become possible due to the intervention of a high Government of India official who had moved his counterpart in Pakistan.

At the meeting Manohar Lal was required to prove that the child was really his. There was a legal angle to it, and he must conform to a set procedure and convince the officials as to his right to the child.

There was tension in the courtyard. The Maulvi sahab was sitting a little apart from the officials. A lot of people had gathered outside Shakur Ahmed's house. Zenab was sitting in the verandah behind a tarpaulin curtain. Her face looked pale, but her eyes were sharp and watchful like the eyes of an eagle guarding its nest. Altaf Husain sat leaning against her, looking tense and

43

bewildered. Zenab squeezed his shoulder again and again.

Before the proceedings started, Maulvi sahab came out with all sorts of threats, perhaps to intimidate Manohar Lal.

"Nobody can take away the child. No kafir can touch him," he kept muttering.

The man heading the Indian party requested the magistrate several times to ask the maulvi to keep quiet. He reminded the magistrate that if the maulvi did not stop interfering, tension would increase.

After the Partition of the country the blood on the roads and streets had long since dried, but its stains were still faintly visible here and there. The fire that had engulfed the houses had died out long since, but the charred frames were still standing. The mad frenzy of the Partition had abated, but its effects still lingered in the minds of the people.

"Call the child!" the magistrate said, starting the proceedings.

"We have not stolen anybody's child," Zenab's agitated voice came from behind the curtain. "Why should I send him out?"

"Produce the child before me," the magistrate repeated his orders. Shakur Ahmed went behind the curtain to fetch the child.

Manohar Lal's heart was pounding hard. The most decisive moment of his life had come. He was eager to have a look at his long lost child. At the same time his mind was assailed by doubts and fears.

The boy was made to stand before the magistrate. Seeing the crowd in the courtyard, he became nervous and clung to Shakur's legs. Putting his finger in his mouth, he looked around at the people as if stupefied.

"Son, come here." The magistrate said. "Look, who is here. Do you know any of them?"

"Nobody should prompt the boy," the police officer said in a warning tone. "Let the child decide for himself."

Manohar Lal himself failed to recognize his own son. An eleven year old boy, a Rumi cap perched on his head, dressed in a muslin kurta and salwar. Manohar Lal's eyes were beginning to deceive him. He stared at the boy for a long time. Then the image of his own child flashed through his mind, and his throat choked with emotion, "Pali!" he cried. "Pali, my son!" But the voice died in his throat. Even otherwise, he was not supposed to draw the boy's attention to himself.

The boy surveyed the people sitting in the courtyard. His expression recorded no change at the sight of Manohar Lal. He was looking scared as before — only a little more so. Manohar Lal watched him intently. He had grown quite tall and fair and handsome and healthy. Manohar Lal felt that the time of decision was gone. The dice seemed to be loaded against him. Shorn of all joys, his life would remain bare and empty like a sandy waste.

Breaking the silence, the maulvi said, "So you have seen it. The child has failed to recognize him. Had he been this man's child, he would have dashed forward to him. And look at this man's audacity — he has come to demand another's child!"

The lady social worker was greatly annoyed. "Come here, son," she said. "Look, who's the man sitting in front of you?"

"No prompting please!" the police officer warned the social worker. "Leave the child alone. Let him find out for himself."

Zenab was sitting inside, holding her breath. She was feeling uncertain.

Addressing Shakur, the social worker said, "You've yourself admitted that he is not your child — that you've adopted him."

Before Shakur Ahmed could reply, the maulvi banged his lathi on the floor and said, "We don't deny that he is an adopted child. But how can one accept this man's contention that the boy is a Hindu child and belongs to him?"

The magistrate nodded his head as if he was in agreement with what the maulvi had said. He looked now at the child, now at Manohar Lal. Manohar Lal felt more and more depressed. His own child was standing before him, and all he could do was to watch him listlessly. The opportunity had really slipped through his fingers.

"The child has become nervous," the lady social worker said.

"Please keep quiet!"

"What more do you want now?" the maulvi said. "It's already decided. You people may go."

The social worker turned to Manohar Lal, "Yes, now I remember," she said. "Where's the photograph you had shown me the other day?"

By way of proof, Manohar Lal had not been able to bring anything except a small photograph. At Kaushalya's request, he had got himself photographed along with her at the Baisakhi fair. Little Pali was sitting in his lap. But the photograph could serve no useful purpose. Pali had now grown quite big and bore no resemblance to the little Pali of the photograph. Manohar Lal took the photograph out of his pocket and passed it on to the magistrate.

"My son is there in this photograph. It's the same child. You can see for yourself."

Shakur Ahmed flared up. "Janab, this photograph proves nothing," he said to the magistrate. "I too have a photograph."

He went in and came back with a framed photograph. Wiping it with his sleeve, he handed it to the magistrate.

"It's the same child whom you see standing in front of you," he said, indicating towards the boy in the photograph. "You can verify for yourself."

"Come here, child." The magistrate placed Manohar Lal's photograph in front of the boy without making any comment, convinced that he would not be able to recognize anybody in the photograph.

The boy looked intently at the photograph for some time. Then, lifting his hand, he placed his forefinger on Manohar Lal's image in the photograph and cried, "Pitaji!" Then his finger slowly moved towards the woman in the photograph. "Mataji!" he exclaimed.

The child's eyes remained fixed on the photograph. A strange restlessness seemed to have seized him.

Manohar Lal burst out crying. He thrust the end of his turban into his mouth to suppress his sobs.

The magistrate placed the other photograph in front of the child. The child beamed. "Abbaji! Ammi!" he exclaimed.

A wave of joy surged through Shakur Ahmed's mind. Zenab peeped out from behind the curtain. Her eyes were brimming with tears.

The maulvi's face had remained taut all this time. But now his expression suddenly mellowed.

"Now he is a Mussalman's son, not a Hindu's. He has read the kalma," the maulvi said with an air of finality.

"Please be quiet!" the social worker cried.

"Why should I remain quiet? This man had thrown him away and disappeared. We brought him up!" The maulvi's voice rose.

Hearing the maulvi's loud and threatening voice, the boy ran and clung to Shakur's legs. Then he ran towards the veranda and hid behind the curtain.

They must have heard what was going on in the courtyard, for suddenly slogans resounded outside Shakur's house, "Allah ho Akbar!"

The lady social worker and the two Indian officials put forward the plea stoutly that, since the child had recognized his father, he should forthwith be restored to him without further ado. But things seemed to be taking an ugly turn. The tension was mounting. While the child was sitting in Zenab's lap with his arms around her neck, the complexion of the problem was undergoing a change. It had become a Hindu-Muslim question. Questions like "Whose child is he? Who had brought him up?" seemed to have become extraneous to the situation.

Finding himself at the end of his tether, Manohar Lal had a brainwave. Getting up, he went and stood near the curtain. Folding his hands he said, "Bahen, I'm not begging you for my child. I'm begging you for my wife's life. She has lost both her children. She is missing Pali very much. His absence is driving her insane. Day and night she keeps thinking of him. Please have pity on her."

The space behind the tarpaulin curtain remained steeped in silence. The officials of both the countries watched the curtain intently. The maulvi rose to his feet. He had no doubt in his mind that Zenab would hurl the choicest abuses at Manohar Lal. Instead, they heard the sound of sobbing from behind the curtain. "Take away the child. I do not want an unfortunate woman's curse to fall upon me. How could I know you have lost both your children?"

Manohar Lal felt like going behind the curtain and falling at the woman's feet.

An hour later the child was given a send off. Amidst tears, Zenab and Shakur helped the child to put on new clothes which had been specially made for the forthcoming Id. They put a new Rumi cap on his head. Then Zenab said, "I will part with the child on one condition. You must send him to us every year on the occasion of Id to stay with us for a month. Do you agree? Then give me your word."

47

Manohar Lal's body tingled. His hands still folded in supplication, he said, "He is your wealth, bahen. I give you my word. I'll remain indebted to you all my life."

The wheel of life started moving again. The same meandering paths, the same turnings, the same ups and downs. If things had ended there, the narration would have assumed the form of a story, holding something of interest for everybody. But nothing ever ends, nothing ever comes to its finality. The powers that be, scored out one more name from the long list of the abducted, and transferred that name to the list of the "Found."

The government jeep was travelling at great speed. By the side of the driver sat an armed guard, and next to him the police officer. At the back of the jeep sat father and son, tightly set against each other, and opposite them the lady social worker. The child looked lost and forlorn. In contact with the boy's body, Manohar Lal's body had again started tingling warmly. The chords of affection which had snapped were again slowly joining together.

They crossed the border in the afternoon. Getting down from the Pakistani jeep, they submitted their papers to the scrutiny of the Indian authorities stationed on the other side of the boundary line. Mahohar Lal, his son and the others then drove off in another jeep towards Amritsar.

The jeep had not gone far when the lady social worker, as if acting on a sudden impulse, stretched out her right hand to whisk off the Rumi cap from the boy's head, and flung it outside the jeep. The red, black tasselled cap, flying in the air, landed in the dust at the edge of the road.

"My cap!" the boy's hand went to his head. "Hai, my cap!"

The lady social worker leaned towards the boy. "You are a Hindu boy. Why should you wear a Muslim cap?"

Manohar Lal did not appreciate the brusque manner in which the cap had been removed from the boy's head and thrown away. "That must have hurt the boy's feelings. He doesn't know that it is a Muslim cap," Manohar Lal said to the social worker. "Why did you throw it away? Stop the jeep. I must retrieve the cap."

The boy had pulled a long face and was on the verge of tears. His hand resting over his head, he kept moaning over the loss of his cap. "Oh, my cap!" he cried again and again.

"He is still a child, ignorant of these things," Manohar Lal explained patiently. "See, he's still crying."

"Let him cry," the woman said. "Crying is not going to do him any harm. You're not going to give him a Rumi cap to wear, are you? He'll stop crying in a short while."

The jeep raced on, raising clouds of dust behind it.

Far away from the border, in a small town, where a lot of refugees had settled down, the news spread at the speed of lightning that Manohar Lal and Kaushalya's son had returned. The impossible had happened. God's mill, they said, grinds slow, but it grinds fine. The boy was returning after seven years. A lucky child indeed! The women kissed the child's head and bowed their heads in gratitude to God. "See, bahen, one who is ordained to live, lives long .... See, bahen, the child you were holding against your bosom was snatched away by death right from your arms, and the one who had stayed away from you and was knocking about lone and forlorn, has come back hale and hearty. Nobody can harm a person who has God's benign protection."

Back home, the child kept whimpering as he had done many years ago on the first two or three days of his arrival in Shakur's house. On the first day of his arrival he kept watching his mother, Kaushalya, from a distance. He saw nothing of those traits in her which he hazily remembered to have marked in her as a mother. The loss of her children seemed to have wrought havoc with her youth. Dim memories of the past were slowly reviving in the child's mind – hazy, nebulous, incoherent. He vaguely remembered his small sister lying in his mother's lap. And the buffalo that stood tethered outside their door, and on whose back he used to have a joy ride. Also the wooden bed that was a permanent fixture outside their house. He could hear a babble of sounds rising higher and higher every moment. The identity of his mother had gradually started returning to his mind. But sometimes he still wondered if the boy who was standing before her, finger in mouth and brazenly staring at her, was really Pali? He would feel more and more confused.

Three or four days passed in this manner.

Then came Sunday. The dholak began beating in Manohar Lal's courtyard from early morning. The women of the mohalla gathered in

49

the courtyard, and sang in tune to the rhythmic beat of the drum. Two small cotton carpets had been spread in the courtyard and there were a few cane seats lined against the walls, and also some cots to sit on in case there was an overflow of guests. Kaushalya was looking her normal self. She was not silent or withdrawn as before. Now she even laughed sometimes. That morning she wore a red chunri bordered with threads of gold – a red chunri, a traditional Hindu symbol of matrimonial bliss and good fortune.

Manohar Lal was all attention to the guests. He was not tired of telling his friends that those people back in Pakistan had taken great care of his son. He could not match the attention and affection they had showered on him. He would indeed remain indebted to them all his life.

The narrow courtyard was filled with guests. Holding a big platter of laddoos, Manohar Lal was about to go round to distribute the sweets, when Pali did something very strange. He had been sitting by the side of his mother, listening to the women playing the dholak and singing, when he got up abruptly and fetched a mat from inside. He spread it on the floor, sat down on it folding his legs under his thighs, and started saying his namaz.

The people sitting in the courtyard watched Pali with curiosity. But their curiosity soon changed into dismay.

"What's going on, Kaushalya?" a woman asked. "What's your son doing?"

Manohar Lal was feeling embarrassed at his son's strange antics in front of his guests. He should have anticipated this and done something to prevent it from happening. He apologetically said to the man standing by his side, "Every afternoon right at this hour he sits down to say his namaz. He instinctively comes to know that it's time for namaz."

"Don't you stop him?" a voice asked.

"He's still a child. He'll learn soon enough."

A man who was regarded as a big shot in the mohalla said in a loud voice for all to hear, "He must at once get rid of this nasty habit. We don't want to have a Muslim among us."

The boy continued with his namaz while the people around him watched with feelings of disgust.

Manohar Lal said as if in self defence, "You know those people didn't have a child of their own. And ..."

"Manohar Lal!" the big shot who was regarded as the Chaudhri of the mohalla, cut Manohar Lal short. "You must know those people have foisted a Muslim convert on you and yet you have nothing but praise for them."

The boy was still sitting on his folded legs and, with his palms raised upwards, repeating his namaz prayers. The Chaudhri went and stood by the boy's side.

His namaz finished, the boy was wiping his face with both his hands when the Chaudhri caught him by the wrist and dragged him to the middle of the courtyard.

"What were you doing?" he asked the boy.

Pali got unnerved. "I was saying namaz," he said in a faint voice.

"We won't allow you to do such silly things in this house," the Chaudhri barked at Pali. "No namaz hereafter. Do you understand?" Turning round to the people standing around him, he remarked, "Those Muslas have planted the poison of fanaticism in his mind. And at such a tender age!"

He stood thinking for a while. "Better call a pandit," he said in a decisive tone to a friend. "And also a barber. We must perform the boy's mundan. And let him keep a proper tuft. Those rascals! They have planted a Musla on us."

Pali stood there looking utterly confused.

"What's your name, boy?"

Pali looked timidly at the massive build of the Chaudhri, and mumbled in a subdued voice, "Altaf, Altaf Husain, son of Shakur Ahmed."

The Chaudhri glared at the boy. With great difficulty he restrained himself from slapping him. The boy felt that the pressure of the man's grip on his wrist had increased. He gave the man a terrified look.

"No, your name is Pali — Yashpal!"

The boy stood silent and then mumbled, "Altaf."

"Repeat that name again and see what happens. I'll pull out your tongue!"

"Have you seen these Musla's doings?" the Chaudhri said, turning to the people standing around him. "They call it conversion —

51

religious conversion. Reform!"

The barber arrived, followed by the pandit. Accompanying the pandit, there was also a man carrying ghee and other ingredients for performing a havan.

The boy was again made to sit on a mat. The barber sharpened the razor on his palm and according to the directions given by the pandit, started shaving the boy's head. As long as the ceremony lasted, the boy kept sobbing with bowed head. Once he got up in fright, and crying "Ammi, Ammi, Abbaji!" ran towards the wall of the courtyard. Standing with his back against the wall, he looked at the Chaudhri like a deer at bay watching a hunter. At the suggestion of the Chaudhri, Manohar Lal went to fetch the boy. He held the boy's hand and gently brought him back to the mat.

A tuft of hair was left in the middle of his cropped head. Pali was bathed, given a brand new dhoti and kurta to wear. To the chanting of mantras, he was given a sacred thread.

"Child, what's your name? Say five times, Pali, Pali, Pali ..."

Some time later, looking every inch a brahmachari, Yashpal, Pali, stood at the door with folded hands, seeing off the guests. The relatives and guests caressed his head and blessed him while departing. Manohar Lal distributed laddoos.

At that time, sitting in their lonely courtyard hundreds of miles away, Zenab and Shakur were making all sorts of conjectures. Zenab said, "He is gone and with him is gone all the gaiety of this house. At this time I used to go out into the street in search of him. He would try to hide from me, running into all nooks and corners. I would never know where to find him. Oh, it was such joy! Well, what do you think? Will he come to visit us for Id? Will those people send him here? I think they will."

"Oh yes, you once told me you had a cousin living in Bareilly. We shall go and stay with him and meet our son. What do you think of that?"

She wiped her eyes again and again.

"Pali" was first published as "Pali" in Hindi in *Pali* (New Delhi: Rajkamal Prakashan, 1989), rpt. in 1991.

COMMENTARY ON PAGE 120

Surendra Prakash

DREAM IMAGES

TRANSLATED BY M ASADUDDIN

That day, I burnt my fingers as I touched the newspaper. Every item of news was an ember. Outside, one could hear a rattling noise, the kind made by moving tanks. There is the danger of an immediate war with Pakistan.

We have already fought three wars with Pakistan. These sporadic wars, each lasting for several days, cast their shadows on the doors, windows and kitchens of our houses. During those dark years I got my elder daughter married. She is happy in her home with a little darling of a son. I have come by many such things which I thought I did not deserve. In my own way I am contented with my life.

I think I have separated myself from society, but as I read the newspaper I feel at one with it and the whole situation undergoes a change. Thoughts get blurred. Embers continue to burn.

It is unaesthetic to talk about inflation, homelessness or a feeling of insecurity, and anything, any sort of behaviour which is unaesthetic, is abhorrent to me. Yet, I remember how the country was divided because of the conflict between two religions. According to a preconceived scheme we were thrown out lock, stock and barrel from the place which has become Pakistan to this side. And many Muslim families from here proceeded towards their new heaven.

I was then a child, but I kept thinking why we had to be either Hindu or Muslim. The answer lay in our birth – because we were born of parents who were either Hindu or Muslim. We were Hindu. So we could not retain even two yards of land in Pakistan. Those of us who survived, came to India. The only things which remained there were memories and shadows. Master Nazir Talib remained there, and so did Akhtar Bhai. Jalal Painter was there, and so was our neighbour Meraj Sheikh, the shopkeeper. All of them were Muslims. They were born to families which were Muslim before their birth. Nevertheless, there must be something common between us that makes me think about them so often.

The Muslims migrating from here did not leave en masse. No one knows what logic made them divide their families. The pain of truncated families must haunt them even today. I have been lucky. Coming here, I have found my own Nazir Talib, Akhtar Bhai, Jalal Painter, Mirza and Meraj Sheikh in Mehmood Javed, Zubair, Anwar and Salam. Alas, what

54

would have happened to those who went there from here?

The day moved on, slowly. With the newspaper hugged to my chest, I lay on the bed littered with embers. And then, I don't know when, my eyes closed.

"... You have done a good thing."

Startled, I looked at my wife who had said these words. We were sitting together on the back seat.

"What?" I asked.

"You've brought the children along!"

I looked at my son and younger daughter who were sitting next to the driver. They were talking to each other in hushed tones, perhaps about the place we were going to. The car was one of those big, ancient Chevrolets. The driver's face looked young, though his beard and moustache were perfectly white.

"I've always dreamt of doing this. The timing too is perfect," I said. "You may put it down to my age."

"Hmm. Tell me, have you even thought of how I'd live without you or you without me, in such a world?"

The car sped along, and we could see everything in front of us through the windscreen. Now I could see bushes along the road, of a kind we hadn't passed earlier. It was dusty all around, and the colours were exactly as I remembered them. The wind was raging. It had an aroma of its own. The stems of kekar and tehli were swinging in the strong wind. I couldn't come up with an answer to my wife's question. Only a supernatural power could have answered it.

We passed by the burning ghat, by Adh Marg where all the water taps were running. Behind Adh Marg we could see hamlets spread out for long stretches. When we reached the bridge on the canal, the car slowed down. We passed the bridge, and entered the market where the car came to a stop on the left. I was the first to get out. I saw Babaji's temple standing there, just as it had before. Outside, under a peepal tree, some sadhus were sucking on a chillum, letting out deep puffs of smoke through their mouths and noses. They had tangled hair, their bodies were smeared with bhabhut, and they wore just a piece of cloth. Near them were cows lazily chewing cud.

I turned to look across the market and saw the clock in the clocktower, but could not see its hands. The market was very crowded. I tried to remember its name, but couldn't. I also couldn't recall the name of the mohalla near which we stood. Yet, I was sure that it was the very same mohalla where our house used to be.

The driver took out the luggage from the car, and my wife paid the fare. The two children looked around with surprise. They looked at me as though to ask, "What next, Daddy?"

"Right here, behind these shops, was our home," I said without much thought.

"Come on, let's have a look," all the three said in unison.

We shared the luggage amongst ourselves and set off. There were thousands of people moving around us, whose faces were invisible. Bodies moving with clothes on. Begging bowl in hand, one of the followers of Baba Kaudi Shah passed by us, nodding his head and begging for alms. Such begging bowls used to be brought from the faraway island of Madagascar. They were made by ripping open a fruit. Several generations could use the same bowl for begging.

We entered the mohalla. The street and the houses alongside them looked the same. Several houses had come up in the open space in front of the mohalla, changing the entire topography. We could not stand for long in front of our ancestral home. Too many eyes stared at us from behind the walls.

All of a sudden I saw Babuji coming out of the house, ready for his daily walk to the shop. Ma came up to the threshold to see him off.

"Who was that, Daddy?" both my children asked me.

"Your Dadaji and Dadiji."

My wife joined her palms in a namaskar from a distance. "How fortunate we are that we could have a darshan of our ancestors!" she said in a whisper, as though she were reciting verses from the Quran.

"Where is Dadaji going, Daddy?" my children asked me once again.

"To his shop."

"Where is his shop?"

"Come, let's find out."

We had left the street, and had moved on to Gol Bagh just behind Regal

Cinema. Then we passed through Changadh and Badru. We saw the shrine of Baba Kaudi Shah where dervishes were ecstatically chanting:

Ali da, mast qulandar,
Ali da, Ali da mast qulandar

They were swinging their heads from side to side while the rat-disciples of Shah Dauley observed them intently, their own heads beginning to move. Clutching their begging bowls, the rat-disciples tried to steady their heads. But in vain. The heir to the shrine, dressed in black, his hair unkempt, gazed at the dome with his bright and beautiful eyes. Then, muttering to himself, he bowed his head and tried to hold it between his knees. The pigeons, perched on the dome, did not stir.

My children watched all this for quite some time, completely absorbed in it till my wife said, "Children, say Allah, Allah." They joined their palms and said "Allah, Allah" as though they were praying before the images of gods.

Far away, the clock in the tower chimed the noon hour. Kites flying in the sky let out a cry. A handcart selling malai qulfi, drawn by four identical looking brothers, went past us. They sang out together:

Qulfi khoye-malai di, piste badam di,
Keode gulab di, khatir janab di ...

In a huge wooden box the qulfi moulds were stabbed into the ice. A white sheet was spread over them. The box was painted light green, the borders deep green. On them was written, "Abdus Shakur and Sons, Qulfiwaley," in black.

The four of us bought a qulfi each, and sucked it. It was great fun.

I said, "The eyes are moist, the heart is soothed."

My wife and children also put on expressions of contentment on their faces. The cart moved along.

We threw away the sticks on the road that leads to Regal Cinema. We followed the road which stretched ahead of us. Soon there appeared a high dome. There was a desolate temple. Sitting on a platform, some people dressed in white dhotis and shirts were talking to each other in low voices. One of them thrust his hand inside his shirt. Putting the other hand under his collar he caught hold of his sacred thread, and started pulling it up and down, so that it became a convenient device for scratching his back. In the ruins in front of the temple there stood a newly built dharamshala. Vendors had stationed themselves near its doors and were selling food. The atmosphere was strangely quiet.

We put our luggage down with a sense of relief, and looked around. A man who was scratching his beard came close to us and said, smiling, "Welcome to the Hindu dharamshala. You can stay here."

It was a happy occasion. Having lived as unwanted tenants in other people's houses all our lives, here at last was a welcome invitation.

"Thank you. We shall stay here," I said with pleasure and relief.

My wife agreed with me.

"Daddy," my daughter said, "Why have we come here?"

My wife and I looked at each other. The question was reasonable enough. Why had we come here? On what errand? After all, we had not hired the car of our own accord. We had not settled the fare with the driver, nor had we told him about our destination. We had not willed these things to happen. We had suddenly found ourselves in a car driven by a man who looked young, but whose hair and beard were completely white. I thought, perhaps we have came to meet Babuji and to see his shop. How energetically he prepares himself every morning for work! How Ma sees him off at the front door! How he sells things at the shop throughout the day, and comes back at night with the day's earning in a bag! Suddenly I remembered how once, while he was returning home, a wayside filcher had snatched his bag from him. There was a total of sixty rupees in it. I am approaching sixty.

"Daddy," my son says, "Where we live, there are five-star hotels. There are neither Hindu dharamshalas, nor Muslim musafirkhanas. Where have you brought us?"

I exchanged a stealthy glance with my wife, avoiding the watchful eyes of our children. I wondered whether we are really like the heir to the shrine, dressed in black, looking at the dome in the graveyard of our past, and when we feel shamed by the meaninglessness of this whole exercise, we sit on our haunches with bowed heads. In the mausoleum, dervishes continue to chant *Ali da*, *Ali da*, swinging their heads from side to side.

In order to evade the question, I said, "Children, stay here for a while. We are going to find out why we have come here."

We passed through a crisscross of broad and narrow roads and streets. When we got tired, we stopped for a while.

"Should we call?" I asked my wife.

"Yes," said my wife. "Let's."

We began to look for a place from where we could make a telephone call. After a long search, we found a telephone in a butcher's shop. Slaughtered animals were hung all over. Blood glistened on their flesh. But the butcher was a perfect gentleman. At our request he allowed us to make the call.

Walking with some difficulty through the hanging carcasses, my wife reached the telephone. She picked up the receiver and dialled a number. Wherever it was that she had called, someone answered and my wife said, "Hello." The person at the other end said, "Wrong number" and the line got disconnected. My wife kept on trying, but the result was the same. She got irritated and turning towards me said, "Wrong number! Wrong number! What the hell! Whom are we ringing up, after all?"

"I don't know."

She rushed out of the butcher's shop, almost stumbling into the carcasses. The butcher warned politely, "Take care, Begum Sahiba. Your clothes may get bloodstained." My wife remembered she had not paid for the calls. She took out a ten rupee note from her purse and held it out to the butcher, saying, "Thank you very much, Bhai sahab."

The butcher gave a cursory glance at the tenner and then looked at us in surprise. "I see! You have come from India."

We were scared as though we had been caught stealing something. "I beg your pardon," he said, "This currency is not in circulation here."

I felt as if I had struck by lightening. "I see. This is at the crux of the matter. It is the currency which separates us and determines our nationality."

My wife leapt to my side. "This is terrible!" she hissed. "We don't have a visa or a passport."

I was scared stiff.

Lifting up my head, I saw the butcher. He was regarding us as a policeman looks at a suspect.

"Listen," I said, "We stand to gain nothing by worrying. Only Anwar Sajjad or Intizar Husain or Kishwar Nahid or Khalida Hussain can get us out of this mess."

"Do you have their addresses and phone number?" my wife asked. "No," I replied, and turned towards the butcher once again. He was a hefty, bespectacled man of middle age. I claimed his attention and said, "Sir, we are in a fix. Do you know Anwar Sajjad?"

"Anwar Sajjad? Who is this Anwar Sajjad?" he asked in surprise.

"He runs a clinic in one of the cities."

"Can you tell me the name of the city?"

"The name of the city ... the name of the city ..." I was muttering to myself, when a young man in a white shirt and trousers, and a beautiful black cap on his head came up to me, and said respectfully, "Salaam alaikum."

"Walaikumsalaam." I returned his greetings.

"I've come to receive you. Dr Anwar Sajjad sent me."

In a jiffy, the young man had put an end to all our difficulties. I felt like hugging him and kissing his forehead.

The next moment, a strange sight flashed before my eyes. He was my own son, standing before me in a different dress. But I asked myself, "Why is he talking to me like a stranger?"

He said once again, "Sir, my name is Abdus Salaam. You can rely on me."

The butcher said from the shop, "Sir, this is my son."

"Okay, let's go."

We went along with him. After a few steps he stopped. One by one, several handsome young men, wearing the same bright dresses and elegant black fur caps, emerged and stood before us.

"Go on, move. Why don't you move?" my wife said impatiently.

"Sure, in a moment. It's just that we are waiting for the car," one of the boys said respectfully.

And then, I was shocked to see that all the boys looked alike.

I said to my wife, "We have no reason to worry now. We'll reach

Anwar Sajjad's clinic by car. He'll let Intizar Husain, Kishwar Nahid and Khalida Hussain know that we have arrived. You'll be delighted to meet Kishwar. She'll arrange to send you to Chakral, the home of your ancestors."

"That's all right," my wife said, "But where have we left our children? They must be waiting for us."

Suddenly, I realized my mistake. We had forgotten the road which would take us back to our children. Before us, there was a broad, transparent road on which bright new cars sped by. Around us were many children who all looked alike. How could we tell them that our children, too, looked the same as them, and that we did not remember where we had left them?

My wife burst into tears.

Praise be to Allah that no one has come to hear of this sad story.

"Khayal Surat" ("Dream Images") was published in Urdu in *Zehn-e-Jadeed,* September-November, 1990.

61

Sa'adat Hasan Manto
TOBA TEK SINGH

TRANSLATED BY M ASADUDDIN

Two or three years after the Partition, it occurred to the governments of Hindustan and Pakistan that, just as they had exchanged civilian prisoners, they should exchange the lunatics confined in the asylums as well. In other words, Muslim lunatics interred in the asylums of Hindustan should be sent to Pakistan, and the Hindu and Sikh lunatics confined in the asylums of Pakistan should be handed over to Hindustan.

It is difficult to say if this was the right thing to do. Anyway, the decision was made by the wise, and accordingly, several high level conferences were held on either side, and a date set for the exchange. A thorough investigation followed. The Muslim lunatics whose families were still living in Hindustan were allowed to stay on. The rest were dispatched to the border. In Pakistan, where most of the Hindus and Sikhs had already migrated, the question of retaining anyone did not arise. All the Hindu and Sikh lunatics were sent to the border under police escort.

It is not known what transpired there, but when the news of the exchange reached here, in Lahore, it evoked some very interesting and intriguing responses. A Muslim lunatic who had been reading *The Zamindar* regularly for the last twelve years, was asked by his friend, "Maulvi Sahab, what is this Pakistan?"

"It's a place in Hindustan where they make cut throat razors," he answered after profound reflection.

His friend looked satisfied with the answer.

In the same vein, a Sikh lunatic asked another Sikh, "Sardarji, why are we being sent to Hindustan? We don't even know the language they speak there."

The other one smiled, "I know the language of the Hindustooras. These Hindustanis are devils and strut about haughtily ..."

A Muslim lunatic, while taking his bath, raised the slogan "Pakistan Zindabad" with such gusto, that he slipped on the floor and passed out. There were some lunatics who were not really insane. Most of them were murderers, whose relatives had bribed the officials to have them sent to the lunatic asylum, to save them from the hangman's noose. These men had some vague notions about why Hindustan had been partitioned and what Pakistan was, but they did not know the whole story. The newspapers were no help. The policemen on guard were ignorant and illiterate – one could make out precious little from their conversations. All they knew was that there was a man named Mohammad Ali Jinnah whom people called Qaed-e-a'zam, the Great Leader. And he had created a new land for the Muslims called Pakistan.

However, they did not know a thing about its actual location and its boundaries. That is why all the inmates of the asylum who weren't completely insane were thoroughly confused about whether they were in Hindustan or Pakistan. If they were in Hindustan, then where was Pakistan? And if they were in Pakistan, then how was it possible that only a short while ago they had been in Hindustan, when they had not moved from the place at all?

One lunatic got so embroiled in this Hindustan Pakistan rigmarole that he became all the more insane. One day, as he was sweeping the floor, he suddenly climbed up a tree. Perched on a branch, he delivered a two hour long speech on the delicate Hindustan Pakistan issue. When the guards asked him to come down, he climbed up even higher. When they threatened him, he said, "I want to live in neither Hindustan nor Pakistan ... I'd rather live on this tree."

After much fuss, when his fits had ebbed, he climbed down, and hugging his Hindu and Sikh friends, began to cry. He was saddened by the thought that they would go over to Hindustan, leaving him here.

A Muslim radio engineer, who held an M Sc degree, usually stayed aloof from the other lunatics, and wandered about silently on a particular garden path all day long. A sudden change in him was manifested by the fact that he took off all his clothes, handed them over to the guards, and began to race around stark naked.

A fat Muslim lunatic from Chiniot, who had been an energetic member of the Muslim League and bathed some fifteen or sixteen times a day, abruptly gave up this habit. His name was Muhammad Ali. One day, he declared in his enclosure that he was Muhammad Ali Jinnah, the Qaed-e-a'zam. Following him, a Sikh lunatic styled himself Master Tara Singh. The imminent bloodshed in the enclosure was, however, avoided by declaring both of them dangerous and confining them to separate cells.

There was a young, Hindu lawyer from Lahore who had turned insane after a failed love affair. He was heartbroken when he learnt that Amritsar had gone to Hindustan. The Hindu girl he was in love with, lived in that city. Though rejected by her, the lawyer could not forget her even in his madness. So he would abuse all the Hindu and Muslim leaders who had got together to split Hindustan into two — turning his beloved into a Hindustani, and him into a Pakistani.

When the talk about the exchange began, a few lunatics consoled the lawyer, telling him not to lose heart. He would now be sent to Hindustan, where his beloved was. But he did not want to leave Lahore because he thought that his practice would not flourish in Amritsar.

In the European Ward there were two Anglo-Indian lunatics. When they learnt that the English had left after granting independence to India, they were deeply shocked. They would now spend hours in secret confabulation about their changed status in the asylum. Would the European Ward be there or done away with? Would they be served breakfast anymore? And, instead of Western style bread, would they be forced to swallow the "bloody Indian chapatti?"

There was a Sikh in the asylum who had been there for the past fifteen years. He would often be heard blurting out a string of strange, unintelligible phrases like "Opar di gurgur di annexe di bay dhiana di mung di daal of the laltain." He slept neither at night, nor during the day. The guards said that he had not slept a wink in the long period of fifteen years. He did not even care to lie down, though he would lean against a wall and take a "tek," now and then.

His feet and ankles were swollen from standing all the time. But despite his physical discomfort, he would not lie down to rest. He would listen intently whenever there was a discussion in the asylum about Hindustan, Pakistan, and the exchange of lunatics. If anyone asked him about his opinion, he would reply in all seriousness, "Opar di gurgur di annexe di bay dhiana di mung di daal of the government of Pakistan."

Later on, however, "of the Pakistan government" was replaced by "of the Toba Tek Singh government" and he began to ask other lunatics where Toba Tek Singh, the place he came from, was. But no one knew whether it was in Pakistan or Hindustan. Those who attempted to explain got entangled in the confusion that Sialkot, which earlier had been in Hindustan, was now reported to be in Pakistan. Who knew whether Lahore, which was now in Pakistan, would not go over to Hindustan the following day, or the whole of Hindustan would not turn into Pakistan? And who could say with certainty that some day, both Hindustan and Pakistan would not vanish from the face of the earth altogether!

The lunatic's kesh had become sparse and straggly. As he seldom took a bath, the hair on his head was entangled with his beard, giving him a fearsome look. But he was a harmless fellow, and had never got into a brawl with anyone during the last fifteen years. The older staff in the asylum knew that he was a fairly well to do landlord from Toba Tek Singh, where he had considerable landed property. One day, without any warning, his brain had gone awry. His relatives had brought him here, bound in heavy chains, and had him admitted to the asylum.

Once a month, his people would come to enquire after his well being, and then go back. This arrangement continued for a long time. But as the disturbances concerning Hindustan and Pakistan began to mount, these visits stopped.

His name was Bishen Singh, but everyone called him Toba Tek Singh. He had no notion of the passage of time – what day or month it was, or how many years had passed. But every month, when it was time for his relatives and friends to come, he would somehow come to know of it. He would tell the guard that his "visit" was on its way. He would give himself a good bath, scrub his body with soap, oil his hair and comb it. He would call for his clothes, which he never wore on any other occasion. Thus spruced up, he would go to meet his visitors. If they asked him anything, he would either stay silent, or sometimes blurt out, "Opar di gurgur di annexe di bay dhiana di mung di daal of the laltain."

He had a daughter who had grown up a little, every passing month, during these fifteen years, and was now a young woman. Bishen Singh could not recognize her. She used to cry at the sight of her father when she was an infant. Now, a grown woman, tears still flowed from her eyes, seeing her father.

When the Hindustan Pakistan controversy started, he began asking other inmates where Toba Tek Singh was. As he did not get any

67

satisfactory answer, his curiosity deepened. Now no one came to visit him. Earlier, he would always know beforehand when the "visit" was due. But now, it seemed as though the voice of his heart, which would foretell him about their arrival, had stilled.

He longed for his people, who used to give him solace and bring fruits, sweets and clothes. If he had asked them where Toba Tek Singh was, they would have certainly told him whether it was in Pakistan or Hindustan, for he believed that they came from Toba Tek Singh where he had his lands.

In the asylum there was a lunatic who called himself Khuda, that is, God. When Bishen Singh asked him one day if Toba Tek Singh was in Pakistan or Hindustan, he, as usual, guffawed heartily, and said, "It's neither in Pakistan nor in Hindustan, for we haven't yet passed the orders."

Bishen Singh begged this "God" to pass the orders, so that the knotty issue was resolved once and for all. But he was very busy, as he had to pass numerous other orders. One day Bishen Singh lost his patience and burst out, "Opar di gurgur di annexe di bay dhiana di mung di daal of Vahe Guruji da Khalsa and Vahe Guruji ki Fateh ... jo boley so nihaal sat sri akaal."

He probably wanted to say that he was, after all, a Muslim God ... He would have surely listened to his request if he had been the God of the Sikhs.

A few days before the exchange, Fazal Deen, a Muslim friend of Toba Tek Singh, came to visit him. He had never come before. When Bishen Singh saw him, he turned away and made to leave, when the guards stopped him.

"This is your friend Fazal Deen. He has come to see you."

Bishen Singh looked at Fazal Deen, and then began to mutter something to himself. Fazal Deen came forward and put his hands on his shoulders. "I've been thinking of coming here to meet you for a long time, but just couldn't find time. Your people have reached Hindustan safely ... I did whatever I could for them. Our daughter Roop Kaur ..." He stopped in mid-sentence.

"Daughter Roop Kaur?" Bishen Singh tried to recall something.

Fazal Deen went on haltingly, "Yes, she too ... is quite well. She too has gone away with them."

Bishen Singh said nothing. Fazal Deen resumed, "Give my salaam to bhai Balbeer Singh and bhai Vadhwa Singh ... to behen Amrit Kaur, too. Tell brother Balbeer Singh that Fazal Deen is happy ... The two brown buffaloes that he had left here have both calved ... one a male calf and the other a female one that died six days after its birth. And tell me if there is anything more that I can do for you. I'm always at your service. And here, I've brought some homemade sweets for you."

Bishen Singh picked up the packet of sweets and handed it over to the guards standing nearby. Then he asked Fazal Deen, "Where is Toba Tek Singh?"

Fazal Deen replied with alacrity, "What do you mean? It's where it always was."

Bishen Singh was persistent. "In Pakistan or in Hindustan?"

"In Hindustan ... No, no, it's in Pakistan." Fazal Deen was flummoxed.

Bishen Singh walked away from there muttering, "Opar di gurgur di annexe di bay dhiana di mung di daal of the Pakistan and Hindustan of the dur fitey munh."

Preparations for the exchange were complete. The lists of lunatics to be sent across had reached from both sides, and the day of the exchange had been fixed.

On a severely cold day, police lorries packed with Hindu and Sikh lunatics proceeded towards the border under police escort. The concerned officials also accompanied them. On the Wagah border the superintendents of the two sides met, and after the preliminaries were taken care of, the exchange began and continued the whole night.

It was indeed a hard job getting the men out of the lorries and handing them over to the officials on the other side. Some just refused to budge from their place. Those who agreed to come out were difficult to manage, as they ran off in all directions. The naked ones among them tore off their clothes as soon as they were made to put them on. If one called names, another burst into a song. While some fought, others cried and wailed. It was difficult to hear anything in the fracas. Female lunatics made their own noises. And the cold was so severe that it made one's teeth chatter.

The majority of the lunatics were against this exchange. This is because they could not make out why they were being uprooted from their homes. Those who could still reason and think, raised the slogan, "Pakistan Zindabad" and "Pakistan Murdabad." They almost came to blows because the slogan incited both the Muslims and the Sikhs.

When Bishen Singh's turn came and the concerned official on the other side of the border began to enter his name in the register, he asked, "Where is Toba Tek Singh? ... In Pakistan or in Hindustan?"

The official laughed, "In Pakistan."

At this, Bishen Singh leaped to one side and ran back to his companions who were still there. The Pakistani soldiers caught hold of him and tried to push him towards the other side, but he refused to move. "Toba Tek Singh is here!" And then he raised his voice, "Opar di gurgur di annexe di bay dhiana di mung di daal of Toba Tek Singh and Pakistan."

They tried their best to persuade him that Toba Tek Singh had already gone to Hindustan, or would be sent there immediately. But he was resolute. When they tried to move him forcibly to the other side, he stood on his swollen legs at a spot in the middle, in a posture that seemed to suggest that no power on earth could move him from there.

Because he was a harmless fellow, they did not use force anymore. He was allowed to stand right there, while the exchange proceedings continued.

Just before sunrise, a sky rending cry emerged from the gullet of Bishen Singh, who till then had stood still and unmoving. Several officials came running to the spot and found that the man who had stood on his legs, day and night for fifteen years, was lying on his face. Over there, behind the barbed wires, was Hindustan. Over here, behind identical wires lay Pakistan. In between, on a bit of land that had no name, lay Toba Tek Singh.

Notes

1   The gibberish – a mixture of Urdu, Punjabi and English words/semantic units – is central to the story, and had to be retained in the original. No English translation could be even partially adequate. However, it must be pointed out that it is gibberish only in the sense that the phrases, taken together, do not make a coherent whole,

though separately, some of them, make sense. It is symptomatic of the utter confusion that lay around in the event of drawing artificial, arbitrary and mindless boundaries between India and Pakistan. It is notable that as the narrative progresses, and Bishen Singh gets more and more politically "aware," his rage increases and the gibberish becomes more comprehensive, strident and desperate. Note the use of the Punjabi "dur fitey munh," (p. 69 and p.ix-x in Gulzar's poem) a damning expression, when Toba Tek Singh names "Hindustan" and "Pakistan."

2   Towards the end of the story, by a brilliant metonymic process, Bishen Singh becomes Toba Tek Singh; the person becomes the place where he was born and had his roots. They merge inextricably with each other, so much so, that towards the end of the story, at least in the Urdu text, it is difficult to distinguish one from the other. To my knowledge, no English translation of the story has endeavoured to retain this tension and ambiguity. I have endeavoured to retain it even if it meant sacrificing a bit of lucidity.

"Toba Tek Singh" was first published in 1953 in an Urdu magazine called *Savera*. It was carried in Devnagari in Balraj Menra and Sharad Dutt, eds., *Sa'adat Hasan Manto: Dastavez*, vol.2 (Delhi: Rajkamal, 1993).

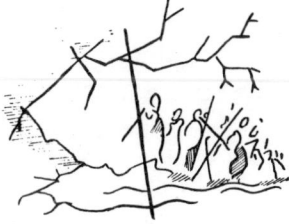

Everyone who lived in the village and the hamlets nearby, knew her. In their minds, they associated her deathless years with the existence of their village. Both were facts accepted without question since the birth of consciousness.

She was so old that she had become static in time, could never be older, had surely never been young. Her dry wrinkled skin was loose around the impatient skeleton. It enclosed her eyes in folds, hiding the yellowed cornea surrounding lustreless pupils. Yet there was vision enough to make her unconscious of its loss.

She used her withered hands for feeble grasping, her crooked fingers for uneasy touching, her bent legs for unsteady shuffling, and not her eyes, but time's familiarity for seeing and recognizing her changeless, circumscribed world.

Through the years, the mud of the walls had not changed, the same wooden arches supported the same sloping thatched roof, the same doll's house sliced off a corner of the small courtyard. And the heavy wooden door leading outside creaked the same warning as it opened and the curtain of matting was lifted.

This was her complete world as she lay in the sun on her string bed — the walls, the arches, the thatch, the courtyard, the doll's house, the curtain, the door to the world outside.

That world had changed, quickening its step in noisy haste. As she lay on her bed, shrivelled lips moving in constant prayer, she heard the impatient sound of a car horn, and the distant desolate screech of an engine's whistle.

Sometimes that alien world stepped through the creaking door. A grandson, a granddaughter, a visitor from the city lifted the curtain. They were self-conscious as they bent towards her for her embrace, lowering their eyes, covering their heads, denying the world that violated her principles, where men and women walked and talked together. Her eyes were protectively dim to new stimuli, her ears dull to new sounds.

Yet they were bright and sharp when the great grandchildren, the little ones, raced through the door. Then there was no conflict of worlds — they shared one created of their bright young love, not flat one dimensional, but given depth and form and colour by their curiosity, amusement and repulsion.

"How old, how old – and don't say it loudly – how ugly is Old Granny."

They would flap the loose hanging skin of her arm, lie on her lap and look,when she chewed an invisible cud, at the fascinating movement of her chin towards her nose, just missing it, then dropping down to begin again its upward drive. They would suddenly scream with high clear laughter, whirl around the bed, somersault to the floor and shout,

"Can you see us, Granny?"

"Of course, of course. An elephant has tiny eyes, but it can pick a needle off the ground."

"Can it, can it really? Tell us the story of the Elephant and the Needle, Granny."

When she walked, her back a broken spring bent to the ground, they laughed.

"What are you looking for, Granny?"

"Looking at the ground into which I must go one day to look for the treasure that is buried there."

"Tell us of the buried treasure, Granny. Tell us a story."

That was their invisible bond, the common language they talked in their own private world. The daughter and sons, the granddaughters and grandsons stood outside it, deaf to its sounds, wrapped in their impatience and hostility, grudging dutiful affection to a parasitic old woman whom time refused to drop into releasing oblivion.

The visible bond between the old woman and the children was the doll's house. They loved it with the same passion. The children hung coloured glass globes in the tiny arches, dug twigs and grass into its small courtyard. Their gaily dressed rag dolls were propped on string beds under the thatch. She cleaned its mud walls with wet clay, her fingers following each curve and crevice with familiar affection. Their interest in it flamed high and burned low, but hers was as steady as her hold on life.

"Tell us a story, Granny."

She dipped into the deep well of her memories. She had no need to stretch in her effortless reaching to draw its constant treasure. The live past was always happily with her, the present an irritating dying burden.

75

The fly that sat on her nose a moment before was as forgotten as the reflex brushing it away, but her nose still twitched with the itching of the one that had sat on it seventy years ago.

Her mother said, "Don't sit there making such faces. The wind will blow on you and set your face forever in that grimace. Kill the fly with your fan, can't you?"

Her mind telescoped life to make it possible for her weak old age to be sustained by the strength of her childhood. She was happy with the children, because she lived in their time.

The youngest one screwed up her face. "Granny, look at me, listen to me. I can whistle."

"Don't do that or the cold wind will blow on you and set your face in that grimace. Don't whistle or the soldiers will get you."

"Soldiers? Which soldiers?"

"The red faced ones, like monkeys in red coats. They whistle to bad women. No village woman is safe when they pass by." Her aged body felt the fear of young girls when old women whispered,

"No woman is safe, no girl is safe."

"Oh, Granny," laughed the children. "How funny you are. The soldiers don't wear red coats, their clothes are dirty. And there are black faced monkeys too. And they did not hurt us. They laughed and threw us sweets from their lorries."

"Don't eat their impure poison," she scolded. Then past memories lashed her present security. "Why," she quavered, "Why did the soldiers come to the village?"

The children did not know, their elders did not care to tell. They could not find time from their own fears to reason why violence had changed its face, why they feared the departure of the soldiers as once she had feared their arrival.

The soldiers had driven into dust clouds that billowed thick over the fields, thinning into an emptiness over distances that held a threat.

She did not feel it nor did the children, but the others lived heavily under its weight. The familiar stillness of their surroundings was an accomplice to their solace seeking minds, as to hers. It could not come to them from out of known distances, to this village, these huts, themselves – the bestiality that was real only to their fear. The village lived uneasily, the breath of its life quickened or caught when some outsider brought chill confirmation. Only Old Granny, who had survived the threats of too many years, refused to believe in its finality.

When the dread moment was upon them, shorn of their disguising hopes, they remembered only the urgency of their frenzied need to escape. Terror silenced the women's wails, tore their thoughts from possessions left behind. It smothered the children's whimpering, and drove all words from men's tongues but, "Hurry, Hurry."

She refused to go with them. Her mind in its pendulum swing, moving from their infecting fear to incredulity that neighbours should turn murderers, rested always at one point. "I am old, I am feeble. I shall slow your flight. It is the children you must save. Besides," she added, drawing conviction from her years, "You will return. In the Mutiny we returned, and our fears were more cruel than reality. Take care of yourselves, give my blessings to everyone in the casbah. It is long since I went there, not since the wedding of ..."

She sat on the string bed, and looked at the door until the curtain had ceased to move before the creaking door, now silent. Soon the outside air was stilled of all woeful noises. She looked around the disordered house, its beloved familiarity ebbing away. Near the doll's house sprawled a rag doll. She shuffled to it and propped it carefully in its proper place. Then she waited in silence, and suddenly whimpered like a lost child until she slept.

The creaking of the door woke her. She could not see who came, how many. She smelt the flaming thatch, and as shadows came nearer across the courtyard, she tried to sit up.

"Mind," she scolded, pointing her bony finger, "Mind you do not step on the doll's house."

"Phoenix Fled" was first published in Attia Hosain, *Phoenix Fled and Other Stories* (London: Chatto and Windus, 1953).

Joginder Paul
THIRST OF RIVERS

TRANSLATED BY ATANU BHATTACHARYA

Bebe is sitting on a cot outside the new house of her only son – alone and absorbed in her thoughts. The wrinkles on her face, burdened and heavy from the course of events, seem to have slid off and embedded themselves into the gnarled wood of the charpoy legs, so much so that one can imagine the age old wood now completely in the clutches of her wrinkles, at the brink of being crushed by them and about to give way.

Bebe raises her head and gazes in front of her, but fails to see anything. She is not quite blind for she can still marshal her blurred vision. But what can one do when a veil of the past perpetually hangs over one's eyes. The ancestral haveli, the doors of scores of rooms that open in a continuous succession, and, and ... Bebe gives a small smile and instantly the edges of her tight wrinkles return to her face from the legs of the cot. She is now mirrored, fully, in her own face. And – her husband frantically searches for her in each of the rooms, and she suddenly bursts out laughing in this room. And her husband, pursuing the tinkle of silver laughter, reaches her and encompasses her tightly in his arms ...

The contours of the haveli are fully etched on Bebe's face, and her laughter ripples through from one room to another ... and ... the creaking cot tries to remind her – Bebe! Think of your age, Bebe. Everyone calls you a lunatic already. But how can Bebe listen to the cot, when she is not herself at the moment?

I was worried that you had lost your way.

I would have been in one of these rooms, even if I were lost. Laughingly she tells her husband.

I will be here, in one of these rooms, even after my death. If you don't find me in one of the open rooms, then the bunch of keys to the haveli are fastened to my pallu. Perhaps, I might fall asleep in one of the locked rooms, as I wait for you to return.

Bebe restlessly spreads her legs on the cot, and pulling her dupatta over her breasts, takes a bulky bunch of keys in her hand. The iron of the keys had grown rounded and fleshy from the weight of the soft abrasion of her fingers for the last fifty years. She can see her soul peering out, in the shape of each key.

This is the key to the kitchen. I've told you a thousand times to come back home before mealtime. But who pays heed to me? ... Is it you? Please wait! Coming ... co-o-ming.

And this key – my Munna studies in this room. Look. The lantern is glowing above his head and your Munna is fast asleep with the book held in his hands.

You unnecessarily reprimand him, perhaps he is studying in his dreams.

No, Bebe. I am the father of a child now, and you still treat me as your Munna. Call me by my name.

When I address you by your name, I feel that rather than my own son, I am calling my bahu's husband.

Then consider me your bahu's husband, and please call me by my name. How can I remain your Munna all my life, Bebe?

Bebe's tremulous fingertips move away from her Munna's reading room key and caress that of her husband's study room.

Come in, Munna's Bebe. Come in. Why have you stopped? Hai! Why are you crying?

The pain is that you are gone forever. Had it been me, I would have looked after you even when dead.

Bebe begins to sob uncontrollably. But for the tears, her shrivelled-up face would not have betrayed her sobs. This key has leapt to her fingers of its own volition, and the door of the room stands ajar. People are carrying out the body of her husband – No! No! Do not take him away! I have lived my entire life in this haveli. I am a stranger to the roads outside. Do not take him away. Do not take him away. Where will I look for him?

People are whispering in hushed voices that Bebe has gone mad.

Yes, I have gone mad. Please let me go mad, otherwise I'll really go mad.

The monsoon has set in in Bebe's eyes, but outside it is parched. Beyond the lawn, in front of the veranda, one tree whispers to another, Look! The hag's tears are drenching the stone floor to no avail. Yes, if it were to rain like that on the soil around us, our thirst would be quenched.

It is as if Bebe, clutching the bunch of keys in her hand, has clasped the old haveli close to her heart.

Bebe is crying in front of her dying husband, her dupatta stuffed inside her mouth to smother her sobs. Don't cry, pagli. I have very little time.

Don't cry. Listen. Stay in this haveli till the end. I will advise Munna to stay here after he passes his law exams. Get him married with all pomp and glory. We have been living in this haveli for generations, and on all occasions of marriage and death, our ancestors have assembled here. I too had witnessed them on my marriage. Among them was my late father – looking just the same. The rest were there too. Are you listening to me? If you stay here, then wherever I may be, I'll be with you. Don't leave this haveli under any circumstance – or we'll be separated. Look, all of them are coming – my father – my grandfather – his father ... Each one of them.

Bebe has really gone crazy. The poor woman is not even sure whether she is still living in the haveli or whether it has been years since she left it and arrived here. The old days are still imprinted faithfully in her mind. They have locked the haveli and are standing outside. Her dead husband and father-in-law, and generations of in-laws, have come to the door to bid them farewell. Her husband's spirit has stepped forward and is patting her shoulders reassuringly. Go, Munna's Bebe! Conditions here have deteriorated so much that it has become necessary for you to leave. Otherwise, these people will spill your blood. No, don't worry about my blood. How can it be spilled when it doesn't exist? But as soon as things get better, come back. Keep the front door locked. We will while away our time somehow, waiting for you to return.

No! It was you, who advised me not to step out of this house. Now it is you who is turning me out.

No, Munna's Bebe! God forbid, if someone murders you, I will have to pursue him even in naraka. And then, I will be unable to return.

No!

Munna's Bebe, leave immediately. No matter where you go, you will return to me. Go, wherever you can – go – or we will be parted forever.

The motherland has delivered a bundle of pain from her womb. And after giving birth to two blood soaked twins, has breathed her last. The Day of Judgement has come – Arre! Why doesn't someone clean these orphans? Put some warm clothes on them? Think of something for them to eat. Where will they rest? But when crisis hovers over our heads, who is ready to listen?

Crowds surge upon other crowds. The exhibition of each dismembered limb has become so commonplace, that only the spectral imagination of a past surfaces from the entire existence of mankind. It is during such days that these two old ghosts – one of a living woman and the other of a dead husband – take leave of each other. Bebe, touching the bunch of keys tied to her pallu, has turned her back to the haveli. She can see clearly. Don't be afraid, Munna's Bebe. You are leaving so you can return again.

Let's go, Bebe, her young lawyer son has extended his hand to help her.

No! No! Bebe pulls her hand back. All my mornings are here ... in this haveli ... She rushes back to the doors of the haveli. And the key sinks in the keyhole and opens the lock – No, Munna's Bebe. Her late husband is still standing at the door, Go!

I won't!

No! Go!

All of a sudden, crazy Bebe falls silent. She follows her son as if she has no inkling where she is headed. With faltering steps, she commences on a journey inside her shrivelled-up nerves. But no matter where she is, she remains here ... right here, in this haveli. Outside the haveli, gunpowder has been laid down in every direction. Fires flare up in succession – deafening explosions can be heard. But how tranquil, secure and alive it is inside the haveli.

Bebe's power of speech has returned. Didn't I tell you, Munna's Bebe? Wherever you go, you'll eventually return here?

Yes, go and take some rest. I have to warm the milk for Munna. He is due to return from the courts anytime.

Bebe, Bebe! How can I explain it to you? If you go on like this, I'll go mad as well.

It's for your foes to go mad, Munna. Am I not here to go mad?

You are, Bebe. How can I convince you that we have left our haveli, village, and country across the border. We've left them several years ago. But you still dwell there.

Where else will I live now, Munna? You settle down anywhere you like, live and laugh, but I have only my ancestral haveli.

Bebe gently caresses the bunch of keys with her fingertips.

Even a lunatic is not as mad as you, Bebe. You still roam with the bunch of the haveli keys fastened to your pallu.

Here. Drink some milk, Munna.

What is the use of drinking milk, Bebe? I often resolve to try each one of your keys and somehow unlock you ... Are you aware that no girl is willing to marry me because of your madness?

Aji, are you listening? Come out of your room. Look, our Munna has brought his bride. What kind of a father are you? Can't you hear the shehnai playing in your haveli? Not even the dead are so deaf. Come on now, come outside. Come Bahu, let me escort you to your sasur. The poor man died hoping to see his son complete his law studies, waiting to see his bride. Come, Bahu! He must be sitting in that room engrossed in his business papers. He will be delighted to see you. He will forget all about his work. Come, Bahu! ... Bahu! Bahu! ... You should spend some time with me. I long for you to talk to me.

How can one speak to a crazy person, Bebe?

No, Munna! I'm not mad.

I'm not Munna. Call me by my proper name.

What is your proper name, Munna? Aji, are you listening? What is our Munna's proper name? Bahu, you have conceived. Stop going to work now.

If I stop working, how will we sustain ourselves, Bebe?

Why are you so anxious about sustenance, Bahu? Our haveli is stacked with grain. Come, let me unlock the rooms and show you.

Bebe ... Bebe! You'll make everybody mad in this house. If not me, at least spare your Bahu.

Who dares equal my Bahu? Aji, are your listening? Look, our Bahu has given birth to our grandson. Look, his forehead looks exactly like our Munna's – even his chin is like our Munna's. Aji, are you listening? What kind of a grandfather are you? You never venture out of your room. Look, who has come to the haveli ...

Don't create a ruckus, Bebe. Let your Bahu rest.

Munna, I was just –

I've told you umpteen times that I'm not Munna.

If you aren't Munna, whose Ma am I?

The way you keep pestering us with your craziness, I've started doubting whether you are my real mother.

Aji, are you listening? Come out of your death chamber and listen to what Munna is saying!

Bebe, lying on the cot in the veranda of her son's new house, is tossing and turning restlessly. The cot creaks and speaks to her, go to sleep, Bebe. Why don't you go to sleep in peace?

Yes, maybe now I should go to sleep. Bebe shuts her eyes, and thinks about her son, Bahu and grandson, who have been out for a long time now. They should be back anytime. Coming back ... Yes!

Bebe! Bebe! Arre, look – Bebe ... Bebe ... Be-be! Her Munna has started crying and her Bahu and her young grandson ...

No, Nanhe don't cry. Bebe snaps open her eyes and extends her arms towards him – but – perceiving no one there, she shuts them again. She envelops herself in an impalpable sensation akin to death; the lunatic begins to believe in her own madness. How can one die by merely closing one's eyes?

Water!

The walls of the veranda retort – If you are thirsty, make the necessary effort, Bebe. What can we do?

Bebe lifts herself up from the cot with some difficulty. She tries to pick up the jug kept on the table nearby, with trembling hands. The empty jug slips from her fingers, and falls to the floor, noisily – like her cantankerous son.

She retreats to her cot, scared all of a sudden. Look Bebe, look at what we have brought for you.

What is it, Nanhe? She has turned quickly, hearing her grandson's voice.

But there is no one there.

Her thirst has increased.

With dry eyes she starts scrutinizing the lock, put up on the front door by her son and wife, that leads to the interior of the house from the outside veranda.

See, his forehead looks exactly like our Munna's. See, even the chin is similar ... Aji, are you listening?

Yes, I am, Munna's Bebe. But who are you talking about? He is our own Munna.

Arre, of course. He really is our Munna.

Come inside, Munna's Bebe. Why are you sitting outside? But come with your face covered with the ghunghat – your sasur is coming this way. No, wait. He has passed – Arre, come in, unlock the door and walk in – come, have a drink of water and give me some too – come.

Who knows from where such energy has come into Bebe? She swiftly moves across to the door that leads inside the house, and tries all the keys of the haveli on the lock, in quick succession. The lock, however, refuses to open.

"Dariyaon Pyas" was first written in Urdu and published in a collection of short stories by Joginder Paul, *Bay Muhavara* (Aurangabad: Kailash Publications, 1978).

Sa'adat Hasan Manto
PANDIT MANTO'S FIRST LETTER TO PANDIT NEHRU

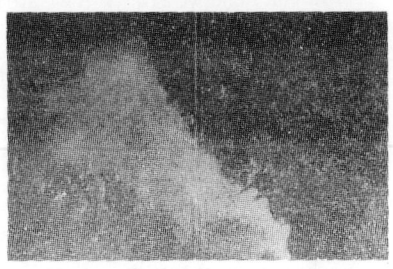

TRANSLATED BY M ASADUDDIN

Panditji, assalamu alaikum!
This is the first letter that I am sending you. By the grace of God, you are considered very handsome by the Americans. Well, my features are not exactly bad either. If I go to America, perhaps I will be accorded the same status. But you are the Prime Minister of India, and I am the famed storywriter of Pakistan. Quite a deep gulf separates us. However, what is common between us is, that we are both Kashmiris. You are a Nehru, I am a Manto. To be a Kashmiri is to be handsome, and to be handsome ... I don't know.

I have a long cherished desire to meet you. (We might yet meet during our lifetime). The older people from my side often meet those from yours. But so far I have not had any opportunity to meet you. What a great pity that I have not even seen you. Of course, I have once heard you on the radio.

As I said, I have long harboured this desire to meet you. Being Kashmiris, we have a common bond. But now I wonder if there is any need for it. One Kashmiri does run into another in by-lanes, or at crossroads.

You settled on the bank of a nahr, a river, and came to be known as Nehru. I ponder how I became a Manto. You may have visited Kashmir a million times. I could just go up to Banihal. My Kashmiri friends who know the Kashmiri language tell me that Manto means "munt," that is, a measuring stone weighing one and a half ser! I am sure you know Kashmiri. If you take the trouble to write a reply to this letter, do write to me about the origin of the word "manto."

If I am just one and a half ser, then there cannot be any comparison between us. You are the whole stream while I am just one and a half ser! How can I take you on? But we are both the kind of guns that ... as the well known proverb about Kashmiris goes ... "Take a shot in the dark." Please do not take it amiss. When I heard this so-called proverb, I felt terrible. But I mention it light heartedly, because it sounds interesting. Otherwise, we both know that we Kashmiris have never accepted defeat in any field.

In politics, I can mention your name with pride, because you know well the art of contradicting yourself. To this very day, who could beat us Kashmiris in wrestling? Who can outshine us in poetry? But I was surprised to learn that you want to stop the rivers from flowing through our land. Panditji, you are only a Nehru. I regret that I am just a measuring stone weighing one and a half ser. If I were a rock of thirty or forty thousand maunds, I would have thrown myself into the river, so that you would have to spend some time consulting with your engineers on how to pull it out.

Panditji, there is no doubt that you are a great personality. You are the Prime Minister of India. You are the ruler of the country that was formerly mine. You are everything. But pardon me for saying that you have never cared for this humble one.

I would like to tell you an interesting anecdote. Whenever my late father – who was, obviously, a Kashmiri – ran into a hato, he would bring him home, seat him in the lobby, and treat him to some Kashmiri salty tea and kulchas. Then he would tell the hato proudly, "I'm also a koshar." Panditji, you are a koshar too. By God, if you want my life, it is yours for the asking. I know and believe that you have clung to Kashmir because, being a Kashmiri, you feel a sort of magnetic love for that land. Every Kashmiri, even if he has not seen Kashmir, should feel this way.

As I already mentioned, I have only been up to Banihal. I have seen places like Kud, Bataut and Kashtwar. I have seen their poverty along with their beauty. If you have removed this poverty, then keep Kashmir to yourself. But I am sure you cannot do it, despite being a Kashmiri, because you have no time.

Between us Pandit brothers, do this – call me back to India. First I will help myself to shaljam shabdegh at your place, and then take over the responsibility for Kashmiri affairs. The Bakshis and the rest of them deserve to be sacked right away. Cheats of the first order! You have no reason to bestow such honours on them. Is this because it suits you? But why at all ...? I know you are a politician, which I am not. But that does not mean I do not understand anything.

---

hato: a derogatory term for a daily labourer who carries goods in the hilly areas. It is an usage that has currency mainly in Kashmir.
koshar: a colloquial term for Kashmiris.
shaljam shabdegh: turnip and meat preparation cooked overnight in a wok.
Bakshi: reference to Ghulam Muhammad Bakshi, then Chief Minister of Jammu & Kashmir.

The country was partitioned. Radcliffe employed Patel to do the dirty work. You have illegally occupied Junagarh, which a Kashmiri could do only under the influence of a Maratha. I mean Patel. (God forgive him!).

You are a writer in English. Over here, I write short stories in Urdu, a language that is being wiped out in your country. Panditji, I often read your statements that indicate you hold Urdu dear. I heard one of your speeches on the radio at the time the country was divided. Everyone admired your English. But when you broke into so-called Urdu, it seemed as though some rabid Hindu Mahasabha member had translated your English speech, which was obviously not to your liking. You were stumbling over every sentence. I cannot imagine how you agreed to read it aloud.

It was the time when Radcliffe had turned India into two slices of a single loaf of bread. It is regrettable that they have not been toasted yet. You are toasting it from that side and we, from this. But the flames in our braziers are coming from outside.

Panditji, this is the season for baggugoshas. What injustice that you have given Bakshi all the rights over them, and he does not send me even a few as a gift! Well, let the gift go to hell, babbogoshas too ... No, on second thoughts, let them be. Actually, I wanted to ask you, why you don't read my books? If you have read them, I am sorry to say that there was no appreciation for them. However, it is more regrettable if you have not read them at all, because you are a writer yourself.

I have one more grievance against you. You are stopping water from flowing into our rivers, and taking a cue from you, publishers in your capital are hurriedly publishing my books without my permission. Is this proper? I thought that no such unseemly act could be perpetrated under your regime. You can find out right away how many publishers in Delhi, Lucknow, and Jalandhar have pirated my books.

Several lawsuits have already been filed against me on charges of obscenity. But look at the injustice of things, that in Delhi, right under your nose, a publisher brings out the collection of my stories and calls it *The Obscene Stories of Manto*. I wrote the book *Ganje Farishte*. An Indian

---

baggugosha: a pear like fruit.
Ganje Farishte: literally, "bald angels."

publisher has published it as *Behind the Curtains* ... Now tell me, what should I do?

I have written a new book. This letter addressed to you is the preface to it. If this book is pirated too, then by God, I'll reach Delhi some day, catch you by the throat and will not let go ... I will latch on to you and make your life hell. Every morning you will have to treat me to salty tea along with a kulcha. Shaljam shabdegh, in any case, will have to be there every week.

As soon as the book is out, I will send you a copy. I hope you will acknowledge receipt of it, and let me know your opinion of it.

You may get the scent of burnt meat in this letter of mine. You know there was a poet in our Kashmir, Ghani, who was well known as "Ghani Kashmiri." A poet from Iran had come to visit him. The doors of his house were always open. He used to say, "What is there in my house that I should keep the doors locked? Well, I keep the doors closed when I am inside the house because I am its only asset." The poet from Iran left his poetry notebook in the vacant house. One couplet in that notebook was incomplete. He had composed the second line, but could not do the first one. The second line ran thus: "The smell of kebab is wafting from your clothes." When the Iranian poet returned and looked in his notebook, he found the first line written there, "Has the hand of a blighted soul touched your daaman?"

Panditji, I am also a blighted soul. I've taken issue with you, because I am dedicating this book to you.

Sa'adat Hasan Manto   27 August 1954

"Dibacha" was first published as a Foreword to Sa'adat Hasan Manto's novelette, *Beghair Unwaan ke* (Lahore: Maktaba Jadeed, 1954).

CRITICAL COMMENTARIES

Essays by

RAVIKANT AND TARUN K SAINT

STUTI KHANNA

ANURADHA MARWAH ROY

M ASADUDDIN

"THE DOG OF TETWAL" IN CONTEXT: THE NATION AND ITS VICTIMS

RAVIKANT AND TARUN K SAINT

"Tetwal ka Kutta" (The Dog of Tetwal)[1] is a remarkable, though often neglected story by Manto. At one level, it describes the tragic end of its protagonist, a stray dog caught in the crossfire between Indian and Pakistani troops. At another, allegorical level, it is a poignant statement about the fatal dangers of human indecisiveness and ambivalence in the war like situation that the Partition had created when national boundaries became sacrosanct, and crossing them involved serious risks.

The post-Partition reorganization was a task of immense magnitude, because apart from the displacement of millions of people on account of the demarcation of boundaries in terms of religious identity, the administrative and military wings had to be regrouped, and the resources of the state redistributed. New administrative structures and military dispensations had to be created, while the existing structures had to be fairly apportioned. This process was speeded up with the preponing of the date of transfer of power. Considerable acrimony and resentment resulted from the subsequent haggling and negotiations.

Troops that were formerly comrades-in-arms now belonged to different national armies, and religious denomination became the key factor for soldiers while exercising the choice to belong to a specific army. This excruciating dilemma is powerfully dramatized in Manto's story "Aakhri Salute,"[2] written a few years after the first Indo-Pak War:

> Earlier they fought an enemy together whom, on account of subsistence, and wealth and honours, they had come to believe was the enemy. Now they themselves were split in two parts. Once they were all Hindustani soldiers: now one was a Pakistani soldier, and the other, a Hindustani soldier. There were Muslim soldiers in the Hindustani army as well. When Rab Nawaz considered this, a strange confusion arose in his mind. And when he reflected upon Kashmir, his mind would give up entirely. Are the Pakistani soldiers fighting for Kashmir, or for the Muslims of Kashmir? If they are fighting for the Muslims of Kashmir, why are they not asked to fight on behalf of the Muslims of Hyderabad and Junagarh? Or, if this war is a strictly Islamic war, then why aren't the Muslims of the rest of the countries in the world taking part? After much introspection, Rab Nawaz came to the conclusion that a soldier should certainly not dwell on such nuances. A soldier should be a numskull, for numskulls make the best soldiers. However, sometimes he was given to secretly cogitating upon such matters and later he would laugh at his own audacity.[3] (Our translation)

The tensions of the period spilled over into actual warfare, as Kashmir became both the battleground and the bone of contention. Initially, Maharaja Hari Singh, the then ruler of the princely state of Kashmir, vacillated, perhaps hoping that Kashmir would be given independence. Meanwhile, Sheikh Abdullah, the founder of the National Conference, was placed under detention for opposing Maharaja Hari Singh's rule. Eventually, however, under Sheikh Abdullah, the will of the National Conference prevailed, and the state of Kashmir acceded to India with certain constitutional safeguards. Jinnah, who according to some versions, had offered a blank cheque to the Maharaja to join Pakistan, was not happy with this turn of events. When the hill tribesmen began making incursions into the Indian side of the Kashmir Valley in 1948, the situation was considered grave enough for Indian troops to be airlifted into the Valley. This led to the first war between the two new born nations, as Pakistani troops managed to occupy what is now Pakistan Occupied Kashmir. Cessation of hostilities took place with the intervention of the United Nations and diplomatic negotiations between the leaders. A cease-fire was declared.[4]

However, in the remote mountainous region where the battle lines were still drawn, an uneasy truce prevailed, and skirmishes still occurred. This would erupt into full-fledged warfare again in 1965, 1971 and 1999 in the form of the Kargil conflict. But even in times of "peace" lives were lost on either side of the border as the troops entrenched themselves in their positions, or sought to improve their line of fire by capturing advantageous terrain.

"The Dog of Tetwal" is set during a period of cease-fire, but could be a story about adversaries locked in a series of skirmishes anywhere in the world. Nevertheless, the story needs to be first understood in its specific context. The description of locales places the story in a geographical area called Tetwal, now in Pakistan. The ironic contrast depicted initially between the seemingly peaceful surroundings on one hand, and the entrenched positions of the opposed army units on the other, sets the tone for the story. The soldiers on both sides live in similar conditions, share the same Punjabi cultural background, speak and behave in an identical military manner, and suffer from the ennui of an uneventful life on the battle front. An undercurrent of difference, however, always runs through their consciousness, finding articulation in the dichotomous "us" and "them," "we" and "the enemy," "this side" and "that side," "Sikh" and "Musalman," and "Hindustan" and "Pakistan."

The allusions to popular songs and the famous rōmance by Waris Shah lend a sense of commonality to the soldiers. Waris Shah composed his version of the Heer Ranjha legend around 1766, though the events depicted relate to the first half of the fifteenth century. This qissa relates the story of Dhido Ranjha, who belonged to a family of Muslim Jats in Takhat Hazaraa. After being dispossessed of his share in the family property, he went to work as a cowherd in the Rajput family converted to Islam, to which Heer Sayal belonged. The tragic story of their unrequited love formed the basis of Waris Shah's elaborate romance, which contributed mystical as well as sensuous elements to the original tale. This narrative poem, composed by a high born Saiyyad of Sufi inclinations, became part of the common corpus of popular Punjabi culture, equally beloved of Hindus, Sikhs and Muslims.[5]

The loneliness and boredom of existence at the front leads Banta Singh to sing the story as a means of solace, a rather incongruous invocation. It is at this point that the dog, a figure of innocence, a free spirit hunting for a stray morsel in these remote parts, makes an appearance on the scene. The Sikh soldiers show immense curiosity in the dog's antecedents; then, in a half playful manner, seek to affix an identity and claim him for their own.

The sardonic remark, "Now even the dogs will have to be either Hindustani or Pakistani," testifies to the absolutization of difference; the logic of national boundaries seems to extend even to the creatures of the animal kingdom. The dog is explicitly described as a refugee, its vagabond status reminiscent of the many refugees wandering about, looking for shelter and food. The poignancy of this exchange is sharpened by our sense of the context in which such black humour becomes possible. The reader can make inferences on the reality of widespread suffering on account of displacement, as personified in the figure of the dog. The soldiers project their own anxiety about belonging and identity, manifesting almost pathological symptoms as they inflict pain upon the helpless dog, which seems to refuse the symbolic weight placed upon its shoulders. Through the use of trenchant irony, Manto makes telling points about the ideology of the Nation-state and its potentially totalizing effects. For, with the advent of visas and passports, free movement across borders is not so easy; citizenship is both a privilege and a limitation. The satirical thrust is deepened, and reiterated in the description of the other side's response to the tag affixed on the dog's neck. Since Nation-states cannot do without fixing identities, the ultimate extension of this logic can be war. Emotions like anger and an unthinking aggression can be thus directed, so as to sustain the tired rhetoric of nationalism.[6]

The Pakistani side, in turn, replaces the tag affixed by the Indians

97

with their own, thus granting the dog a new identity. The absurdity of this mirrored act is captured in the rhyming names bestowed on the dog —"Chapad Jhunjhun" and "Sapar Sunsun," even as the bewildered dog shuttles between the opposed military camps. However, loyalties must be unambiguously declared; not to do so can be a risky business.

In his ironic piece "Pandit Manto's First Letter to Pandit Nehru," Manto wrote:

> Panditji, there is no doubt that you are a great personality. You are the Prime Minister of India. You are the ruler of the country which was formerly mine; you are everything. But pardon me if I say that you have never cared for this humble person (who is also a Kashmiri) ... Between us Pandit brothers, do this: call me back to India ...[7]

Manto retained a strong attachment to the land of his birth, though he may not seriously have considered returning as did Qurratulain Hyder and Josh Malihabadi.

At the story's end, the dog is sent on a mission; its new identity is meant to be a lesson to the "Sikhras" in the Indian camp. The dog, trapped in no-man's land in the crossfire, runs helter-skelter in a state of panic before being shot and killed. The dog thus acquires martyrdom for Himmat Khan's Pakistani cause, or meets poetic justice in the proverbial "dog's death" in Harnam Singh's contemptuous, but telling phrase.

The dog's situation, thus, embodies the dilemma of all people who faced such a closure of choices because of the Partition. There could be no more room for uncertainty, and their allegiance had to be demonstrably firm and unalloyed. Through the refraction of his own experience as well as the general experience of liminality, Manto achieves a searing critique of the oppressive structures that came into being with the division of the subcontinent.

The story operates at several levels, allegorizing the predicament of the uprooted and exiled people, and also commenting on the resultant dehumanization of war as mutual hatreds became irreconcilable. Aijaz Ahmed has pointed out in his criticism of Frederic Jameson, the fallacy of attempts to categorize all Third World narratives as national allegories.[8] Manto's narrative bears this out; the vantage point is not that of nationalism, but of its victims. The accompanying militarization of consciousness is brilliantly dissected in an analysis that is prophetic in nature. Neither side is spared as Manto represents the breakdown of trust, the atmosphere of suspicion and paranoia, the hostility and rigidity of thought that percolates down even to the common man.

As translators, we were dissatisfied with the earlier translations of this story, and faced an obvious problem: neither of us reads Urdu. We thus worked with the Devnagari transcription. Furthermore, the passages from "Heer" in the original were virtually untranslatable, carrying with them specific allusions and associations. In this brief note we will refer to some of the difficulties in finding cultural equivalents. For example, the description of nature and landscape with which the story opens, sets a particular tone of langour and ennui. Take for example the sentence,

"Hawa mein phoolon ki mahak nahin thee jaise ki rat ko unhone apne itradan band kar liye hon, albatta chir ke paseene, yani biroze ki bhi bu thee magar yeh bhi kucch aisi nagavar nahin thi."[9]

Manto uses an extended simile here, drawing upon local knowledge of flora and fauna. The imagery of the closed case of perfume to connote flowers which cease to exude scent at night even while the pines emit their resinous odour, conveys atmosphere and local topography. We have chosen to be fairly literal, preferring accuracy in such cases. However, an altogether different problem arose in the case of the Punjabi songs, in particular, "Heer." The verses from Waris Shah's romance are oblique and suggestive, and share both romantic and mystical grounding. For instance, the allusion to the one who has left, never to return, is an image both of a lover as well as a dead person. In the mystic sense there is an emphasis on inward attainment, the intimacy of the self's encounter with truth. Ranjha is the divine beloved, and Heer the lover who seeks him. The quest is for a final unity of the self and the Ultimate, the seeker and the sought, the lover and the beloved:

> *Heer herself at last became Ranjha.*
> *Rare is the man who realizes this.*[10]

This ultimate truth is a transcendental one, and the imagery used to describe its attainment is often very colourful, and drawn from the natural surroundings. Our own paraphrase merely hints at the multiplicity of layers of meaning in the Punjabi original that is sung unto this day. The well-known passages sung by Banta Singh appear in the section of the "Heer" narrative when Heer, having been forcibly married against her will to the crow-like husband, meets Ranjha (the falcon lover), who dons the garb of a fakir and comes seeking alms at her doorstep. The pathos of separation and unrequited love, and the beauty and necessity of self-sacrifice is condensed in these lines. In the last few lines recited, there is a reference to Waris Shah's decision to renounce his status as a high born Saiyyad and become a poet in the mystical tradition, donning the "garb of sorrow."

The elliptical quality of the allegorical exchange between Heer and Ranjha, at a time when there seems little hope of union, and the gentle melancholy and acceptance of the need for renunciation, puts into sharp relief the grim reality of staccato commands being issued and obeyed in the military hierarchy. The above imagery recurs in the phrase,

"Aisa maloom hota tha ki khakistari pahariyon ne bhi udasiyan pahan li hain."[11]

For "khakistari" or "matiyali," our translation was "soil-tinted." "Earthy" did not suit the purpose, and in our translation it reads as:

"It appeared as if the soil-tinted mountains too had taken on a mantle of grief."

As Waris Shah wrote elsewhere:

> *Love is a sickness full of woes,*
> *All remedies refusing.*[12]

Such philosophical insights come to the soldiers through their common heritage, and are recollected in this time of boredom and loneliness. However, it is as if the verses of Waris Shah are drained of significance and value in the context in which they are being recited. Though "Heer" might provide solace for a while, such a rendition can only seem grotesque, given the overarching reality of war, even as the two Nation-states flex their newly acquired military might. Manto's unsparing honesty and psychological insight is borne out here. He himself loved the folk culture of Punjab, and planned to compile the songs of the region, a task that remained incomplete.[13]

In other instances, it was difficult to convey the colloquial humour of the dialogue between soldiers: "Oye anpadh, tere saath to bat karna pichanave ka ghata hai"[14] becomes "Oye, ill-read lout, there is no gain talking to you." Such a flattening out of cultural idiom was inevitable, as trying to make soldiers speak in the Cockney dialect would have seemed ludicrous. These exchanges add an element of comic relief.

It is ironical that the Devnagari transcription by Menra and Dutt, which was the basis of our own translation, should omit a reference to the script in which the message on the cardboard piece was written. Subedar Himmat Khan notes with derision that the statement, "This is a Hindustani dog" is written in Gurmukhi (the Punjabi script) and asks Bashir to write his reply in the same "keera makoras" (literally worms/ insects) in Manto's original. The elision of this reference to the long-standing politics of language and identity in the Punjab, which can be traced back to the nineteenth century, is quite inexplicable.[15]

This is a reminder of the need to cross-check every version of Manto with the original, or else the text may lose much of its radicality.[16] The humour and scorn implicit in the original usage, through which a boundary premised on the absolute identification of language and community[17] is drawn, was difficult to capture in translation. Yet an element of this must be retained in order for us to grasp the brilliance of Manto's critique of the processes that led to language itself becoming a casualty, as nationalist jingoism prevailed.

Manto's primary focus, though, is on the human tragedy of the Partition, which comes alive in the depiction of the bleak antagonism and absurd situations that the war brought about in its aftermath. He voices through his tales the infinite suffering of the dislocated and the dispossessed, the victims of the nation.

Notes

1   Balraj Menra and Sharad Dutt, eds., *Sa'adat Hasan Manto: Dastavez*, vol. 2 (New Delhi: Rajkamal, 1993) 226-33. Jagdish Chander Wadhawan, *Mantonama: The Life of Sa'adat Hasan Manto*, trans. Jai Ratan (New Delhi: Roli Books, 1998).

2   Menra and Dutt, eds., *Sa'adat Hasan Manto: Dastavez*, vol. 2, pp. 234-42.

3   Menra and Dutt, eds., *Sa'adat Hasan Manto: Dastavez*, vol. 2, p. 235.

4   Ajit Bhattacharjea, *Countdown to Partition: The Final Days* (New Delhi: HarperCollins, 1997) 42-43, 71-72, 87-93.

5   R K Kuldip, *Waris Shah, 1730-1790: A Critical Appreciation of the Poet and his Only Heer* (Calcutta: Inter Trade Publications, 1971). Also Gurcharan Singh, *Waris Shah* (New Delhi: Sahitya Akademi, 1998).

6   B Anderson, *Imagined Communities: Reflections on the Origin and Spread of Nationalism*, 2nd ed. (London: Verso, 1983) 1991.

7   Abdul Bismillah, "A Reading of Pandit Manto's Letter to Pandit Nehru" in Alok Bhalla, ed., *Life and Works of Sa'dat Hasan Manto* (Shimla: IIAS, 1997) 178.

8   Aijaz Ahmad cogently refutes Jameson's argument that in the moment of decolonization, Third World writers necessarily produce "national" allegories. See his "Jameson's Rhetoric of Togetherness and the 'National Allegory'" in *In Theory: Classes, Nations, Literatures* (London: Verso, 1992) 95-123.

9   Menra and Dutt, eds., *Sa'adat Hasan Manto: Dastavez*, vol. 2, p. 227.

10 R K Kuldip, Cited in "Foreword" by E T Lombardozzi, vi, in *Waris Shah 1730-1790: A Critical Appreciation of the Poet and his Only Heer* (Calcutta: Inter Trade Publications, 1971).

11 Menra and Dutt, eds., *Sa'adat Hasan Manto: Dastavez*, vol. 2, p. 228.

12 Cited in R K Kuldip, *Waris Shah 1730-1790: A Critical Appreciation of the Poet and his Only Heer* (Calcutta: Inter Trade Publications, 1971) 15.

13 Jagdish Chander Wadhawan, *Mantonama: The Life of Sa'adat Hasan Manto*, trans. Jai Ratan (New Delhi: Roli Books, 1999) 136-39.

14 Menra and Dutt, eds., *Sa'adat Hasan Manto: Dastavez*, vol.1, p. 231.

15 For a detailed analysis of this phenomenon, see A Sethi, "The Creation of Religious Identities in the Punjab, *circa* 1850-1920," Ph D diss., U of Cambridge, 1998.

16 For an analysis of Khalid Hasan's English translation of the story, see M Asaduddin's "Manto in English: An Assessment of Khalid Hasan's Translations," Alok Bhalla, ed., *Life and Works of Sa'adat Hasan Manto* (Shimla: IIAS, 1997) 159-71.

17   Urdu had become the national language of Pakistan, identified with Islamic identity. In the process, Punjabi, written in Gurmukhi was erased, as it came to be identified with the Sikhs in India. Baluchi, Pushto, and Sindhi were declared provincial languages, unlike Punjabi which was now written in Urdu script, known as Shahmukhi. A similar process of linguistic hegemony and partial erasure in India contributed to the movement for Khalistan, as Hindus consciously

decided to distance themselves from Punjabi. In their effort to propagate "Hindi-Hindu-Hindustan," Urdu, of course, had become the "other" language for Hindu nationalists. For a fresh and passionate account of Hindi versus other languages, see Alok Rai, *Hindi Nationalism,* Tracts for the Times Ser. 13 (New Delhi: Orient Longman, 2001), and also Anil Sethi, "The Creation of Religious Identities in the Punjab, *circa* 1850-1920," Ph D diss., University of Cambridge, 1998." For recent dialogue on the politics of language and identity in Pakistan, see http://is.rice.edu/~riddle/mlists/ SASIALITS, the internet discussion forum on South Asian Literature, especially the exchange on Urdu, Oct 2000.

"HOW MANY PAKISTANS?": AN OVERVIEW

STUTI KHANNA

Some stories have strange histories. Kamleshwar's "How Many Pakistans?" was written in the late sixties – between 1966 and 1967 – and subsequently got "lost." It was unearthed in 1990 by an admirer of the author, and reprinted in *Kohra*, a recent collection of his short stories. A persistent theme running through the stories that make up this collection is that of the nation, which becomes a highly charged category, both in the political and the personal, emotional realm. In the Preface to *Kohra,* Kamleshwar writes, "About this short story collection of mine I have only this to say: most of the stories in it have a foreign setting. However, to me, these stories are deeply Indian, because every foreign country also has another country in it and my country has a foreign country within it!"[1] (author's translation).

Our story invokes the themes of the nation and nationality in the context of the Partition of India – the sundering of one nation into two. Comparable in magnitude to the World Wars in Europe, it was an event that killed millions of people and, more tragically perhaps, displaced millions of others, rendering an entire generation homeless and leaving indelible scars on its collective psyche. Such a momentous event could not but become the subject of literary inquiry. While the first generation of writers and poets – Sa'adat Hasan Manto, Josh Malihabadi, Qurratulain Hyder – tried to grapple with immediate and pressing issues such as: "To which country did they belong? ... What were their links with their erstwhile homeland? ...,"[2] the writers of the sixties and later, necessarily took a more distanced, potentially more objective look. Bhisham Sahni, Rahi Masoom Raza, Krishna Sobti and many others, all sought, in their different ways, to exorcise the ghost of that event.

Kamleshwar writes in the Nai Kahani tradition, a movement which gained momentum in the 1950s and 60s. A new world, a new order of things had arrived – first, the country's independence, quickly followed by the Partition – both being the outcomes of immense socio-political upheaval. The old ways of writing, of representing "reality," simply would not do. Language used in the same way as before was incapable of communicating the complexity of emotions generated by those turbulent times. At a time when received norms and given "truths" were so demonstrably at odds with the collapsing world order, the only means of authentic portrayal of life was through a focus on the individual consciousness. This group argued that "Hindi literature of the preceding years was too didactic, too romantic, too tendentious."[3] They wanted a fiction that explored a variety of real life experiences and that had no explicit political commitments. As a group they promoted critical discussion and self-conscious interest in form.

While wrestling with the same concerns in his work and focusing on the individual's angst-ridden consciousness, Kamleshwar is distinctive as a writer in that he chooses to root this exploration in the context of specific socio-political events, giving his work a keener edge, as it were. A recent short story of his, titled "Apne Desh Mein," has as its protagonist a Belgian, who is trying to grapple with the history he has inherited – a history of brutal colonization in Africa, and excesses committed there, all in the name of civilization – the burden of which does not allow him to sleep when he is in his own country. In his words, "You can never know how much I love my parents and my country ... but I also fiercely hate those very parents and that same country ... because I am unable to sleep in my country."[4] This tortured, divided self, unable to come to terms with the repercussions on the personal level of larger historical events, can be traced back to the story we are dealing with, "How Many Pakistans?" in the specific context of the Partition and its aftermath.

A recurring theme in Partition literature, though evoked in distinctive ways, is that of loss – the loss of the homeland leading to a similarly irrecoverable loss of selfhood. In "How Many Pakistans?" the motif of the journey with which the story opens, links up with that of the dervish – the lonely protagonist as a homeless wanderer, constantly on the move. In this case, the journey is also on the mental plane – a journey into the past, an attempt to recover one's sense of self by coming to terms with the past – an attempt doomed to failure, since the past has not stopped, and perhaps will never stop impinging upon the present. The story ends with an acknowledgement of failure: "Where can I run to escape from Pakistan? Is there any place where there is no Pakistan? Where I can become whole ..." (28).[5]

This psychic state of "half-ness" is also elaborated in the story at the formal level, as the past is not available as an unbroken continuum, but in stark imagistic flashes of pain and loss. One of the most noticeable narratorial techniques put to use in the story is the constant use of images – physical, sensory, and tactile. Memory is split into three compartments, each of which is given an appropriate heading, almost like chapter headings. These are also intensely imagistic photographic flashes, evoking a range of sensory reactions. The first of these is "Mehandi Flowers," where the narrator reminisces about the budding love between him and Banno, a brief interlude that ends with his being forced to leave his hometown and Banno behind. The second "part" is titled "The Night was Moonlit and Banno was Naked," with a graphic visual of Banno's agony and Mangal's equally anguished witnessing of it. Finally, the third phase elaborates on the chant-like words, "Anyone else?" reiterated all through the story. It ends with Banno standing half-dressed in the doorway of the brothel, asking if there are any more customers. Each of these parts end with the realization of separation, distance, and of a Pakistan between the two lovers. The narrator comes up against different manifestations of the same divide at each of these three landmarks in his life, which ultimately lead him to conclude that the logic of division, once set in motion, proliferates endlessly and seeps into each and every aspect of life.

Dismemberment is another image in the story that gains significance through iteration. The narrator works for a while in a "limb factory" in Poona, which manufactures artificial arms and legs. Time and again, he sees grotesque visions of decapitated bodies walking the streets. Master sahab gives a graphic description of the fight in which Mangal's grandfather's arms were cut off. This pervasive sense of physical fragmentation is mirrored by psychic fragmentation: "These few people who looked like human beings – were they for real or part of a sinister dream? Only broken, torn men seemed real now. People with complete, whole bodies struck terror in the heart" (25). The protagonist is an emotional amputee, a man without volition or a sense of purpose. Needless to say, physical dismemberment becomes an enactment on the individual level of the larger socio-political reality of the Partition.

Another image which the author invokes repeatedly, is that of an untrammeled flow, a spurting out. In the phantasmagoria that life seems to have become for Mangal, blood is seen to be gushing forth from decapitated bodies. Again, "a torrent of blood" flows from his grandfather's amputated arm. This image of death mingles with the image of life – milk, dripping from Banno's breasts – to coalesce into an image of raw pain, of life and beauty gone waste, and literally going down the drain that Ammi squeezes her soaked odhni[6] into.

Personal relationships become impossible to sustain under the castrating shadow of socio-historical events. While both Mangal and Banno are trapped in "Pakistan" together, it is a "painful togetherness," a togetherness that lacks the potential to unite them in any satisfying manner. More frightening, perhaps, is the notion that personal relationships have become redundant in this scenario. Mangal's words on leaving Chunar, "After all this, it didn't really matter whether or not I got Banno. What had to happen, had already happened ..."(17) are perhaps the saddest comments possible on the disabling potential of communalism, the insidious creation of rifts between two communities that have lived together all along. The "pulsating Pakistan" within the narrator only threatens to erupt, but finally does not. It remains with

107

him, inside him, as an enervating abyss, an apathy, a "lessening of feeling." The only source of enablement comes unexpectedly, when one accidentally stumbles against cherished fragments of the past in the horrific present. Kamleshwar uses the image of the peepal tree in a telling way, to highlight the devaluation of religion and religious totems in a situation emerging from communal strife. The rustling of the peepal tree is comforting to Mangal, not because it is a tree sacred to the Hindus, but because it "sounded like the clerk typing on his typewriter in the hospital office .... This was the only familiar sound. Everything else was now frightening, of another world" (23).

Kamleshwar's protagonists are not men of action. They, in fact, do not act, but are acted upon. They are not heroes in the way Mangal's grandfather, for instance is, plunging headlong into the fray, emerging physically disabled but spiritually triumphant. They are tortured, anguished, lonely, and ultimately, defeated souls. What redeems them is their heightened consciousness, their agonized awareness of their defeat. What also redeems them is their poetry. Kamleshwar's prose style poses more than the usual problems for the translator, largely because it encompasses many different styles of writing. On the one hand, his writing displays the restraint demanded by the Nai Kahani mode – a detached, ironical, understated tone. On the other, however, Kamleshwar the scriptwriter emerges to the fore, making for stylistic excess that is hard to reconcile with the tone of restraint. So, while we have passages like the one where Master sahab tells Mangal about Banno, and where the impassivity of the tone is conspicuous, "... the women were asked to jump off the second floor to save their lives. The children were thrown down too. There were nine women. Two died. Five infants died ..." (24), we also come across statements the highly wrought tone of which seems to preclude any genuine emotion – "Shame, fear, anger, tears, blood, exhaustion, madness, love – were boiling, seething inside me" (17). Again, the starkness of the images that frame the story is juxtaposed with a lushness in the narrative – the emotional address to Banno, the keen detailing, the lingering memories, like those of the mehandi flowers, and the tortured awareness that there is now no one to blow on them, and make their fragrance waft up.

This leads us to a difficulty inherent in the process of translation itself, the supposedly straightforward rendering of a "source language" into a "target language." As we are aware, no two languages have exactly corresponding words in them. In "On Language and Words," Arthur Schopenhaur writes: "At times, a foreign language introduces a conceptual nuance for which there is no word in our own language ... Thus, in learning a foreign language one must map out several new spheres of concepts in one's own mind that did not exist before."[7] These elusive "conceptual nuances" largely relate to culturally specific terms. A look at the opening passage of our story will make this clearer. The word "mehandi," in the oft-repeated phrase, "mehandi ke phool" can be translated to "henna" fairly accurately. Yet a moment's thought will reveal how inadequate such technical accuracy is in this case. "Mehandi" has very specific Indian/Eastern connotations that cannot be conveyed by a literal translation. I have therefore chosen to retain the word "mehandi." Again, conveying the flavour of the idiomatic phrase "hawa lag gai" in translation posed a problem. Translating it as "... you said there was something in the air ... that it had gone to my head," comes closest in meaning to it.

In addition to such specific instances that abound on every page, there is also a more fundamental linguistic difficulty – that of rendering a mellifluous, uninflected language like Hindi into the inflected English language. English has a staccato rhythm to it that makes it ill-suited to render effectively the wordiness and lyricism – the "emotionality" – that comes naturally to the Hindi language. This perhaps accounts for the slight awkwardness in the translation into English of Hindi rhetoric and high emotion.

The Sanskrit classic *Bhartriharinama* plays an interesting role in the story. There is no general consensus on the dates of Bhartrihari's reign or whether he was a king at all, but he is, without doubt, considered to be the author of the three *Shatakas* – the *Shringara Shataka*, the *Niti Shataka* and the *Vairagya Shataka* – three collections of a hundred verses each, expounding three different aspects of life. It also becomes, in our story, the locus of a cross-cultural amalgamation – as Bhartrihari's fort, which becomes the physical location that brings the two lovers, a Hindu and a

109

Muslim, together, and as a reworked cultural signifier in Master sahab's colloquial Urdu rendering of it. This branching out – apbhranshization – of classical works to enter the mainstream, is a characteristic of the pluralism the country has always generated. (Kamleshwar's use of the apbhranshized name of the *Bhartriharinama* – the *Bharatharinama* – becomes relevant in this regard.) It is this pluralism that becomes the first casualty wherever communalism rears its head. Texts which have belonged to the common corpus suddenly become markers of difference, so much so, that "if [Master sahab] hadn't been writing the *Bharatharinama*, there might not have been so much opposition ..." (16). Interestingly, the concerned parties – Mangal, his grandfather, Banno and Master sahab – seem to be nothing more than mere pawns, used to further communal antagonisms that they have no interest in. Each of them is bewilderingly caught up in a historical process they have played no part in, and which ultimately destroys them. Master sahab is writing the *Bharatharinama* till the end, but it has driven him insane.

The three *Shatakas* of the *Bhartriharinama* bring out the tension between worldliness and asceticism that is so integral to Indian thought. Vairagya, or renunciation, is traditionally the ultimate goal of a life in which both Shringara, or sensual pleasure, and Niti, or civic life, have played their allotted parts. The two verses in the story are from the *Vairagya Shataka* and talk of renunciation of worldly pleasures, and ultimately of the mortal shell, the body, in order to release the immortal soul, the Atman, to its ultimate destination, the Paramatman. The *Vairagya Shataka* also links up interestingly with our protagonist, the self-styled dervish, whose half-hearted attempts at renunciation, in the last resort, fail. These are examples of "conceptual nuances" that become difficult to convey in translation. Kamleshwar

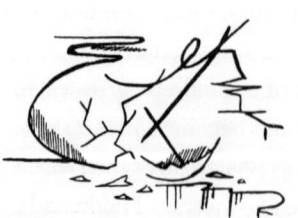 brings out in his story the tragic consequences that arise from the refusal to understand such conceptual nuances, to accept and maintain a composite ethos. True culture has within itself the capacity to be all-encompassing, and its enrichment is in direct proportion

to this capacity. This innate capacity is foreclosed by the advent of communalism – perceiving the different as the "other," and therefore as a threat. This perhaps has been the most damaging legacy of the Partition. "How Many Pakistans?" is an appeal to undo the damage, to create a more humane and inclusive ethos.

Notes

1   Kamleshwar, "Preface," *Kohra* (Delhi: Rajpal, 1994).
2   Mushirul Hasan, ed., *India Partitioned; The Other Face of Freedom,* vol.1 (New Delhi: Roli Books, 1997) 31.
3   Cited in Susie Tharu and K Lalita, eds., *Women Writing in India: 600 BC to the Present,* vol. 2 (New Delhi: Oxford UP, 1993) 344.
4   The author's translation from Kamleshwar's *Kohra* (Delhi: Rajpal, 1994).
5   All citations from "How Many Pakistans?" are from this volume, pp 12-28.
6   Odhni is a long scarf worn by women in North India.
7   See Rainer Schulte and John Biguenet, eds., *Theories of Translation: An Anthology of Essays from Dryden to Derrida* (London: U of Chicago P, 1992) 32-33.

"PALI" AND COMMUNALISM TODAY

ANURADHA MARWAH ROY

During 1947 and 1948, our erstwhile colonial rulers drew random lines on the map, splitting the country into two. Mayhem followed. Countless lives were shifted and taken like pawns on the chessboard of subcontinental history. Partition Literature is about this period, and can be roughly defined as the creative attempt to make sense of one of the worst pogroms in human memory. In trying to grapple with the enormity of misery, writers dealing with this period obsessively deployed imageries of rape, violence and destruction. As a result, if read as a collection, the baggage of calamities gets too heavy in Partition Literature. Amidst this lot, Bhisham Sahni's "Pali" has proved to be memorable, revealing a fine and delicate sensibility at work. The image of Pali, a little innocent boy, first shorn of his foreskin, then of his hair by carping zealots, is infinitely moving.

The story's achievement is especially remarkable, as the main action in "Pali" isn't directly about the carnage. It is the story of a child who is first converted to Islam and then "purified" into Hinduism. Religious observances and symbols – the circumcision and the shaving of the head – are foregrounded as diabolical rituals, eroding the primal image of innocence.

The story gets its emotional power from this profanation – the inversion of the conventionally accepted role of religion from a faith that sustains, to an instrument of torture.

Bhisham Sahni is one of the foremost writers of the country. His work is imbued with a sense of social responsibility. "Pali" is not only tense and moving, it also has a message. It might be added here that, in the face of aggressive Hindutva, this message is especially relevant. Does "Pali" give us an insight into what makes religion the vexed thing it is today? I will now critique "Pali" as a story about communalism. This kind of reading, not strictly literary, is inevitable for a literature that deals with such a strongly resonant historical event as the Partition.

The Pessimistic Determinism of "Pali"

The critique of religion offered in "Pali" has its mainspring in the author's progressive leanings. In the story, religion only serves communal interests, firmly locating itself in the social sphere, and playing absolutely no role in the psychological lives of the characters. The pandit and the maulvi, the perpetrators of the diabolical rituals, are selfishly narrow in their attitudes in contrast with the two sets of parents who are capable of universalizing their pain. Therefore, to recreate the sense of waste that the historical carnage had left in its wake, Sahni deploys twin poles of good and evil: secular humanism versus deadening religion being the first pair, and the nucleus of family love versus the dispersed hatred of mass hysteria being the second.

It is a stark and unclouded night vision, made sharper by authorial interjections that convey naturalistic notions. The story begins:

> Life goes on and on. Its ends never meet. Neither in the mundane world of realities, nor in fiction. We drag on drearily in the hope that some day these ends may meet. And sometimes we have the illusion that the ends have really joined. (30)[1]

The suggestion of life held hostage by hostile external forces, the fortuitousness of events, and the powerlessness inherent in the

113

human condition is unambiguously made in these opening sentences. Throughout the story, blind chances and mysterious all-powerful forces guide the affairs of mankind, without allowing agency to human beings. Kaushalya and Manohar Lal's family, one can safely presume was a happy one, is uprooted by the Partition, much in the same way that little huts are washed away by floods; Pali is lost because of the crowd, not abandoned by his parents. There is no space for any choice, not even of the agonizing kind that made the film *Sophie's Choice* a searing psychological drama about the limits of human endurance.[2] The lorry moves, even as Kaushalya is screaming for her husband and child, and then, just as fortuitously stops to take in only Manohar Lal; their convoy is attacked, whereas many other lorries have passed safely. The couple is bereaved yet again: their baby dies. The child could have as easily been made to survive, but the author reiterates:

> There are some wounds which heal with the passage of time, leaving a mark on the mind. But there are certain griefs which slowly eat into the heart like termites, completely ravaging the body. *There is nothing a man can do about it.* When Kaushalya reached India with her husband, her lap was bereft of a child. (40, emphasis mine)

This is pessimistic determinism at its best – or worst. Humankind is buffeted again and again by overwhelming forces. It cannot be denied that the vision of the powerlessness of individuals in the face of circumstances is particularly appropriate in recreating the tragedy of Partition. However, in doing so, Bhisham Sahni is also affecting a sharp divide between human beings and their environment, positing the latter as "given" rather than what is continuously created. And therein lies much of the dissatisfaction one may feel with the story as a text about communalism. The main characters in "Pali" never display the harsher side of life. Feelings of anger, selfishness and revenge are always located outside them, and so is religion.

The lost Pali floats into a childless Muslim couple's life. Zenab and Shakur, tolerance personified, are mirror images of Kaushalya and Manohar Lal. A maulvi – not the couple themselves – insists on the child's conversion to Islam. It is to be noted that the change of name initiated by Zenab is a personal preference, not a religious consideration. Ironically, her good hearted intentions destine her to further travails in Bhisham Sahni's naturalistic universe. If anything, her final heroic action – giving up her adopted son for the sake of the grieving Hindu mother – only serves to darken her life for all times to come. The heartrending sequence coalesces into twin images in the end: Hindu parents watch helplessly as a sobbing Pali is shorn, and the Muslim parents grieve the loss of their son. The story reaches out to an even bleaker future as Zenab's Pollyanna plans of meeting Pali at least once every year, we know, will not materialize, for very soon the borders between the two countries will harden and grow like walls precluding any contact.

In some ways, "Pali" is reminiscent of the art cinema[3] of the seventies in which the heavy boot of establishment repeatedly trampled underfoot the aspirations of the ordinary man. Call it establishment, or religion, or destiny, in films like *Ankur* or *Nishant* as in "Pali," the image of the common man defined by poverty, simplicity and helplessness, comes up against looming incomprehensible forces, and any possibility of successful combat is foreclosed by the first shot. It might be relevant to add that Bhisham Sahni's *Tamas* has been televised successfully by Govind Nihalani, one of the exponents of art cinema.[4]

How does the romanticization of the common man and the foreclosure, affect the reading of "Pali"? This question is tied up with more political ones. Is the conjunction of naturalism with communalism in the story historically justified? Is the complicity of the common man not an issue at all in the tragedy of Partition? Recent researches point in the opposite direction.

Women and children, researchers have proved, suffered the worst between 1947 to 1948, and not all attacks on them were from the outside. Besides macabre community decisions like urging all women to commit suicide to escape dishonour, there were reprehensible individual acts like husbands refusing home to "defiled" wives, or senior male members "sacrificing" all the women members of their family to avoid "dishonour." The abandonings and the murders – often constructed as heroic acts by the individuals themselves – are indicative of a complex interplay of individual motivations around community or religious feelings.[5]

In "Pali" – a story where all tension is due to communal enmity – there is no such internal drama. The characters, whether they play minor or major roles, are posited either as victims or heroes. Significantly, Zenab's final heroic act of giving up the child she was living for, is devoid of any spoken or unspoken hatred for those who are taking him away from her. Similarly, Manohar Lal feels no indignation against the Muslim couple that has made him knock around for three years in search of his own son. In both cases the warring, hatred-filled communities are the villains; the attacks on the protagonists are only from the outside.

To conclude, the story is dramatic and effective in that it makes an emotionally charged case for humanism devoid of religious falsities. However, at an analytical level, it may raise certain doubts in the reader's mind. Present political events – the demolition of the Babri Masjid and subsequent large-scale justifications of the act, could serve as an example – have proved beyond doubt that the evil of communalism continues to exist as much within us, as outside. Not many of us today can recognize ourselves in Manohar Lal and Zenab.

The Hindi Original

I have been moving freely from the Hindi original to the English, as though they were a single text. But there are significant differences. In the original Hindi version, the thematic contrasts are offset by a far more nuanced language. The power of the story as a literary piece is thus more evident in the original. To a certain extent, this is inevitable because every language carries with it a rich fund of associations situated in its own cultural context, which cannot easily be conveyed into another language within the space of a single literary work.

In "Pali" some amount of transposition is evident even in its original form. The action of the story is situated specifically on either side of the India-Pakistan border, within a span that can be traversed by jeep in a few hours. Presumably, the language spoken in this part at the time of Partition and even today, would be a dialect of Punjabi. Bhisham Sahni's Hindi, without actually moving into the dialect, successfully conveys the feel of the language spoken in this region.

Sahni achieves this effect mainly with his vocabulary. As an example, I will look at the use of the word "gunjhal" in the second paragraph (which has been translated as "knots" in the English version):

> Manohar Lal and his wife had also once lived under a similar illusion. They believed that a great calamity had at last passed over their heads. That the knots that had formed in their lives had been untied. But knots of life never get fully resolved even in stories, much less in one's life. No sooner is one knot untied, than another knot forms in its place. The story thus never comes to an end. (30)

In Punjabi, the word "gunjhal" is used to connote both problems of life and matted hair. Bhisham Sahni uses it here in the context of life, juxtaposing it with the word "suljhana" ("untangled," therefore, might have been a better choice of word than the "untied" used by the author in the translation). The human desire to run a comb through life is at once revealed to be a self-defeating one, as this usage ties up with the opening metaphor of life as an implacable strand. The suggestion is deft and economical, and the text abounds with such examples. Not only is Sahni enriching the Hindi lexicon, but he is giving his language the regional flavour that makes it the distinctive feast it is. Coloured heavily with exclamations and sayings specific to Punjabi, that blend masterfully in the easy flow of his mellifluous narration, Sahni's dialogue too is consistent with his regional sensibility. "Pali" is a very finished literary piece.

However, much of that beauty is lost in the English translation. The imagery of hair, for instance, is dispensed with altogether. The complex interplay between "life," "story" and "knots" of the Hindi original is flattened and made bipolar by using "life" and "story" interchangeably. In the Hindi version it is clearly the "gunjhal" that leads to the story, and it is "life" that *mercifully* goes on in spite of the "gunjhal."

The English translation is simplified further by a collapsing of characters. In the Hindi original, Zenab emerges as a far more easy-going character than Shakur, who is God-fearing and prone to doubt. In the English translation, Shakur's interior voice is transferred to Zenab, leading to a certain blurring and interchangeability. At a

117

crucial point in the story – while deciding what to do with the child who has walked into her heart – Zenab (in the Hindi original it is Shakur) rationalizes:

> The tailor, Mahmud, had kept a Hindu woman in his house and no one had bothered to investigate. Mir Zaman had ransacked the Hindu tailoring shop next to his, and had kept the stolen things in the shop for all to see. Nobody had taken him to task for it. And as for her, she was only giving refuge to a child – a lost child whom her husband had picked up on finding him in the street. What was wrong with it? (36)

Some of the loss in the English version could have been avoided with care, and a more felicitous choice of words. But there are other instances where the author has chosen to leave out an observation altogether, as it does not contribute to the forward movement of the story. The following example is from a crucial point in the story where Manoharlal reappears without his son.

The suggestion is that, had he not appeared at that particular moment, Kaushalya would have ignored conventional wisdom and got down from the lorry, and Pali's fate as well as that of "Pali" would have been very different. At that point, the narrator observes (I am translating the omitted pieces): "Who can tell which of the following constitute the decisive factor – events, individuals, or fate? Mishaps shatter lives and from the cracks discrepancies peep in like urchins, provoking the hapless individual."

I may have over-translated by emphasizing the image of the urchin. In my view, in this case an added complexity works better than a glossing over. That Bhisham Sahni chose the option of simplifying the text, leads to some general questions I am going to raise about the translation.

What is it that gets translated when a story is rendered from one language into another? Is it the content, devoid of any form? Or is an equivalent form sought in the other language? Who is the story being translated for?

The target reader might provide the key to the other answers. When a story is translated from Hindi into English, it is targeting a more diverse, if not a more numerous readership. Gaps of culture and history may be safely presumed. What might serve to fill that gap is literariness. The reader of English in this country and the Western reader who buys an Indian book are likely to be sophisticated readers. A case for a more nuanced and complex translation in English follows from here.

Too often, and as in the case with this story, translation in our country is a labour of love. It thus seems unfair and ungracious to pick holes in a translation that the author has conceded to do, investing time and energy in the project. My protest is thus directed at those who edit, compile, and commission translations. The process of creation is a fairly untheorized one, but to make a journey once again on the trodden path would hardly provide inspiration for an author. Besides, along with familiarity, translation perhaps also requires distance from the subject matter. Joyce prescribed silence, cunning and exile for the artist in his novel *Portrait of the Artist as a Young Man;* a listening ear, skill, and engagement with the original, while placed in another context, might be the attributes to look for in a translator.

Notes

1   All references to "Pali" in this essay are from this volume, pp 29-52.

2   William Styron's novel *Sophie's Choice* was first published in 1979. It was made into a film directed by Alan J Pakula (1982), starring Meryl Streep. It tells the anguished tale of a mother, a concentration camp survivor, who was forced to make the choice of life and death between her two children.

3   The term "art cinema" is used to describe a movement that was a revolt against the glossiness of commercial films. As contrasted with the pancake make-up and cabaret sequences that had become the staple fare, Shyam Benegal, Saed Mirza, and Govind Nihalani — to name a few directors associated with art cinema — focused on the ordinary faces of peasants and workers, and the travails of the common man.

4   Bhisham Sahni's novel *Tamas* was first published in 1973. Govind Nihalani serialized it for Doordarshan in 1988.

5   For a detailed analysis of the violence perpetrated on women and children, and on the criminal behavior of ordinary people during the Partition, see Urvashi Butalia, *The Other Side of Silence: Voices from the Partition of India* (New Delhi: Viking, 1998).

AGAINST FORGETTING:
MEMORY AS METAPHOR IN "DREAM IMAGES"

M ASADUDDIN

It comes from the whole of his sensitive life since early childhood. Why, for all of us, out of all that we have heard, seen, felt, in a lifetime, do certain images recur, charged with emotion, rather than others? The song of one bird, the leap of one fish, at a particular time and place, the scent of one flower, an old woman on a German mountain path ... such memories may have symbolic value, but of what we cannot tell, for they come to represent the depths of feeling into which we cannot peer. We might just as well ask why, when we try to recall visually some period in the past, we find in our memory just the few meagre arbitrarily chosen set of snapshots that we do find there, the faded poor souvenirs of passionate moments.

T S Eliot in *The Use of Poetry and the Use of Criticism* (1930)

The human predicament is to remember. It is remembrance or this ability to remember that helps one make sense of one's life, and reconstruct the past in a coherent way. The survivors of holocaust, genocide or political oppression – be it the Stalinist purge, the Jewish

Holocaust, or the Partition of India – have tried to reconstruct past events through memory – both voluntary and involuntary – and these attempts at reconstruction have given birth to some of the most enduring works of literature. History cannot tell us the whole truth. It conceals more than it reveals. Every generation negotiates this tension between closure and disclosure in its own way. As regards India, the spate of books that have appeared on the theme of Partition in recent years demonstrates that the culture of remembrance is at its peak, and that story-telling has come to be validated as one of the ways in which individuals try to grapple with the past in an age when the canons of historiography and political thought fail to put the past in order. The presence of the past is now more potent than ever before, leading to a multi-pronged discussion of the Partition and its aftermath.

An act of remembrance is always subjective, partial and fragmentary. Yet it contains moments of truth that illuminate significant facets of life and historical reality. Though societies discover their own ways of dealing with the past and its unbearable memories, their manner of retrieval and commemoration of them shows convergence as well as divergences. What is common in all societies, however, is a longing to transform the memories of the past culturally, through a multitude of artifacts. Commenting on the way Holocaust memories have been sought to be kept alive in Israel, America and Germany through monuments that evoke different emotions in individuals confronting them, depending on their cultural and national identities, Gabriel Motzkin points out: "Cultural translation is then not a tangible process between languages or styles, but rather an intangible one between conflicting historical experiences as contexts for similar artifacts. The styles have converged, but the histories have not."[1]

Remembrance and retelling are important and crucial devices used by Surendra Prakash to weave plots, and offer oblique and ironical comments in a number of his stories, most notably, in "Jamghorah Ulfram," "Bazgoi," "Dream-like"[2] and "Tadposaiyan."[3] These narratives help him to retrieve a significant segment of his past through memory and recollection. Surendra Prakash was born in 1930 at Lyallpur, where he spent the most impressionable and formative period of his life. The shared community life between the Hindus and the Muslims helped him imbibe the composite ethos of that time, and it became an inalienable part of his experiential world and literary consciousness. The Partition, which overtook him, sounded the death knell for such a shared life; he had to migrate to India soon. However, the memories of his early life at Lyallpur, and his experiences during the days of Partition and its aftermath, inform a significant part of his writings. "Dream Images" needs to be studied in the context of the author's life and oeuvre, and its historical moment.

"Dream Images" is about the disjunction and rupture created by the Partition in a tradition of a long and communally shared social and cultural life, the disintegration of composite community life, and its imaginative reintegration through memory and dream. It is a story of exile, loss and imaginative reclamation. In fact, the story collapses the distinction between the notions of "exile" and "home," rendering their meanings interchangeable. What was home before is no longer so in terms of geographical space. And the geographical location where the protagonist lives now cannot be home in its most comprehensive sense, because he does not feel the same affinity with it.

The memory of a mutually interactive Indo-Muslim culture, and an inherent, deeply felt religiosity of the people form the texture of the story. Its opening lines remind the reader of the immediate historical past and the genesis of India and Pakistan's enmity that caused sporadic violence and unrest, and cast its baleful shadow on the life of the common people in both the countries. The rumbling of tanks on the road outside the author's house can have just one, unmistakable message. The deprivations of social life, such as a price rise, lack of water, and other basic amenities, highlight the failure of the State to provide the bare minimum to its people. Their juxtaposition with the needless battles that must be fought to keep alive hostility between the two nations, drives home the utter absurdity of political life in India and Pakistan. It highlights the fact of liminality that still haunts the life of the people, particularly of those displaced during the Partition. Thus the story is, at one level, subversive of the politics of attrition, hatred and vilification that has been ongoing in both countries.

The narrator directly confronts the alleged "causes" and "legitimacy" of the Partition. Apparently, the country was partitioned because of "religious incompatibility." To some, the partition of India is the most damning statement about the impossibility of a synthesis of the two ways of life, Hindu and Muslim, and of a shared meaningful and mutually enriching inter-community life. The narrator recreates an exact picture of such a community life in pre-Partition India that belies the above premise. It would be unrealistic to expect that he would give us a full-blown account of the causes – the so-called agency/agencies – and fix culpability. Nevertheless, the ironic stance adopted by him stands as a devastating indictment of Partition, and the insensitivity of political leaders to the human tragedy that it entailed. With the benefit of hindsight, the narrator and his readers know that mere religion proved to be too flimsy a basis for the creation and sustenance of a modern day state like Pakistan, which could barely hold itself together for two and a half decades. The aspirations of the people of East Pakistan and their love of Bangla, their mother tongue, proved a more potent force than religion.

The story raises some fundamental questions about religion and politics, and their bearing on identity formation – the identity of the individual and the community to which the individual owes allegiance. Identity – largely a social construct – addresses issues of language, culture and religion that cohere and coalesce inextricably. The narrator questions, "Why were we Hindus or Muslims?" and gives himself the most clear-headed and sensible answer, shorn of any shibboleths: "The answer lay in our birth – because we were born of parents who were either Hindu or Muslim. We were Hindu. So we could not retain even two yards of land in Pakistan. Those of us who survived, came to India. The only things which remained there were *memories* and *shadows*" (54, emphasis added).[4] Very few people practise religion because of deep personal conviction. They are born into some religion or the other, and begin to practise it uncritically and unquestioningly. Now the question arises – why do people resort to violence and why are they driven to kill one another on an issue which involves such little personal effort or conviction, and into which very little deep reflection or thought may have gone? Besides, if all religions basically preach human love and brotherhood,

123

then why should they lead to the dismantling of institutions and dismemberment of countries and peoples? All this is germane to a full understanding of the subtext of the story.

The largest forced migration of population in human history, and the demographic dislocation it entailed, had its own complexities. While Hindu families from Pakistan migrated en masse and reintegrated themselves into the newly emergent India, Muslim families from India remained divided between the two countries. If one half of the family migrated to Pakistan, the other half stayed back in India. "The pain of truncated families must haunt them even today" (54). As though the physical vivisection of the country was not enough, they were internally divided as well. Straddling two warring states and two politically incompatible worlds caused them deep anguish. That which essentially was a human problem, and needed an imaginative and sensitive treatment, was sought to be solved by a single stroke dividing the land. The greatest mistake that the Indian leaders committed while agreeing to the division, was to think of the land only in terms of geographical territory and moveable property. How could one divide the heart and the memory?

There is no escape from memories. During a catastrophe, there is no time to reflect; reflection is needed later for "coping," for coming to grips with the inevitability of loss and displacement. Exile is an ontological condition to be grappled with on a daily basis. For the exiles, it is impossible to exorcise the past. Even those who cannot remember accurately because of the suddenness of events and the attendant shock, are still haunted by the lost places, abandoned photographs and other recollections. And they try to recover some of that lost density of life through imaginative recreation. Literary narratives tell us of exiles who live entirely in the past, and even try to replicate the old world in all its physical details. Joginder Paul's Urdu novella "Khwabrau"[5] deals with a group of people in Lahore who try to replicate the whole of Lucknow – its topography, the manners and customs, speech patterns and so on. In "Dream Images," the narrator has built up a new life in India on the ruins of his former life in Pakistan, and is fairly content with his domestic successes. He gets his elder daughter married, and she is happy in her new life with a son. He can even recreate a part of his former life because he has found his "... own Nazir Talib, Akhtar Bhai, Jalal Painter, Mirza and Meraj Sheikh in Mehmood Javed, Zubair, Anwar and Salam" (54). But memories continue to haunt him. He wonders what invisible bond binds him to his former place and lost friends.

The past can be relived only in dream, because the real world is too hostile, and entails the negotiating of a "passport," "visa," and "a different currency." However, once the narrator is free from the fetters of realpolitik, and is transported into the world of dream, things move at a faster pace. Events and scenes from his past life flit across like images on a screen; the bridge they had to cross, Adh Marg, Regal Cinema, the clock tower, kites flying in the sky, the handcart selling malai kulfi, saints and sadhus taking deep puffs at their chillums, the grandfather and his shop, and the shrine of Baba Kaudi Shah. The interweaving of these visual details and the narrator's associative perceptions recreate the past in all its variety and complexity. The dream journey takes place as though it were a common occurrence of daily life. Everyday reality and the world of imagination fuse, so as to become almost indistinguishable.

The mythopoeic imagination of the author encompasses the past and the present so that they merge into an uninterrupted continuum, and a kind of continuity of life is envisioned through subtle symbolism, though ruptures have taken place in that continuity. The author's use of the magic-realist mode and real life characters like Intizar Husain, Anwar Sajjad, Kishwar Nahid, Mehmood Javed, Zubair, Anwar and Salam in an essentially imaginary recreation, underscore this element of continuity. However, the narrator-dreamer is unconsciously aware of the disjunction that has taken place between the past as memory recreated it, and the present that he "sees." Though the general geographical contours of the locality remain the same, new structures have come up that signify the changes that have taken place. Hence, though the places are familiar, the narrator cannot make "connections" with the people. Each telephone number his wife dials, evokes the response, "wrong number." This difficulty in establishing links, symbolically represents a lack of communication, resulting in a lack of empathy. And empathy is essential to enter other cultures and sensitivities. It is significant that the narrator can get out of the quandary in which he has placed himself and his family, only through a kind of messianic leap, which, even if one makes allowances for the mode he has adopted, seems somewhat gratuitous.

The children of the narrator are strangers in the familiar world of their parents, and express their mild resentment at the seemingly communal nomenclature of the boarding house, that is, the Hindu dharamshala. But as they glimpse and internalize a way of life that thrived on communal sharing and interconnectedness, their hostility gradually melts away. This is why when they "visit" the shrine of the Sufi saint Baba Kasaudi Shah, they take a cue from their parents as they intone, "Allah, Allah as though they were praying before the image of gods" (57).

Thus, in "Dream Images," the author deftly fuses documentary reality and fictional material to evoke a slice of his past from his memory; to salvage, as it were, whatever he can of the culture before it is irretrievably lost. It is a fervent plea against forgetting, and for the preserving of a memory – however fugitive – of an epoch, before time and history have placed it beyond our reach.

If the original story is about the crossing of borders – both geographical and metaphorical – the translation of it into English can be seen, as all translations essentially are, as a crossing of linguistic borders by the translator. "Indeed, if the translator's task is to cross the divide of linguistic borders, the status of the translation itself is defined by its suspension between two cultures, two languages, and two texts."[6] Thus, in its broadest sense, a translation is also an interpretation of historical and cultural codes and idioms, and translators are interpreters and critics who stretch and transgress the limits of linguistic boundaries and cultures.

A literary text not only creates meaning, but also contextualizes the meaning. "Dream Images" creates the context of a shared communal life, and the author uses words, expressions and symbols that acquire additional meaning in that context. He takes for granted the reader's knowledge about the nature of such a life. The effortless ease with which the narration shifts from the quotidian, realistic level to that of the magical and the dream world, would require some effort on the part of the reader to assimilate all its implications. The elusiveness and the sense of mystery that characterize Surendra Prakash's prose, are, in fact, difficult to translate. Yet, it was a great challenge to render the quiet, understated, almost hushed tone of the lyrical Urdu prose into a similar prose with varying registers, to convey the liminality of experiences.

As a translator, my other concern was to retain the cultural nuances of the original as far as possible. Words do not come to us emptied of meaning, but carry with them cultural memory, rich with a connotative context. For example, words and phrases such as "mazar," "sajjada nashin," "kashkool," "jenew," embedded in the composite religious and cultural tradition of India, do not have exact or approximate equivalents in English. One alternative was to explain them in the body of the translated text, which would have robbed them of much of their density. So I have decided to retain them. Those who are interested can always probe further to know more about them. If not, the context will help the common reader to grasp the meaning. The same can be said about "Hindu dharamshala" and "Muslim musafirkhana." Their translation as "guest house" or some kind of "hostelry" would have taken away much of the resonance of that culture where people practised exclusivity based on the notions of purity and pollution, and yet could create an inter-community life of mutual enrichment, respect, peaceful co-existence and inter-dependence. Besides, I believe these terms would be generally intelligible to a pan-Indian audience.

The chanting by devotees of expressions such as "Ali da mast qalandar" in the Sufi shrine and the kulfi vendors' sing-song cry, "Qulfi khoye-malai di, piste badam di, keode gulab di, khatir janab di ..." to sell their wares, illuminate aspects of the shared socio-cultural life, and the tenor of that life at a particular historical moment. They too are embedded in the quotidian of that culture so as to make any rendition of them into English grossly inadequate. Then, the sudden shift in the linguistic register in the sentence, "Aap is Hindu dharamshala mein nivas kar sakte hain," with its insistence on the use of Sanskrit tatsama[7] words, cannot be replicated in English without sounding pompous. Hence, it had to be rendered in plain English with a neutral register.

I would also like to use this opportunity to point out an omission in the earlier translated version of the story. The line – "The disciples of Shah Dauley were looking at them intently" should be read as – "The rat-disciples of Shah Dauley ..." The phrase as it occurs in the original text is "Shah Dauley ke chuhe." In my preliminary reading of the story, I could not make out what it meant. However, as I probed deeper, I discovered that the shrine that the narrator describes had a large rodent population. These rats, considered the protégés of the saint, caused no trouble or harm to anyone. Couples without children would visit the shrine, seek the saint's blessings, and pledge their firstborn to the saint. According to popular belief, the first child of such couples would be born with a small head, like that of a rat. All such children, given away to the saint after their birth to become his disciples, would be known as "Shah Dauley ke chuhe." Sa'adat Hasan Manto has a short story with the title "Shah Dauley ke Chuhe," that deals with this theme. My probing further revealed that there are quite a few shrines, both in India and Pakistan, that have an overwhelming population of monkeys, donkeys, and even scorpions. The reigning saints of such shrines invoked God's blessings not only on their human disciples, but on their devotees in the animal kingdom as well. In this and other senses too, translating "Khayal Surat" into English was an act of cultural recall and retrieval for me.

Notes

1   Sanford Budick and Wolfgang Iser, eds., *The Translatability of Cultures: Figurations of the Space Between* (Stanford: Stanford UP, 1996) 266.

2   These stories are available in English translation in Avtar Singh Judge, trans., *Retelling* (New Delhi: Sahitya Akademi, 1997).

3   Translated into English as "Shadowlines" by M Asaduddin in Mushirul Hasan, ed., *India Partitioned: The Other Face Of Freedom*, vol. 1 (New Delhi: Roli Books, 1997).

4   All refererences to "Dream Images" are from this volume, pp 53-61.

5   Translated into English as "Sleepwalkers" by Sukrita Paul Kumar and Sunil Trivedi in Keerti Ramachandra, ed., *Sleepwalkers* (New Delhi: Katha, 1998).

6   Mae Handerson, ed., *Borders, Boundaries and Frames: Cultural Criticism and Cultural Studies* (New York: Routledge, 1995) 9.

7   Sanskrit words that have passed into Hindi.

PARTITION OVERVIEW

Essays by

NAIYER MASUD

ARJUN MAHEY

RAVIKANT

SAUMYA GUPTA

BODH PRAKASH

PARTITION AND THE URDU STORY

NAIYER MASUD

TRANSLATED BY DEEBA ZAFIR

After the Partition in 1947, the people of the subcontinent could be categorized as follows:

1. Non-Muslims, who after the Partition, migrated to India from those areas which came to be called Pakistan.
2. Muslims, who lived in India and after the Partition migrated to Pakistan.
3. Non-Muslims who were already resident in India.
4. Muslims who already belonged to Pakistan.
5. Non-Muslims who belonged to Pakistan and continued to live there even after the Partition. These were few in number.
6. Muslims in India, who even after the Partition, remained in India. These Muslims, perhaps, outnumbered those that had stayed back in Pakistan as well as those who had migrated from India.
7. There are hardly any, and if at all, very few instances of non-Muslims belonging to India and migrating to Pakistan, or for that matter, Muslims belonging to Pakistan, migrating to India after the Partition. However, in some short stories such characters have been portrayed.

In this list, according to age and temperament, three other categories can be added, which are, those people who at the time of the Partition:

8   Had spent most of their lives at one place – that is, the aged who were essentially nostalgic or had a wealth of memories, and would find it difficult to adjust to the new situation.

9   The young – for whom to start afresh was not difficult.

10   Children – for whom knowledge about matters relating to Partition and the causes leading up to it was received from their elders.

And finally,

11 &   People belonging to areas of divided Bengal and divided Punjab,
12   who migrated to a different city within the same region. For instance – those who migrated from Amritsar to Lahore, or from Dhaka to Calcutta. They found a familiar cultural environment despite having migrated to a new city, and did not experience the sense of alienation which was the share of those who migrated from Uttar Pradesh, Hyderabad and the Northern areas to Bengal and Punjab, or of those belonging to Sindh, Punjab and Bengal, who had to leave their land for distant areas, the cultural and linguistic ethos of which were entirely removed from their own.

The Urdu short story has authentically represented all the above categories, and its authenticity derives from the fact that most of the short story writers were representatives of one or the other category.

A major difference marked the situations of the Muslims in India and the non-Muslims in Pakistan. A large section of Muslims in India were nationalistic, and therefore opposed to the Partition. They, as well as many other Muslims, had chosen to remain in India. Despite this, they had to, at every step, face the notion that with the formation of Pakistan, they must leave India and that it had no place for them. They could have argued, and they did, that India was their country; they would continue to live there and exercise their constitutional rights as any non-Muslim. However, the non-Muslims in Pakistan faced an entirely different situation. Pakistan was created for Muslims, not for them. And in this new country they would be relegated to the status of Kafirs or non-believers, as in any Islamic State. It was not possible for them to say that the Partition (or the formation of Pakistan) was unacceptable to them and they could hardly assert their rights as first class citizens. Even this brief outline is sufficient to reveal that the Partition provided Urdu fiction with ample material for some very fine and powerful short stories. There were many issues, experiences and reactions connected to the Partition, and these themes were appropriate for colourful fiction of a high quality. But the horrifying communal riots that followed the Partition, temporarily eclipsed other aspects of the Partition. The literary scene was flooded with short stories about Partition-related communal violence; the Partition and riots were considered synonymous. Just as the riots had destroyed many lives, the stories related to them robbed Partition of its various other aspects. Like the Urdu language, Urdu fiction also performed the task of bringing hearts together rather than stressing factionalism. Both Muslims and non-Muslims had crossed the extremes of barbarism. However, the Urdu short story, instead of stressing on these barbaric acts, focused mainly on human friendship and courageous acts of rescuing each other.

When the period of riot-related fiction came to an end, other aspects of the Partition were foregrounded. For instance, the problem of settling down in a new place, the struggle for employment and the establishment of a new business, the reversal of class/ fortunes, adjustments to a new and strange milieu and so on. Many short stories were written on these issues, even in a humorous vein. However, these issues are not Partition-specific. Communal riots have occurred both before and after the Partition. The search for a house or new settlement is an issue that may accompany emigration, and may arise even without the event of the Partition. The search for employment, the rise and fall of fortunes due to a revolution in history (or even without it), getting acquainted with strangers or adjusting to new surroundings, are all issues which are independent of the Partition. Nor can the Partition and its implications be confined to these. These themes offer but a glimpse of a few simple and obvious aspects of the Partition. The Partition of a huge country or the division of a large nation is a vast topic. In fact, it befits the scope of a novel, and it is difficult for the short story to deal with it in its entirety. It is for this reason that the Urdu short story has broken up this vast area and addressed it in sub-themes.

However, there is a theme that deals exclusively with the Partition, and on which there is an abundance of short stories where it is more powerfully evoked than in novels – the theme of the division of families as a result of the formation of Pakistan. There were innumerable Indian Muslim families from which the majority of its members migrated to Pakistan while some preferred to stay back in their homes and country. Some were left behind out of necessity, compulsion or a sense of expediency. Thus, there was an abundance of such desolate houses that had once brimmed over with prosperous and happy residents, and now had only the aged or the idle left behind. A number of floors of these big houses would remain empty and were gradually demolished. The houses acquired a haunted, ghostly appearance, and their portals sang the elegy of a bygone era. It was not possible for the short story writer to remain unaffected by this scene. On the whole, the best short stories on the Partition were written on this theme. The short stories of these divided families and desolate homes drew their strength from the comparative narration of the past and present situation. The families that came from Pakistan were not divided thus, but even they were haunted by the spectre of the past. The stories written under the influence of this phantom of the Partition captured the various colours of the cultural history of India before the Partition. This important task could not have been undertaken, or at least, not on such a large scale, had the Partition not taken place. This can be seen as the most positive influence of the Partition on Urdu fiction.

The enumerated categories given at the beginning of this discussion reveal the novelty of the stories related to the Partition in Urdu, but it is difficult to quantify the number of such stories, several of which are of a very fine quality. Therefore, it is not surprising that when we compile a list, mentally, of the best Partition-related stories, we include the following four – "Gadariya" by Ashfaque Ahmed, "Housing Society" by Qurratulain Hyder, "Lajwanti" by Rajinder Singh Bedi and "Toba Tek Singh" by Sa'adat Hasan Manto. "Gadariya's" Daoji Sufi is Hindu by temperament, but his personality incorporates elements of Muslim culture. However, the Partition relegates him to the status of a Kafir. The head-plait labels him as a Hindu and Hindu alone. "Housing Society" contains within it the scope of a novel. The revolution in the economic and social status brought about by the Partition and migration is depicted in this novella. The exchange of populace is taken up in "Lajwanti" which is a story of an abducted woman, who after living in an alien country with a man of another religion, returns to her husband. The exchange of populace is also the theme of "Toba Tek Singh" though its subject concerns the exchange of lunatics, and not abducted women. The exchange of populace (or even the event/act of the Partition) is something that the insane mind cannot accept as well. Exasperated by the altered political geography, a lunatic in "Toba Tek Singh" takes refuge in an imaginary landscape of the mind and climbs a tree. Time and again, the central protagonist reacts to the Partition in broken, elliptical, nonsensical words from which no meaningful and coherent sentence emerges. Perhaps it is for this reason that so many meanings have been attributed to these utterances.

PARTITION NARRATIVES: SOME OBSERVATIONS

ARJUN MAHEY

Prefatory

I submit the following set of observations ("essay" would be too ponderous a word) with a certain amount of hesitation. In the first place, I am neither a historian nor a social scientist, and my encroachment on both these professional territories may seem somewhat precocious. In the second place, many of my observations will seem anachronistic: that is to say, they will seem to be statements which can be nuanced more substantially in the light of the enormous (and enormously good) recent material available on the Partition of India. In the third place, these observations appear to leave a very large question, which they implicitly bring up, unanswered.

Briefly, therefore, I need to take account of these arguments.

Regarding the encroachment into other territories, I can only offer the reasoning of the educated layman: which is, that I will try to wrest to my purpose whatever tools I can find to hand, in this case sociology and historiography, in an attempt to try and understand the phenomenon called (for want of a better phrase) the Literature of Partition. To remain perfectly consistent, therefore, I am only too happy when as a teacher of literature and an incipient student of an obscure branch of Indology, others encroach upon my territories in an attempt to get a surer purchase on literature or on India's pre-modern past. There are many things, and the Partition is one of them, which escape the rational grasp; and as Indians, it is surely imperative – whether one is in the academic profession or not – to try and absorb the full meaning of what occurred fifty or so years ago.

As for the anachronism, these observations were jotted down almost a decade ago; they were meant neither for publication, nor for more than four people to read; in effect, they were a set of amateur forays into a foreign territory. If I have not updated them, it is only because there is so much, and so much that is remarkable, that has been published since I wrote, that my contribution to any new perspective is bound to be miniscule. I offer this piece, therefore, as an indication not of any larger insight into the Partition, and certainly not as a more coherent or recent one, but as a personal testament, necessarily dated as all such testaments are, to an act that transformed my future before I was born. In larger terms, it may be understood as an indication that my generation (the first born in Independent India) has had to carry the consequences of an event not created by it, and which, though near enough to feel the wounds of the event, is nevertheless far enough from it for me to attempt, in whatever manner I can, a personal understanding of (a part) of it.

About the "implicit large question," I need to make a few clarifications. Among other things, the Partition of India was, it seems to me, an unprecedented event; and unprecedented events of this enormity become inexplicable, precisely because the language we use up to the point of the event is serviceable only for the incidents that have occurred *prior* to it, and are inadequate in understanding the event itself. In a condition of such absolute social breakdown such as the Partition was, language – itself a symptom and cause of solidarity – is *also* in a condition of breakdown. The social body repairs itself after a while (inadequately well, as the current jingoism in the body politic demonstrates), but is no longer what it used to be since the trauma has modified it; my "large question" (which I nowhere answer, but which is implicit in the piece that follows) is: How come a similar alteration did not occur to the languages of Northern

India? How did our vernaculars survive, if not linguistically, at least in literary terms, without a transforming convulsion? Why do we still write and think and talk, if we do, as if the Partition did not fundamentally rearrange the languages, and hence the meanings within which we conceive what it is to be an Indian (or a Hindu, or a Muslim, or whatever one perceives oneself to be)?

I cannot pretend to answer this question; and therefore, to the third of my self-arraignments, I can only say that it falls outside my range of analysis. Perhaps it is not within the domain of literary thinking to address this issue; perhaps it needs a philosopher of history, particularly the history of language, to address it with anything like competence; or perhaps (as my intuition tells me) our tool of investigation, which is language, is simply too fragile an instrument with which to reach out over the abyss without snapping.

The observations that follow, sketch out in broad brush strokes how the Partition of India in 1947 has been portrayed by three sets of narratives: one, narrative histories; two, short stories in Hindi, Urdu and Punjabi; and three, Sa'adat Hasan Manto's short piece entitled "Toba Tek Singh." This last has usually been considered a short story, but I shall contend that is not merely what it is, and does indeed afford us a view of the Partition which neither history, nor other short stories attempt. In effect, I hope to redefine it.

In other words, I shall compare (and sometimes contrast) two or three ways in which events have been assembled to form a narrative, each of which manages to say what the others cannot. Analyses of these three narrative strategies will take up approximately a third of the paper each.

History

> History does not repeat itself. Historians repeat each other.
>
> *Lord Balfour*

In the summer of 1947, the Partition of India, and of the Punjab in particular, was effected with catastrophic results. Ten million people (mostly Hindus, Sikhs and Muslims) had to leave their homes and ancestral holdings, and a tenth of them were slaughtered in the most

137

singular civil war in recent history: there were no leaders, no armed forces, no plans, only a spontaneous and visceral ferocity whose possibility was unanticipated, and whose legacy is more than evident even today.

If nations could suffer trauma, the Partition certainly ignited one in both India and Pakistan. And, as in some traumata, the victims dissolved into catatonic shock that displayed itself as silence. For a number of years after the event, no writer of any renown on either side of the new border rescued an adequate sense of lucidity to approach the issue. Something had been permanently lost, and the inadequacy of mere words was discerned throughout the north of the country in an understood code of silent mourning.[1] The brutality of the trauma was compounded by the detail that there was no adequate way to transmit this collapse to those who hadn't undergone the ordeal: very few photographs survived, and fewer journalistic first person accounts were possible. Unlike the rigorously and officially documented Holocaust of European Jewry a few years earlier, there was nothing to chronicle the severity of human torment.

Nor was it evident that the writers could invoke the capacity to write of such things.[2] Relative to the wealth of Urdu, Punjabi and Hindi writings which existed before, and since the Partition, the Partition itself is little represented: at best only a handful of stories, novels and poems. The reason is more than obvious: any "non-factual" (or non-statistical) account of the event is apparently capable of re-exploding into another full-scale civil war.[3] This does not imply, however, that no writing was accomplished upon the Partition; on the contrary, the social scientists and the historians – the usual analysts of trauma – were more than bounteous. Histories, biographies, autobiographies, statistical surveys, a positive sweep of "factual" narratives usurped the stretch. As is usual in such cases, narrative history attempted to define what narrative fiction declined to even contemplate. It is to such narrative histories that I now wish to turn, so as to analyze their component parts, and unwrap how they assemble our current impression of India's Partition.

History, as Hayden White has demonstrated untiringly,[4] retains the rhetorical tropes of narrative fiction, creating a plot where the Antecedent (or villain) generates the Consequence (or victim), and it plays with variations of this plot, so that one may have a historical narrative dealing with several Antecedents, generating several Consequences. Thus all history is moral in intent, and necessarily plays out the chronicle in the rhetorical tones of an inevitable genre (for example tragedy, or melodrama, or farce). Furthermore, and this Hayden White nowhere mentions, since History's rhetorical tropes are inadequate to the substantiality of suffering, it deals with anguish by quantifying pain: statistics and numbering the dead appropriate the unique status of grief.

Narrative histories of India have thus used the following rhetorical signals to chronicle the Partition:

(i)   *Cause-Effect:* a series of events (intended and unintended) set off a series of consequences, one of which is massacre.

(ii)   *Moral inflection:* if intended, the villain can be located in either a person or a group who/which has intentions other than a peaceful transfer of populations. If unintended, morally reprehensible ignorance is seen to be the cause, in which case ignorance itself becomes an unmeritorious liability. In other words, the leaders have a vested interest. If they do not, past experience should have directed them to be wary. In either case, they are culpable.

(iii)   *Statistics:* as a mode of gauging affliction.

(iv)   *Genre/Icon:* seen as a particular *kind* of recognizable human behaviour familiarized through literature; that is, plotted (and identified) as either a tragedy, or a farce or a melodrama et cetera.

A survey of representative narrative histories that dealt with the issue of the Partition displayed/revealed the following details:

(i)   *Cause-Effect:* The effect was the Partition, but almost no historian seems to focus on the same cause or causes. Each historian focuses on one particular cause as being of prominent consequence which turns out to be either one of the following: political mismanagement (Khan, 1987),[5] the Muslim League's inordinate demands (Singh, 1990),[6] unavoidable haste (Raza, 1989),[7] Gandhi (Chandra, 1984),[8] Mountbatten (Sherwani, 1986; Hamid, 1986),[9] Hindu Nationalism (Wolpert, 1982),[10] Jinnah (Das, 1982; Spear, 1961)[11] and Nehru (Wolpert, 1982).[12] Only two historians dare dodge the issue, the one by simply not speaking of it (Chandra, 1988),[13] and the other by taking the cause-effect to its narrative limit by asking the question in the very title of his sensationalist booklet "Was India's Partition Avoidable?" (Mukherjee, 1987; in other words, "Could the causes of the effect have been controlled"?).[14] Interestingly, the answer is a qualified "Yes."

(ii) *Moral Inflection*: This becomes evident in the Cause-Effect issue. Once the "victim" and the "villain" are located, the moral tone inevitably becomes apparent in the following terms: since X caused Y, if X had not occurred, Y would not have occurred. Needless to add, historians are rarely as crude as that; nevertheless, since there was a willed cause, avoidance is possible. Only very rarely is human agency removed from cause, but even there some vestigial sense of ethical misgovernment is imputed in the account.[15]

(iii) *Statistics:* Little needs to be adduced as testimony here. Without exception, the fact that one million people died is cited in histories. Not a single historian conceives of using the idea of narrative perspective to make clear exactly how large a figure a million is in the scheme of things. The number allows the figure to stand as one without meaning, since audiences in India may possibly conceive of large numbers in a somewhat dissimilar way from their non-Asian counterparts.[16] Inevitably, too, government documents of both India and Pakistan advance numbers as a record of the dead, but these latter statistics are not history proper, merely registers: involved in a narrative, they may take on historical status.

(iv) *Genre/Icon*: This is by far the most visible, and the most intriguing of rhetorical tropes that history shares with fiction – the trope, that is, of giving the narrative a meaning that is already available, and will thus find an echo in the aesthetic sensibilities of the social body. In Hayden White's phrase:

> Viewed in a formal way, a historical narrative is not only a *reproduction* of the events reported in it, but also a *complex of symbols* which gives us directions for finding an *icon* of the structure of those events in our literary tradition ... [it] *tell us* what images to look for in our culturally encoded experience in order to determine how we should feel about the thing represented ...[17]

And what does this complex of symbols present? What icon or icons are presented in these histories? How are we supposed to feel?

Unstated but assumed, every history bargains on the sense that there is a common human code of conduct that has been desecrated. The causes for getting people to the point of ignition may have been various, but once they reached that point, the effect was the violation of the brotherhood of man. Time and again, this is the icon accepted, and the suffering and anguish are made subservient to this perfidy.[18] What supports this acceptance is the fact that narrative histories enact the Partition as a tragedy[19] with the appropriate literary language. Thus, titles can immediately alert us to the aesthetic desired even before we have begun to read, and every title is a rhetorical indication of tragedy, that is, of immense suffering consequent upon moral error. A few titles are sufficient intimation of what is going to follow; titles such as *Disastrous Twilight*,[20] *The Roots of Confrontation in South Asia*,[21] and *The Endgames of Empire*.[22]

Even more than the titles, however, the language of historical narratives begins to forfeit its self-imposed neutrality when it comes to the Partition. This is true not only of those histories that are pointedly lurid, and of which, like Collins' and Lapierre's bestsellers, there is no scarcity, but of the responsible chronicles as well. Thus graphic expressions take the place of bland facts: the hordes of forcibly migrating peoples are "fiery" and move across the Punjab "like a dark cloud of locusts" (Wolpert, 1982),[23] are "ablaze," "frenzied" and "raging" (Das, 1982),[24] and are "tempestuous" and "blinded" (Chandra, quoting Nehru 1971).[25] The otherwise sober Chandra even slips at one point into appalling journalese and cliché: "... the dream of Indian Unity had been shattered" and everywhere there was an immense "communal orgy" resulting in "indescribable brutalities" (Chandra, 1971).[26] The irony of historians using this genre is that it was pre-empted by the military: we are told by Auchinlek's second-in-command that in the possibility of the Indian Army becoming inefficient, a plan officially called "Madhouse" had been instated, as had another plan called "Bedlam" in case the army turned hostile.[27] For historians to narrate the Partition as a national tragedy was, it seems, not merely possible or useful. It was inevitable. There was no other stylistic currency available.

Literature

Literature is not sickness, but rather a response to sickness.

Sa'adat Hasan Manto

If the histories of the Partition were intent on characterizing the event as an irresponsible and avertable tragedy, novels were intent on using similar tropes to focus on the consequent affliction which history could not arrogate. Needless to add, using the same tropes only gave novels a comparable focus: they too, like history, used the notions of cause and effect, of tragedy and of morality, and of numbers. In effect, the two methods reflected and complemented each other; they accepted, by and large, the terms of reference that the other had used.[28] To take only the most obvious example, Bhisham Sahni's *Tamas* is a story in which an entire village goes up in flames because a single, minor episode (a pig slaughtered and left outside a mosque) invites revenge, which in turn attracts counter-revenge. The police force called in is helpless, and in the end the British send out the army to put a stop to the continuing devastation. In the meantime, everything worth fighting for has been lost. Here present are cause, effect, morality, tragedy and icon.

Short stories, on the other hand, have used slightly different emphases, and thus set themselves off from history as a method of staging the Partition. To make my meaning clearer I will analyze some, and tease out such stylistic and tonal displays as can be applied across the spectrum of the Partition stories.

In Agyeya's "Muslim-Muslim Bhai-Bhai,"[29] a number of women are waiting for a train to take them out of the town where they have lived all their lives. Over the course of the account, we slowly learn that the women are not really friends, and have gathered together only because they are Muslims, and it is unsafe for them to remain in this largely Hindu locality any longer. The train they are waiting for will take them to the newly formed Pakistan. The wait is long, and when the train arrives, very full and very hostile, the women manage, against all probability, to scramble into a swarming cabin where they are accosted by another bunch of women, and asked to get off. An argument ensues; we learn that the unfriendly women too, are Muslims; that they consider these other women who have just got onto the train to be perceived as lower class women (perhaps prostitutes; this is left deliberately unclear); that the exclusivist disposition of class snobbery is more forceful than the sisterhood of religion (the title becomes ironic at this point); and that finally the women have got off the train, defeated by the overbearing malevolence of difference. The story ends with them standing, helpless and tired, by the edge of the station, knowing that the train that left was the last one out of there.

The irony is doubly fierce: on the one hand, given the fate of most trains that crossed the new Indo-Pakistan border, the class-conscious women will probably meet the same end as the women they abandoned at the station, and on the other, they will do so *because* their victimizers will see them as *not* different from those whom they have abandoned.

What are the gestures used here, and what is the effect? There is no death and much is understood, but primarily two important moves are accomplished. I shall call these the structural focus, and the epiphany.

The structural focus is something that Agyeya's story shares with practically every short story, namely that it is structured in a way in which a single point becomes both the focus and the reason for the existence of the story. The beginning (what in classical rhetoric would be the thematic "laying out of the scene") leads to the event itself, which in turn leads to the reinforcement of the theme at the end (called the "epanalepsis"). Sometimes the event and the epanalepsis are conjoined, a factor familiar to readers of "surprise ending" stories. A single *tone* as well as a single *plot* unites these three structural elements, and so the short story is designed as much to suggest a mood, as it is to detail an event. In the case of Agyeya's anecdote, the waiting comprises the procatascue (i.e., the laying out of the scene) the rejection comprises the event proper, and the later despair comprises the epanalepsis.

The epiphany is the event itself. The reason I call it an epiphany is that, in short stories about the Partition, a complex moment of recognition occurs at a focal point. A person (or people) finds herself in a position where her entire identity is being defined by the rules of somebody else's game. Since the stakes include death – and since choice is excluded from the game – the horror of the moment of focus becomes, in effect, a betrayal – a betrayal of the promise of history, a betrayal of self-possession, even a betrayal of individuality, since the person is defined, usually, as part of a collectivity. It does not matter that her self-perception does not include the definition that others have foisted upon her, nor even that it may have been invisible to her: the moment of betrayal is an internal tectonic shift in which death and the recognition of her loss of identity are glimpsed simultaneously with the comprehension of irreversibility. It does not even matter that she does not die: a transformation has developed, definitive in nature, and she cannot recapture the integrity of the past again, any more than she can rescue the future. It is evident that the epiphany or burst of recognition is infernal and has no saving grace.[30]

All Partition stories have such an epiphany, such a moment of impact, and all such moments are dense with the moral intuition of what it means to undergo an act of betrayal. Such is Agyeya's story "Badla"[31] in which living through the Partition unsettles a Sikh's sense of rootedness so completely that he spends the remainder of his days on a train from Aligarh to Delhi, and back again. So is Mohan Rakesh's celebrated "Malbe ka Malik"[32] in which an aged Pakistani Muslim gentleman visits his now ravaged house in India where his son had died at the hands of his closest friend, and speaks to the friend with affection, ignorant of the part he played in his son's murder, and in which the irony is sharpened to the point where the betrayal (or epiphany), the murder itself, recounted for us, becomes unbearable in the light of the subsequent courteous conversation.

The finest short stories make the point of impact doubly distressing by ironizing its meaning: thus in Manto's "Khol Do"[33] the movement which tells a man that his daughter is alive even though comatose, is the unconscious gesture she makes to pull down her trousers, surrendering herself to rape. Thus in Maheep Singh's "Pani aur Pul"[34] a woman, passing through her old village in a train, remembers its people with simultaneous nostalgia and anxiety, aware, when some of them crowd at her window in a demonstration of affection, that they can be both supportive and malevolent, and that she will never be certain what roles they will take up at any time. Thus too, K A Abbas's impeccably controlled "A Debt to Pay"[35] in which a first person jingoistic account of religious hostility is dismantled at the point of impact when a parochial Muslim scholar witnesses a Sikh dying in the act of protecting him. The Sikh's reason for such a sacrifice is that a Muslim friend had once saved him, the same Muslim friend who was responsible for planting the jingoistic judgment in the scholar's head in the first place. And finally, Sheikh Ayaz's finely wrought portrayal of village frailty in Sindh, entitled "Neighbour"[36] in which the reader is allowed to glimpse the sham neighbourliness of Hindus and Muslims on the eve of Partition, swearing total devotion to each other, allowing for the hollowness of their claims to resound louder with the increasing pitch of their disclaimers.

Some short stories have tried to add a narrative disclaimer to the usual historical option of either/or (*either* Muslim *or* Hindu) by exploiting the possibility of both/and (*both* Hindu *and* Muslim). The Hindu-Muslim antagonism thus becomes a strange form of internal dissonance and confusion, and one that can only lead to duplicity towards a part of oneself. Such a story is the sketch Manto entitled "Tetwal ka Kutta,"[37] in which a stray dog on the Indo-Pakistan border, adopted by the peace-keeping border forces of both countries, is killed by soldiers from either side who out of boredom, and for a bit of fun, take stray shots at it and accuse it of treachery. The irony is that, the only time when the enemies agree about something, is when they want to kill a creature which has been an unselfish friend to both; the indictment of treachery is one that can only recoil back onto them. The tones of pathos and savage frivolity are balanced and captured by the simple tactic of overlapping images of the dog's wounded bewilderment with the soldiers' indifferent brutality, counterbalancing simultaneously the ideas of death and a diversion.

The finest such story, however, is Bhisham Sahni's "Pali."[38] The plot is rudimentary, yet very forceful. A Hindu child loses sight of his parents during the tumultuous disorder of abandoning what is now Pakistan, and is adopted by a childless Muslim couple who, in mild defiance of the community, decide to bring him up as they would their own child. He is circumcised, accepted by the neighbours, and brought up as an orthodox Muslim boy who finally blends in with his new environment. Circumstances devise a method, however, by which the Hindu father finds out about his son, makes a trip to Pakistan, watches on as the child recognizes a very old photograph of his wife and himself, and entreats the Muslim couple to let his son go back to India with him. Reluctantly they agree on the prerequisite that the child be brought up Muslim. The man is hesitant but acquiescent. He and the child leave for India. According to the man's commitment, the child is allowed to say his namaz howsoever he pleases, and to attend Muslim festivals. Thus far, however, he has been a pawn in a game of adults. Now we sense his own individuality which is baffled by the Hindu adults trying, despite his father's support of him, to constrain his non-Hindu behaviour into something more like what the story goes on to suggest is their own provincial Hinduism. The perplexity is further sharpened when the question of his identity becomes a community matter, as it had earlier in Pakistan, and his father has no concrete rejoinders to offer to the bluster of parochialism that the other adults demonstrate. The sketch ends with the child reprehensibly distressed, and traditional enemies are seen to be nowhere more alike than when they are proclaiming difference. It is the child, fostered by both, and a menace to neither, who is victimized for being, as it were, non-sectarian.[39]

Fable

> History is the recital of facts represented as true. Fable, on the other hand, is the recital of facts represented as fiction.
>
> *Voltaire,* Philosophical Dictionary

The iconoclastic author of Urdu short stories, Sa'adat Hasan Manto, who lived during what may be called the Age of the Progressives, a golden period for Urdu Literature and one to which he was a substantial contributor, was among the Partition's most violently distressed voices. His own life, tangential as it may seem in the litany of numbers and atrocities that marked the event at the border of the two new countries, performed a brutal internal re-alignment which finally propelled him to a premature and romantically self-inflicted death.[40]

Manto's stories have, by and large, been noticed against two

146

contemporary backdrops: that of the Progressives, a cluster of ideologically motivated writers deeply responsive to European and Anglo-American intellectual trends, and that of "realism," a propensity which has been commented upon repeatedly in any analysis of his tales that one is likely to come across.

Let it be said at once, that his place within both these grids is not in the least simple. The Progressives, who came into existence in the early 1930s, partly in response to European anti-Fascist trends which they wished to emulate — and which included such stalwarts as Mulk Raj Anand and Sajjad Zahir — were always ambivalent towards Manto. At some points, he was hailed as a fellow Progressive, and at some others, denounced as destructively obsessed with carnality.[41] The best that can be said about this equivocal affiliation is that there were periods of overlap between the aims of the Progressives (a broadly left-of-centre writing) and the aims of Manto (undefined, and experimental).

The assessment of realism is problematic for other reasons. Despite the fact that at least one of his contemporaries regarded him as an anti-realist reactionary, he has come to be seen increasingly as a realist. Thus in a recent overview of his work, Leslie Flemming praises him for his "realistic exploration of themes"[42] and Salim Akhtar remarks that he "was a follower of the tradition of realism in the Urdu short story."[43] All three estimations use the word "realism" to mean "the unpleasant." Thus, to say that Manto was a realist, is to say that Manto's characters and situations are drawn from the grittier, or the more sordid margins of life, and that he centres his tales around the poor, the foolish, the deprived and the marginalized. Prostitutes, victims, and the debased certainly *were* the fodder for his plots, but this does not necessarily make him a realist. Gopi Chand Narang is closer to the mark when he says that Manto's characters are "drawn from the lower strata and are marked by stark *reality*."[44] Manto seems to be — and this is admittedly an atypical understanding of him — a moralist. That is to say, his stories are constructed in such a way, as to manoeuvre his central characters into a false moral position — and one that is usually self-inflicted — and to dismantle their fragile moral foundations in a lamentable crisis which is finally self-destructive. The moral thematics of such a structure has no particular fondness for any one specific strata of society (after all, false moral positions are even more dramatically visible when money or power are involved) and so the only *literary* worth of Manto's fondness for the coarse and the deleterious aspects of existence was that they afforded him a rich and untapped source of moral ambiguities, and thus allowed him to make one single and unpleasant comment upon human behaviour again and again. Nor can this comment be reduced to the simplicity of a moral or an apothegm: Manto was not a writer of allegories or parables: his territory was the rich and variable kingdom of moral uncertainty.[45] In any assessment of his thematic skills, it would probably be just to call him a social moralist who owes more, whether consciously or not, to Pushkin and to Maupassant, than to any of his literary contemporaries.[46]

And yet, despite this difference between himself and the more "realist" Progressives of his time, and despite the quite clear distance between himself and other North Indian writers generally, Manto's stories, for which he is known very widely indeed, used the identical tropes of narrative that I have outlined above: tropes of narrative used by the historians, novelists, and with a change of emphasis, other short story writers of the time and later. Inevitably, there is a cause, an effect, a betrayal and a crisis of tragic division in which the promise of the past is placed beyond reclamation. Manto, like the rest, places his story in the recognizable tenor of his times.

With one exception – "Toba Tek Singh." A marvellous little anecdote which appeared in the collection *Phundne* published in Lahore in 1955, it is a miracle of creation during what may be termed the dry period of production in Manto's life, narrating the reaction of one man – a Sikh landowner incarcerated in a mental home – to the Partition. Abidingly popular,[47] the story is less a developed plot than the unfolding of a sketch which outlines the immense internal changes, a fact that we can only infer but never directly glimpse, occurring inside Toba Tek Singh. The strength of the story lies in a series of cleverly plotted devices which are used to establish an image of the Partition that is unlike any other that we have been given thus far. A brief analysis of some of the most visible ones may be in place to see exactly *what* picture of the Partition is being represented here.

The fact that the fiction takes us to an asylum[48] takes the notion of victimhood to its extreme. There is no creature more forlorn than the insane, unthreatening human being who is bewildered, and in a state of constant confusion about how to deal with the world. Apart from perfunctory acknowledgements that there are also other kinds of insanity available – the violent, for instance, or the macabre – Manto nevertheless focuses on the mild, baffled, and wholly endearing figure of Toba Tek Singh whose constant little acts of harmless lunacy and surprising normalcy (such as dressing up in advance when guests arrive, or reacting to the incomprehensibility of the Partition by altering his equally incomprehensible pidgin speech) are reminders that the consequences of political absurdity can reach the utter outposts of the world.

This political absurdity is nowhere actually mentioned. The Partition happened at some previous time; the story takes place a few years after; who takes the decision to transfer the insane is left vague and is possibly a political gesture of no importance whatsoever ("... it occurred to the Governments of Hindustan and Pakistan ...")[49] and the decision is framed in a jargon that parodies the pomposity of certain journalese visible even in latter day India ("... Anyway, the decision was made by the wise and, accordingly, several high level conferences were held on either side ..."). The unsettling nebulosity of authority is aggravated when we, the readers, come to understand that this is a story plotted to tell us nothing, or very little, of the effects of Partition in cause-effect terms. It moves by focusing on the slow and stupendous changes occurring inside Toba Tek Singh's mind as he tries to deal with what the Partition means. In other words, its story is the story not so much of a willed betrayal, nor possibly, of betrayal at all, but more a tale of anxiety resembling Kafka's meditations on the vacuous but overwhelming pressure of forgotten political gestures.

As the narrative moves along, exploring the alteration in the minds of the insane inmates, a parallel becomes increasingly apparent to us: a parallel between the greater world out there, which committed these people to both the asylum and the pressures of the Partition, and the little world before us of terror and confusion. In effect – by wielding the vigorous narrative skills of metaphor *and* metonymy (we are both reminded of, and find a miniature of, the world in this deranged

149

microcosm) – the lunatics become echoes, or mirrors, of what is happening to humanity at large during Partition. This is signalled in many modest sketches: such as when there is a political rift within the asylum and several inmates set themselves up as either gods or statesmen;[50] such as in Toba Tek Singh's breaking a lifetime's habit of speaking one unintelligible sentence and confusedly politicizing it;[51] such as, at the very end, in the location of the very plot of land that gives Toba Tek Singh his political, legal, and self-conscious identity.[52] The initially comic tone of the piece, betrayed to such great effect through the narration itself, ends in a statement of death as absolute as it is poetic, compressing as it does the very limits of language, politics and identity. For Toba Tek Singh to die is tantamount to his land being stuck in no-man's land, and of India and Pakistan losing all sense of themselves. And this can be expressed, in the end, by nothing more primal and meaningful than a shriek that (in one translation) "pierces the very sky."

To recapitulate and condense: "Toba Tek Singh" is a mirror of the very world that produces it. Refusing to posit itself as an "effect" or "consequence" of a cause, it sees itself as echoing the world in which it reproduces the act of the Partition, as well as its moment of impact, in smaller, profounder ways by concentrating on the penetrating transformation and anguish of one man in a condition of definitive solitude, plundered of whatever ideal he had retained in his troubled mind to keep himself alive. *It must be a monstrous thing indeed, the Partition,* the story seems to say, *which can rob even an insane man of his fragile hold on reality.* Indeed it must; and such a story, such a mirror, can be nothing less than an act of moral condemnation. Metaphorically, *becoming* the world which produced it, the story seems to express itself less as a consequence than as a logical cause of the kind of temperament needed to set off monstrous behaviour. The Partition did not cause it; on the contrary, it needs this kind of deranged political sensibility to create something like the Partition; the Partition is the consequence of our country being no saner in the end than Toba Tek Singh and his many fellow lunatics. The world out there *is* the world in here.

Metaphor and suggestion, then, not allegory nor political morality play,[53] is how the story presents itself. Its narrative tactic declines the

150

expedient four-fold rhetorical tropes outlined above;[54] it represents unreality through other tropes. The question is: do these fresh tropes form some new kind of writing in this story, some original genre, or can they be gathered into something that allows us to see the piece as a familiar genre? I believe the latter is true: that Manto has, whether calculatedly or not, committed his story to the stylistic keeping of one of the oldest genres in the world.

That is to say, the fable. Since "Toba Tek Singh" is, by my estimate, fabulous in the most vital sense of the word, and since my understanding of the fable has been refined and developed by R J Blakham's admirable essay on the subject,[55] it is to this essay that I now turn to help situate Manto's little masterpiece in its scheme of clarification. A story needs very few procedures to qualify as a fable, and the methods it needs, "Toba Tek Singh" seems to possess.

"To start with, a fable is a narrative fiction in the past tense ... [and is] basically a metaphor."[56] Having already clarified the metaphoric mode of Manto's story, let me add to this initial attribute of the fable — that although the story is situated in the past, its *meaning* is transferable. By this I mean that it cannot, to use Harold Bloom's memorable phrase, be folded back into its own time. This is not to say that it "transcends" its situation; more likely, having arisen from a specific situation, it revitalizes itself every time that situation is repeated. Thus "Toba Tek Singh," arising as it does from the particular fact of the Partition of India in 1947, nevertheless dwells in every situation of political segmentation that occurs subsequently. Without any but the most facile changes, such as those of names, it can address itself meaningfully, to take only the most blatantly obvious examples, to the division of post-war Germany, to the division of post-war India, and to the dissolution of the Soviet Union. The story searches out and lays bare, as it were, the profoundest human consequence of political territorial divergence in a *single* such act, and somehow touches the lowest common denominator of *all* such acts which, on coming into contact with it, continue thus to revitalize the meaning of the story.[57] This is not, however, to make some puerile claim to "universality"; it is, more modestly, to claim that wherever political division exists, this fable

151

gathers meaning: it will vanish on the day that political divisions vanish. It is the skeletal meaning of any such division, and is profoundly non-historical in the moral meaning that it generates out of such a situation.

Secondly, the "medium is the message. The message is not delivered – certainly not in the 'morals' tagged on to the Aesopic fables: it is embodied. It is in this sense that [a] fable is a conceptual artifact, which remains to be used."[58] Little needs to be said here, articulating how Toba Tek Singh, the man, bodies forth the fact of the Partition in his perplexed and partitioned self, and how the story connects his biography to the story of his sundered village and country. Moral as it is, Manto's tale is not moralistic: it is impossible to distill succinct apothegms out of it that may be "universally applicable."

And finally, "The action is the whole of the invention [and] inhabits the ambiguous borderland of the aesthetic and the ethical ... [Moreover] as a demonstration [it] is not a policy but a cry, so the truth pictured by a fable is a statement that jolts, not a statement that settles ..."[59] Again, little needs to be adduced as evidence: the story ends both literally and metaphorically as a jolting cry; and the fine borderland between the aesthetic and the ethical – an appropriate metaphor for a story about borderlands – is drawn in the sensitive use of the name of the story, which is also the name of the village and a metaphor for the central character's state of mind, as well as the state of the country.

Manto's fable, then, inhabiting the aesthetic territory that appeals across boundaries because of its link with a political anxiety shared by all divided people, makes its transition into non-historical meaning, precisely by virtue of this aesthetic. In a sense, it is a distillation of the best of several Partition stories. If I may be permitted a critical conceit, it is the Partition story that all Partition stories aspire to be. Slowly, over the years, it has achieved the magisterial and immaculate status of an archetype.

Notes

1   Ramesh Mathur writes: "... the literature of Hindi, Punjabi and Urdu languages is confined to the pre and post-Partition events which took place in the Punjab ..." In *Writing on India's Partition* (Delhi: Sumant, 1976) 17-18.

2   Sa'adat Hasan Manto may be cited as an instance of civilized response to the event. We are told that his "first shocked reactions to the violence of Partition ... [were] essentially a collection of anecdotes, some as short as two lines ..." and were drawn out "... with the barest distant third person narration ... in the ... most stripped down language possible ...." See *Another Lonely Voice: The Life and Works of Sa'adat Hasan Manto*, ed. Leslie Flemming, trans. Tahira Naqvi (Lahore: Vanguard, 1985) 73. Later Manto was to recount that "The Partition of the country and the changes that followed left feelings of revolt in me ... When I sat down to write I found my thoughts scattered. Though I tried hard I could not separate India from Pakistan and Pakistan from India ... my mind could not resolve the question: what country did we belong to now, India or Pakistan?" The above lines are quoted in Khalid Hasan, "Sa'adat Hasan Manto: Not of Blessed Memory," *Annual of Urdu Stories* 4 (1984): 89-90.

3   Recent literary events have gone on to justify this idea. To take the most exceptional example, Bhisham Sahni's popular Hindi novel about Partition, *Tamas,* (Darkness), first published twenty-three years after the event, although the author lived through the phenomenon, was turned into an immensely celebrated television serial aired by the Government of India during prime time a few years back. In the Introduction to the English translation of the novel, the director of the film, Govind Nihalani, wrote that there was an extensive attempt to put a stop to production, because it was feared that the film might aggravate concealed hungers and re-start a settled enmity between Hindus and Muslims. See Bhisham Sahni, *Tamas*, trans. Jai Ratan (New Delhi: Penguin,1988)

4   See Hayden White, "The Historical Text as Literary Artifact," *Tropics of Discourse: Essays in Cultural Criticism* (Baltimore: Johns Hopkins UP, 1978).

5   See Wali Khan, *Facts are Facts: The Untold Story of India's Partition* (New Delhi: Vikas, 1987).

6   See Braj Kishore Singh, *The Indian National Congress and the Partition of India* (Delhi: Capital, 1990).

7   See S H Raza, *Mountbatten and the Partition of India* (New Delhi: Atlantic, 1989).

8   See Sandhya Chandra, *Gandhi and the Partition of India* (New Delhi: Sterling, 1984).

9   See Latif Ahmed Sherwani, *The Partition of India and Mountbatten* (Karachi: Council for Pakistan Studies, 1986). Also see Shahid Hamid, *Disastrous Twilight* (London: Leo Cooper, 1986).

10   See Stanley Wolpert, *Roots of Confrontation in South Asia* (New York: Oxford UP, 1982).

11   See Manmath Nath Das, *Partition and the Independence of India* (New Delhi: Vision Books, 1982). See Percival Spear, *India* (Ann Arbor: Michigan UP, 1961).

12   See Stanley Wolpert, *Roots of Confrontation in South Asia* (New York: Oxford UP, 1982).

13   In all fairness, he does speak of the Partition of Bengal in terms of the response to its suggestion by the British Government. Interestingly, the response is measured statistically: the majority of the population that voted did not desire the Partition. See Bipan Chandra, *India's Struggle for Independence* (New Delhi: Viking, 1988).

14   See Hiren Mukherjee, *Was India's Partition Avoidable?* (Calcutta: Munisha, 1987).

15   S H Raza, for example, comes close to pointing the finger at nobody in particular, and R J Moore effectively focuses on the (un-unified) administrative machinery of British

India in the forties. According to Moore, no single – or even organized mass – move to halt the blunder could possibly have taken place. See S H Raza, *Mountbatten and the Partition of India* (New Delhi: Atlantic, 1989) ; and R J Moore, *Endgames of Empire* (New Delhi: Oxford UP, 1988).

16   It would not be unfair to remark that readers of histories and newspapers in India – that is to say, the literate, urban middle-classes – are far less moved by numbers than their kinsfolk elsewhere in the world. In a nation of such a large population, hundreds and even thousands of deaths (which occur every year, steadily and regularly) leave an unusually weak sense of disaster. In an essay about the Buddha legend, Jorge Luis Borges mentions that in their scriptures, Hindus and Buddhists have become used to large numbers of celestial and terrestrial beings, and are skeptical of numbers (which are "... large bubbles, emphases of nothingness ..." See Jorge Luis Borges, *Other Inquisitions (1937-1952)*, trans. Rith Simms (New York: Simon and Schuster, 1968) 153. Whether this is correct or not, it certainly pertains to the issue of statistics as a form of rhetorical procedure designed to invoke some sense of enormity and magnitude. Very often it may not.

17   See Hayden White, "The Historical Text as Literary Artifact" *Tropics of Discourse: Essays in Cultural Criticism*, (Baltimore: Johns Hopkins UP, 1978) 88-91.

18   Both Stanley Wolpert and Bipan Chandra view this betrayal, however, as a special case of an ongoing tension rooted in a tradition of similar betrayals of Hindus by Muslims and vice-versa. See Stanley Wolpert, *Roots of Confrontation in South Asia* (New York: Oxford UP, 1982); and Bipan Chandra, *India's Struggle for Independence* (New Delhi: Viking, 1988).

19   Shahid Hamid, *Disastrous Twilight* (London: Leo Cooper, 1986).

20   Stanley Wolpert, *Roots of Confrontation in South Asia* (New York: Oxford UP, 1982).

21   R J Moore, *Endgames of Empire* (New Delhi: Oxford UP, 1988).

22   See Stanley Wolpert, *Roots of Confrontation in South Asia* (New York: Oxford UP, 1982).

23   See Manmath Nath Das, *Partition and the Independence of India* (New Delhi: Vision Books, 1982).

24   See Bipan Chandra, *Modern India* (New Delhi: NCERT, 1971).

25   See Bipan Chandra, *Modern India* (New Delhi: NCERT, 1971).

26   There are a few exceptions, but these are so rare that it is practically impossible to locate them. Although history refuses to transgress the trope of tragedy in this instance, once in a while, an ironic or farcical phrase alleviates the horror into a kind of grim parody of itself. One such example occurs in Shahid Hamid's *Disastrous Twilight* when the author quotes an unknown British Magistrate as saying: "The British are a just people. They have left India in exactly the same state of chaos as they found it." See Shahid Hamid, *Disastrous Twilight* (London: Leo Cooper, 1986). It would, however, be just as well to keep in mind Hayden White's warning regarding the innate status of history-as-tragedy: "No historical event is intrinsically tragic; it can only be conceived as such from a particular point of view, or from within the context of a structured set of events of which it is an event enjoying a privileged place ..." See Hayden White, "The Historical Text as Literary Artifact," *Tropics of Discourse: Essays in Cultural Criticism* (Baltimore: Johns Hopkins UP, 1978).

27   See Shahid Hamid, *Disastrous Twilight* (London: Leo Cooper, 1986) 54-100.

28   It should be clarified, however, that my statements here are descriptive and not prescriptive. A novel written about Partition may, in future, use different rhetorical gestures or even ironize existing ones. None that have appeared so far seem to do either.

29   S H V Agyeya, "Muslim-Muslim-Bhai-Bhai," *Writing on India's Partition*, ed. Ramesh Mathur (Delhi: Sumant, 1976).

30   It is possible to see this epiphany as embodying what C M Naim has ventured to notice in Indian Muslims, a self-image of "undifferentiated, consolidated community," with the minor difference that the self-image of undifferentiation is not voluntary but inflicted forcibly. See C M Naim "Being a Muslim in India: The Challenge and the Opportunity" *Contemporary Indian Tradition*, ed. Carla M Borden (Washington: Smithsonian Institution Press, 1989) 57-65.

31   S H V Agyeya, "Badla," *Writing on India's Partition*, ed. Ramesh Mathur.

32   Mohan Rakesh, "Malbe ka Malik," *Writing on India's Partition*, ed. Ramesh Mathur.

33   See Sa'adat Hasan Manto, *Kingdom's End and Other Stories*, trans. Khalid Hasan (New Delhi: Penguin, 1989). The author was considered a sexual pervert for writing this piece. His own response was typical and accurate: "If you cannot bear these stories, that means that this is an unbearable time." See Sa'adat Hasan Manto, *Another Lonely Voice: The Life and Works of Sa'adat Hasan Manto*, ed. Leslie Flemming, trans. Tahira Naqvi (Lahore: Vanguard, 1985) 32.

34   Maheep Singh "Pani Aur Pul," *Writing on India's Partition*, ed. Ramesh Mathur.

35   K A Abbas, "A Debt to Pay," *Writing on India's Partition*, ed. Ramesh Mathur.

36   Sheikh Ayaz, "Neighbour," *Writing on India's Partition*, ed. Ramesh Mathur. The story was banned in Pakistan.

37   See Sa'adat Hasan Manto, *Kingdom's End and Other Stories*, trans. Khalid Hasan (New Delhi: Penguin, 1989).

38   See Bhisham Sahni, *We Have Arrived in Amritsar and Other Stories*, trans. Jai Ratan (New Delhi: Penguin, 1998).

39   With regard to the distinctions between historical and fictional narrative representations, the latter have treated of the anxieties of women, children and animals – the non-threatening part of society – as *also* created by the same psychological forces that inspired the rioting. Need I add that it is invariably male?

40   I used the word "romantic" in its literary sense. Manto died of excessive drinking – which he indulged in despite his doctor's directives – at the age of 42, having composed his own epitaph five months earlier. The epitaph reads: "Here lies Sa'adat Hasan Manto. In his breast are buried all the secrets and nuances of the art of short story writing. Even now, weighted down by earth, he is wondering if *he* is the great short story writer or God!" More to the purpose, Manto could never decide which country he belonged to after 1947. He spent a number of years after Partition in India, but went over to Pakistan later and died in Lahore, a citizen of Pakistan. Since he was not particularly religious, it seems clear that his decision was motivated by expedience rather than sectarian inclination, and that he was never wholly comfortable with it. His final years, lacerated as they were by the sense of dual belonging, comprised of

the most forlorn and unproductive time of his life. See Sa'adat Hasan Manto, *Another Lonely Voice: The Life and Works of Sa'adat Hasan Manto*, ed. Leslie Flemming, trans. Tahira Naqvi (Lahore: Vanguard, 1985) 21.

41 It is astonishing, in retrospect, how puritanical this movement was. One of the Manto stories which came under this particular kind of fire was "Mozel," the story of a Jewish prostitute – though this is never made explicit – and a besotted Sikh lover of hers who goes to enormous lengths to fulfill her outlandish demands. Somewhat hackneyed, it is nevertheless an erotic story of great charm. Another such story, subsequently banned in Pakistan, was "Khol Do," a chilling tale of the absolute pitilessness of gang-rape which Ali Sardar Jafri, a Progressive himself, initially applauded as "the masterpiece of this period" (see Sa'adat Hasan Manto, *Another Lonely Voice: The Life and Works of Sa'adat Hasan Manto*, ed. Leslie Flemming, trans. Tahira Naqvi (Lahore: Vanguard, 1985) 28. Later Jafri had occasion to change his mind, but most today concur with his earliest verdict. Over time, several writers broke off from the Progressives because of their restrictive, increasingly left-wing dispositions; Manto himself came to scorn them and broke off ties with them after a public denunciation of one of his stories in Hyderabad. His own words are perhaps the best indication of his position vis-á-vis this movement: "... At first, progressives made my writing known and were proud that Manto was one of them. Now they say that Manto is not one of them ... If anyone should ask me what group I am in, I will say that I am alone, in every respect alone ..." See Manto, *Another Lonely Voice.* Needless to add that such a self-evaluation is by no means the whole truth. He learnt from several European masters, notably Freud, Chekhov, Pushkin and Maupassant, and began his literary career in the early thirties by translating into Urdu, Victor Hugo's *The Last Days of a Condemned Man* and Oscar Wilde's *Vera.* Later he was himself to be compared, with some fairness, to Maupassant, and in recent times he has been equated with Gorky. See Frederick I Kaplan and S S Dulai, "Humanity at Bay: The Conflict Between Man and the Word in the Stories of Gorky and Manto," *Journal of South Asian Literature*, 13 (1977-78): 1-8.

42 See Leslie Flemming, "Foreword," *Journal of South Asian Literature*, 20 (1985): iii.

43 See Salim Akhtar, "Is Manto Necessary Today?" *Journal of South Asian Literature*, 20 (1985): 1.

44 See Gopi Chand Narang, "Introduction," *The Best of Manto*, ed. and trans. Jai Ratan, (New Delhi: Sterling, 1989): vi.

45 Leslie Flemming is closer to the truth of this view when she uses the word "realism" – as she does – to mean something other than "focussing upon the sordid." In a later publication she says that realism is a plot that "deals with a single illuminating event in the life of a single character." See Sa'adat Hasan Manto, *Another Lonely Voice: The Life and Works of Sa'adat Hasan Manto*, ed. Leslie Flemming, trans. Tahira Naqvi (Lahore: Vanguard,1985): 95. Yes indeed. This is what I have called the epiphany or, in the case of Partition stories and much of Manto, the instant of (sometimes self) betrayal.

46 Nor am I the first to feel so. For other reasons, both Mumtaz Shirin and Gopi Chand Narang have indicated Manto's resemblance to Maupassant. Why this is so may be understandable in the light of Rashid Ahmed Siddiqui's suggestion, made as early as

1945, that Urdu was the first Indian language to react nationally to foreign ideas. For reference to Mumtaz Shirin, see Leslie Flemming, "Foreword," *Journal of South Asian Literature*, 20 (1985). For reference to Gopi Chand Narang, see Gopi Chand Narang, "Introduction" *The Best of Manto*, ed. and trans. Jai Ratan (New Delhi: Sterling, 1989). For reference to Siddiqui, see Rashid Ahmed Siddiqui, "Urdu Literature" *The Indian Literatures of Today*, ed. Bharatan Kumarappa (Bombay: The International Book House Ltd., 1947).

47   The most articulate among dozens of attestations about its popularity, Leslie Flemming mentions that "the story has profoundly moved not only Indian and Pakistani readers, but American University students as well" and adds in a footnote that it has " been a perennial favourite." See Sa'adat Hasan Manto, *Another Lonely Voice: The Life and Works of Sa'adat Hasan Manto*, ed. Leslie Flemming, trans. Tahira Naqvi (Lahore: Vanguard, 1985). This is part of a wider appreciation of Manto who is considered to be "... the most controversial and most widely read Urdu short story writer ... [there is]." See Gopi Chand Narang, "Introduction," *The Best of Manto*, ed. and trans. Jai Ratan (New Delhi: Sterling, 1989).

48   Manto had first-hand experience of a mental home; he voluntarily confined himself to one in 1952 to try and rid himself of his destructive alcoholism, to no avail. He left some weeks later and recalled the episode with some bitterness afterwards. See Sa'adat Hasan Manto, *Another Lonely Voice: The Life and Works of Sa'adat Hasan Manto*, ed. Leslie Flemming, trans. Tahira Naqvi (Lahore: Vanguard, 1985) 18.

49   All quotations from the story are from the translation by M Asaduddin. See this volume, p. 64-71.

50   One inmate declares himself God – only to be later accused of sectarianism by another inmate – and two unfortunates set themselves up as leaders of the Sikh and Muslim communities, one calling himself Jinnah, the other Tara Singh.

51   From "opar di gurgur di annexe di bay dhiana di mung di daal of the laltain" it becomes "opar di gurgur di annexe di bay dhiana di mung di daal of the government of Pakistan," and later, in a fit of pique against "God" who turns out to have parochial Muslim sentiments to the detriment of the rest of the inmates, becomes "opar di gurgur di annexe di bay dhiana di mung di daal of Vahe Guruji da Khalsa and Vahe Guruji ki Fateh ... jo boley so nihaal sat srı akaal. "

52   The idea is conceived in a delicate and brilliant device of conflation: Toba Tek Singh is so named because that is the name of the village to which he belongs. Thus, at the end of the story when we discover that the village is nowhere to be located, the sense of dislocation extends to Toba Tek Singh, the Sikh inmate. At his cry at the end, when he collapses to the ground, several narratives converge. The last line of the story reads: "In between, on a bit of earth *which had no name*, lay Toba Tek Singh." *Which* Toba Tek Singh, we ask, the man or the village? The implication is *both*. In other words, in a demonstration of violent irony, Toba Tek Singh has collapsed in

his own village, not only ignorant of that fact, but only when it, like himself, has been robbed of identity and, extended between India and Pakistan, has been plundered of a name. See Leslie Flemming, "The Post-Partition Stories of Sa'adat Hasan Manto," *Journal of South Asian Literature* 13 (1977-78): 99-109.

53 Flemming has called the story an allegory. See Sa'adat Hasan Manto, *Another Lonely Voice: The Life and Works of Sa'adat Hasan Manto*, ed. Leslie Flemming, trans. Tahira Naqvi (Lahore: Vanguard, 1985) 83. An allegory, however, asks for an exact point-for-point resemblance to the world of moral ideas, such that, for instance, X character would stand in for Y virtue (or vice). To do this to "Toba Tek Singh" would be to force its characters into curious categories simply to prove a point.

54 See the discussion on Cause/Effect, Morality, Statistics, Tragedy on p. 139

55 See H J Blakham, *The Fable as Literature* (London: Athlone, 1985).

56 See Blakham, *The Fable as Literature,* p. xi.

57 Thus "[a] fable will not merely express a truth graphically and memorably, but mainly will generate and store new meaning in the conception it represents ..." See Blakham, *The Fable as Literature*, p. xi.

58 See Blakham, *The Fable as Literature*, p. xix.

59 See Blakham, *The Fable as Literature,* pp. 225-52.

PARTITION: STRATEGIES OF OBLIVION, WAYS OF REMEMBERING

RAVIKANT

Hai kaun satya? Patte jiske jharte rahte?
Ya vah jisme nit nutan patra nikalte hain?
Do roop, ek se naash hame avgat karta,
Doosara, mrityu par hami panv de chalte hain.

Ramdhari Singh Dinkar

Those who forget history are condemned to repeat it.

The *Tamas* reminder

History lies not by misrepresenting reality but by exiling emotions.

Ashis Nandy

One can easily hear the narcissistic nation's optimistic voice at its "moment of arrival" in the nationalist poet, Ramdhari Singh Dinkar's "Ek Bharatiya Atma ke Prati," a poem he wrote on his sixtieth birthday. The poet's free nation was then a baby which had not even completed three years after an unimaginably painful birth that took place in the most vicious of circumstances – amidst death and destruction, loot and arson, en bloc migration and dislocation, molestation, abduction and rape, fear, insecurities and untold miseries of refugee life. The Indian freedom came – anticlimactically for many – with Partition. The occasion for celebration was also one for mourning. The irony and pathos of the predicament was underlined by Faiz in an oft-quoted couplet:

Yeh daag daag ujala, yeh shab gazida sahar
Vo intezar tha jiska, yeh vo sahar to nahi[1]

Here, less obvious than the almost total rejection of the night bitten dawn, is a sense of disappointment, even lamentation. This heart broken, disillusioned couplet stands in sharp contrast to the confident statement from Dinkar, exhorting the Indian soul to forget the destruction and move ahead, trampling down even death. Nehru, the quintessential visionary of progress, or Sardar Patel, the pragmatic nation builder, could not have said it better – not in any case, in as muscular a poetry as that of the virile poet Dinkar.[2] These concerns of the nationalist poet were strikingly similar to those of the first prime minister and the first home minister of independent India. This essay will elaborate upon the less-than-coincidental nature of this similarity while making a broad argument about national memories – "historical" and "fictional."

Till recently, we as a nation, in fact, have been sleepwalking through these decades until an odd film or a novel, or the actuality of a riot awakens us to momentarily remember and refer back to the nightmare of the Partition. The nation has grown up, ritually counting and celebrating birthdays – its own and of the great souls that won it the freedom – while systematically consigning the Partition to oblivion.

Given our preference for collective – and selective – amnesia, it is hardly surprising that the unusually strife-ridden, violent times we are living in, have jolted many scholars and intellectuals out of inertia. The Partition has managed to become an agenda for at least some of them.[3] In this context, it is perhaps a justifiable lament that we do not have rich archives in terms of historical, literary or biographical documentation. Alok Bhalla, the editor of a useful collection of stories relating to the Partition, feels that "there is not just a lack of great literature, there is, more seriously, a lack of great history."[4] A newspaper essay that tried to gather views of painters, writers and theatre personalities representing "two generations" recorded these ideas, concluding that we Indians have been unable to come to terms with what is the most catastrophic moment in our recent history.[5]

To be sure, this widely felt sense of dearth is not about any kind of discursive production on the Partition. For there has been a constant flow of well-researched volumes on different aspects of the subject. Historians, for one, cannot be faulted with having ignored the Partition as such. What has, rather, become the issue is the question of ways of seeing. A historiographical review essay correctly points out that one predominant concern with historians has been to see and explain the Partition as nothing more than a mere "transfer of power." And the nationalist approach in this respect has been no less "whiggish" – hence "elitist" – than that of colonial historiography represented by Percival Spear and later by Gallagher, Tomlinson and others.[6] The narrowness of such constitutionalist approaches is too obvious to be repeated here.

Even the histories that cannot be bracketed in the above categories are marked by similar limitations. An obsessive concern with causation has led them to an analysis of the goings-on in the domain of high politics.[7] It is from that domain of high politics that heroes and villains have been created or demolished to answer the nagging question: was the Partition inevitable? A permanent favourite with the university examination systems, the question invariably produces examinees' resolution in one variant of apologia or the other. In other words, at least a couple of generations of historians, and those who read these histories, produced and digested superficial, apologetic literature. Superficial, since there always had been easy villains to lay the entire blame on, and feel relieved. Historian's history could never show in any significant detail the Partition as a great human tragedy, simply because the ordinary men and women – except as an amorphous mass – were always kept out of it.[8] Viewed in this way, Bhalla's complaints about "lack of good history" make a lot of sense.

It is possible to explain this lack in terms of limitations inherent in the craft of history writing. But there is more to it than History's innate helplessness in representing pain and suffering. How can one, for example, account for the perennial refusal of historians to treat Partition

161

as part of Indian history, as part and culmination of the same processes that resulted in the Independence which they are so fond of. The dominant view with regard to Partition as "aberration," as "nationalism gone awry"[9] and the "other" of Independence amounts to nothing less than a form of self-denial, a flight as it were, a tendency to run away from the harsh realities of the past.[10]

The problem of coming to terms with a harsh past is further complicated by the continued state of tension and conflict between "Hindus" and "Muslims" on the one hand, and India and Pakistan on the other. Riots inside and wars on the front are occasional yet violent expressions of the uneasy – and I shall argue, unequal – relationships between the communities and the nations. Partition – the event, memory and metaphor – indubitably remains central to this long history of strife and warfare. As a result, there exists a liberal consensus whereby issues of communal violence in general, and the Partition in particular, are disallowed any serious space not only in the children's histories, but also in adult discourses.[11] The device of declaring certain issues as "sensitive," and therefore taboo, has meant, for all practical purposes, an undeclared ban on them, making writing or any other practice a difficult exercise.

I wish to illustrate this point by a brief recall of the fierce controversy the tele-serialisation of *Tamas* provoked in January-February 1988. The six hour long film, based on Bhisham Sahni's Sahitya Akademi award winning Hindi novel of the same name, and a couple of stories – "Sardarni" and "Zahur Baksha" – was broken up and shown on six consecutive Saturday nights, 10 pm onwards. This clearly was not a prime time slot, since for the Mandi House the film apparently belonged to the suspect domain of the "sensitive." Though recreated by an able and sensitive team led by no less a director than Govind Nihalani, the film did not exactly attract wide publicity or rave previews. But once the first episode was shown, it caught the imagination of an estimated 3.5 crore viewers. That was a poignant moment of collective encounter – brought about for the first time in the nation's history by an immensely powerful and unique audio-visual medium, leaving a countrywide audience stunned. The film was widely acclaimed by critics as a landmark, a "true to life" production, and an eye-opening account that helped understand what had hitherto remained by and large incomprehensible. The importance of *Tamas* was also sought to be underlined in its reformatory role in the present, which in turn came to be seen as a mere extension of that gruesome past.[12] Yet this is only one side of the success story of *Tamas*.

On the flip side, newspaper editors received angry letters complaining that *Tamas* disturbed and caused insomnia, the import being the futility and cruelty of showing something that was painfully real and still very much a part of existence. *Tamas* evoked actions even more angry and violent. The Hindu Right, more precisely one "Javed Siddiqui, fronting for the Shiv Sena," challenged the validity of the telecast in the Bombay High Court, claiming that the serial distorted history and was lopsided in implicating the Hindus alone in the scenes depicting violence. The BJP, together with its mass fronts, carried out violent demonstrations at various Doordarshan Centres in Punjab, Delhi and Bombay, demanding the serial to be taken off air. Bhisham Sahni and Govind Nihalani received anonymous life threats, with the result that they "began moving out with a ring of pistol-packing security men."[13]

The point in going over the controversy about *Tamas* is not to restate the obvious that memories of the Partition are troublesome and unpleasant. Not even that some of these images are eerily topical today, rendering the subject "sensitive," making forgetting pragmatic and silence sensible. On the contrary, the telecast of *Tamas* was an explosive moment. The debate around, and the protest against *Tamas* exposed the hollowness of many truth claims – for example, the inherent presence of tolerance and democracy in Hinduism. Secondly, the State betrayed its own political preference by giving a marginal timeslot to the telecast, assuming a priori, the "sensitive" nature of the film. In the seventies, M S Sathyu's *Garam Hawa* had generated similar controversies, and was cleared for public screening only after the prime minister and the cabinet watched and approved it. Neither *Tamas* nor *Garam Hawa* led to any riot. Yet the representations of the Partition have regularly been suppressed in the name of the ever-lurking fear of a possible riot. This fear, in its myriad political and cultural avatars,

163

constitutes our "oppressive present." Here, even writing about the historiography of riots invites serious accusations of indulging in "emotional balkanisation" and "disintegration" of India.[14] There is thus a definite politics responsible for not being able to write meaningfully: there have been conscious strategies of oblivion.

In order to historically establish and nuance this statement, it is necessary to revisit the early years of Indian Independence. Partition wounds were fresh then; migration to and from the other side of the newly created border was still on. Partition was not a distant memory, but a quotidian experience being lived out. The State was understandably busy dealing with the expediencies arising out of the Partition. The elaborate exercise, however, was seen as pragmatically unavoidable and transitional administrative work of preparing the stage for the real dramatis personae – progress and national reconstruction.

This is the sense one gets reading the speeches of Sardar Patel, the busy home minister and "Iron-man," responsible for dissolving princely states and integrating them into the Indian nation. He was in a Dinkar-like hurry to clean the nation's air, polluted by bad faith and bad blood, that accompanied the evil called Partition. Patel saw communal tensions as mere hiccups in the way of national progress – a far cry from the endeavours and appeals of a fasting Gandhi. In fact, Patel believed that the government deserved a word of admiration for the unparalleled ease with which the daunting task of the transfer of power was achieved. Partition is reduced in Patel's discourse to a tough but ultimately manageable, administrative exercise. Consider the following extract from one of his speeches:

> Even though we were overwhelmed by the disturbances after the Independence Day, we have accomplished a great deal. We have carried out successfully and effectively the separation of armed services, stores, both civilian and military, and of many other large undertakings incidental to Partition ... We have settled all this out of court. In addition we have carried out an exchange of forty to fifty lakhs of people on each side. Any government in the world would have been overwhelmed by such tremendous responsibilities, but thank god we have weathered the storm and turned the corner.[15]

Patel's voice here appears like one coming from above – from the chief of the family who had to carry out his responsibilities in a moment of crisis, and hence, trial. Patel's "we" is not the people of India and Pakistan, but their leaders and/or governments. Patel takes pride in the fact that problems were sorted out internally – by dialogue and mutual agreement; they, the heads of two nations, did not go to any court. Thus, the Partition gets naturalised as another sad but ordinary quarrel between two brothers in a Hindu undivided family.

However, Patel knows that the explanation is *not* convincing enough, for it is not as if the Partition just happened. Therefore, he is under some pressure to explain why the Partition plan was accepted:

> I can tell you that if we had not accepted Partition, India would
> have broken into bits. The country is saved from fragmentation
> by the accession of States. Otherwise, a Raja-sthan would have
> been something worse than Pakistan.[16]

He rationalises the Partition as inevitable, indeed, a wise solution in the existing circumstances. Nothing much was thus lost in his opinion. On the contrary, if Indians helped the government in its endeavours, a greater integrationist dream could be realised:

> Now that we have been able to salvage a major part of India and
> have been able to build it up into an extensive single unit, let us
> make it powerful. If we become prosperous and powerful, I have
> no doubt that small bits of territory round India would themselves
> take our shelter.[17]

The people therefore need not worry, concluded Patel. They only had to strengthen the government. It may be argued that the Sardar was trying to instill confidence in his "subjects" who had gone and were still going through a painful experience. What is interesting is that he goes to the extent of suppressing the truth with respect to the patriarchal attitude towards abducted women:

> I have not come across any who is not anxious to claim them [the
> oppressed and suffering women] back into his home.[18]

One could ask, if men had been magnanimous about "their" abducted women as Patel has it, why on earth the appeal? Patel obviously was more interested in painting a rosy picture, reducing the Partition to a non-problem.[19] And from the Muslims who chose to stay back in India, Patel demanded an unalloyed loyalty to the nation, their only saviour. Patel's speech at Lucknow had different messages for Hindus and Muslims. While the RSS was exhorted "to use their wisdom and work judiciously," Muslims were given a candid admonition by their "true friend":

> Mere declarations of loyalty to the Indian Union will not help them at this critical juncture. They must give practical proof of their declarations ... Those who are disloyal will have to go to Pakistan. Those who are still riding on two horses will have to quit Hindustan.[20]

Understandably, some Muslims of Lucknow came running to the Mahatma, who in his turn tried to defend his colleague by saying that he was good at heart, while accepting that Patel should not have spoken in the manner he did.[21] This only further irritated Patel. In an anguished letter to Gandhi on 13 January, 1948, Patel made his sentiments explicit, "... you have again and again to take up cudgels on my behalf. This ... is intolerable to me." On another occasion, referring to Gandhi's "compulsions" to defend him, he said, "I am not a weak person who should be defended by others."[22] Clearly, Sardar Patel was no longer the Mahatma's "yes man" he used to be. Himself being isolated and helpless, Gandhi was forced to speak in the State's voice, demanding loyalty from the Muslims:

> Let them prove that they can be trusted and they must understand that they must be loyal to the Indian Union and not to Pakistan. I shall judge them by their conduct ... since I have undertaken the fast in the cause of the Muslims, a great responsibility has come to devolve on them.[23]

This was a few days before Nathuram Godse killed the Mahatma. And the news that a Hindu committed the act was received with a sense of relief in Muslim households.[24]

Now I will turn to the text written by Rajendra Prasad, the first President of India. The text which is an introduction to a collection of Gandhi's essays – most of which relate to Partition – on communal harmony, pays glorious tribute to Gandhi for his indomitable courage, and expresses hope that the readers will learn from these writings. In a short space of nine pages, Rajendra Prasad squeezes in Gandhi's biography and a history of Hindu-Muslim relations from Khilafat to Partition. Khilafat, to him, represented the first and the last occasion when Indian Muslims actively participated in the Indian national movement after which,

> ... [they] gradually drifted away from the Congress and the Congress movement and with the exception of a small number of stalwarts amongst whom the most prominent was Maulana Abul Kalam Azad, practically the whole community became indifferent, if not hostile, to what the Congress was doing. Before the Muslim League emerged as a power demanding division of India into Muslim and non-Muslim India, there were some who had been working in their own silent way and carrying on propaganda among Muslim intellectuals. But Mahatma Gandhi did not lose faith and continued to work for unity and especially for Hindu-Muslim unity ... It is remarkable how by his honest and fearless advocacy of communal unity he has *enraged many of the Muslims and a negligible few among the Hindus; the Muslims as a body, with a few exceptions, looked upon him as an enemy* ... (emphasis mine)[25]

Gandhi was killed, Prasad goes on to say, by those Hindus who did not like his indefatigable efforts to give protection to the Muslims. In this telescoped history of the quarter of a century, he equates the national movement with the Congress movement, and "communalism" with the Muslim League's efforts at dividing India into two. Quite clearly, the Gandhian project of uniting communities into a whole is far from finished – the text not only reproduces some of Gandhi's thoughts on the subject, but also by putting a preface imposes a certain

167

reading of Gandhi, "communalism" and Partition:

> This is the long and tragic history of Mahatma Gandhi's attempts to establish Hindu-Muslim unity which ended with the establishment of Pakistan on the one side and his supreme sacrifice on the other. The *problem* has, however, not been solved inspite of the creation of Pakistan. We have *still some 40 millions of Muslims in this country*, spread all over the vast area of what is called India today.[26] (emphasis mine)

While Prasad's lamentations about the creation of Pakistan not delivering the required goods could be that of any Congressman's, what is striking in his narrative is the fact that the Muslims living in India, by the very *act* of their living, constitute a problem. The unstated implication in the statement is an open violation of the principles of the Congress-led national movement and the grounds (rejection of the two-nation theory, acceptance of minorities, etc.) on which Partition was accepted: Prasad chooses to go against the very constitution he is supposed to uphold. And all this is done in the preface of a text intended to promote communal harmony!

The statements of Sardar Patel and Rajendra Prasad represent different voices of the State, concerned to create "normal conditions" so that the nation could achieve and preserve unity and integrity, and move unobtrusively on the path of progress. The project of unity is sought to be accomplished by a certain homogenizing drive by including a sense of oneness among different communities of India. This discourse is remarkable for the selections it makes from history, as for the reified vision it presents for the future. The vision, both about the past and the future, either ignores or blames, but ultimately marginalizes the minorities, especially the Muslims. It unilaterally blames all the Muslims – with certain exceptions – for the Partition, by telling us that most of them wanted Pakistan.

There are nevertheless certain literary texts that do not speak in the State's voice: the Partition in these texts is more than mere physical vivisection of India into two enemy states. The Partition here is not just lamentation – though it is that as well – for, what can be termed

"Partition Literature" is grounded in a sense of loss, terror and uncertainty. It also points towards the ambivalence and the conflicting pulls of loyalty which the people experienced, and for which the State had hardly any sympathies. In certain significant ways, this literature tries to show the ways in which violence was perpetrated on men and women. There are also recent alternative secondary readings of communalism, nationalism, Independence and Partition that focus on the memories and oral narratives of the victims, survivors and perpetrators of sectarian atrocities during the Partition.[27] Literature – written in Hindi, Urdu, Bangla, Punjabi and several other languages – forms another huge archive. Taking forms ranging from fictional genres such as stories, novels, poems to intimate autobiographical narratives, literary memory is treated as a mandatory source for reflections on the Partition. Krishna Sobti registers one such fragment revisiting the Partition after forty years:

> *Balle-balle Jawaharlal*
> *Tune kar diya kamaal*
> *Tujhe sau-sau sisen de raha*
> *Har Punjabi lal ke jo*
> *Lut-put ke aaya hai*
> *Saath mein kuch nahi laya hai*
> *Dariyaon ke paani cheer-char*
> *Tune kar diya bada kamaal*
> *Dharti phad Punjab ki*
> *Hame de diya ek rumaal*
> *Kis kar ke?*
> *Is kar ke*
> *Chahe mathe peeten*
> *Chahe mar-khap jaayen*
> *Kis kar ke?/*
> *Is kar ke*
> *Aazadi Khoon chahti hai*
> *Tabhi vah rang lati hai*
> *Tere chehre ka kamaal*

169

Balle-balle Jawaharlal
Ab arz karen ham milke
Laakhon haal behaal
Sambhalo raj apna,
Sambhalo desh apna,
Sambhalo mohar apni,
Sambhalo fauj apni,
Balle-balle Jawaharlal. [28]

This fragment, overheard on the streets of Delhi, in Sobti's words, was "neither a song nor a story. It was an answer to the question that time had pasted" on the victims of the Partition. This peculiar intractable fragment might not be a great piece of literature, but it contains, in spite of its cynicism, a sense of pain and deja vu. The ironies of the Partition are writ large in the mock celebration that Nehru receives in the text. The Partition was as impossible as separating the waters of the rivers of the Punjab. The handkerchief that Jawaharlal offered them is little consolation in the face of indescribable miseries that fell to their lot. And now that the impossible had been made possible, they completely disassociate themselves from the act of Partition. They dedicate the raj, the "desh," the "mohar" and the "fauj" (literally, the rule, the nation, the insignia, and the army, in that order) to the one who has created them.

I do not need to emphasize the stark contrast between statements made by Prasad and Patel on the one hand, and the statement recorded by Krishna Sobti on the other. If the former represents the State's concern and is a voice from above, the latter originates in an undefined elsewhere. It is a voice that cannot be harnessed into the meta-narratives of progress and unity. The Partition, here, is not just a clinical, administrative exercise: it is the price some people have paid for freedom. Independence and Partition are not two mutually exclusive tropes, but are linked with each other in an inseparable manner, products of the same historical processes. Literature, in this sense, represents a space where voices resistant to the elite national narratives find expression.

It is not my intention to glorify literature as a preserve of popular memory, hence as resistance against State power. There are voices in it that can be easily identified with concerns of the State. In fact, Partition as a metaphor has often been deployed by both the State's secularist agenda and by those fighting sectarian forces in post-Partition India. Here the Partition is generally divested of its historicity and equated with conditions of riots of which India has had one too many.[29] *Tamas* was defended in the press on precisely these grounds. Representations of the Partition are celebrated for their reformatory contents because the Partition for many is a lesson that Indians should have learnt.[30]

The post-Partition context of Indian cultural production bears the distinct mark of hegemonizing discourses. It is a context marked by diminishing Muslim characters in Hindi novels,[31] a gradual decline in "Muslim socials" in Bombay films,[32] and the slow, painful journey of Urdu and Hindustani towards oblivion.[33] This is a context in which growing up Muslim means growing up facing both the stereotypical expectations, as well as the charge of identifying with Pakistan.[34] Kashmir, Ayodhya, Bhagalpur, Pokhran, Kargil, or even a cricket match becomes an occasion for the nationalist surveillance and scrutiny of the ever suspect Muslim loyalty. For "proven defaulters" Pakistan represents a ready-made dustbin to which they can with impunity be consigned. The Partition and the metaphor it represents is implicated in all such omissions, erasures, and stereotyping. The shadow cast by the Partition has indeed been a long one. As Kedarnath Agrawal prophetically and poignantly wrote in August 1946:

> *Aah! Dharti bant gayi hai!*
> *Ek Hindustan ab do ho gaya hai.*
> *Aag, paani aur gagan tak bant gaya hai.*
> *Aadmi ka dil, kaleja kat gaya hai ...*
> *Bhool ek aisi hui hai,*
> *Jo aneko peedhiyon tak dukh hame deti rahegi*
> *Hum karaha hi karenge.*
> *(Alas! The earth stands divided*
> *And the unity of India partitioned*

Fire, water and even the sky is divided,

The human heart has been cut up ...

Such a blunder has been committed,

That we'll suffer for many generations

We'll continue to writhe in pain. (Translation mine)

Notes

1 Faiz Ahmed Faiz, "Subah-e-Aazadi," *Saare Sukhan Hamaare* (Delhi: Rajkamal, 1993) 163.

2 To be fair to Dinkar's poetry, it represents a whole range of voices but its popularity rests particularly in those poems that try to evoke a sense of nationalist valour. See *Chakraval* (Patna: Udayachal, 1950) for many such poems.

3 A significant sign of the shift is the unprecedented attention showered on the Partition by almost all the leading English dailies and weeklies in 1997; the fiftieth year of Independence witnessed substantial commemorative coverage on Partition as well. See for example the special issues of *Outlook,* 28 May 1997, *India Today,* 18 Aug. 1997 and *Frontline,* 22 Aug. 1997.

4 See Pamela Philipose, "Unfinished Journey," *The Indian Express*, New Delhi, Aug. 14 1994.

5 Pamela Philipose, "Unfinished Journey," *The Indian Express*, New Delhi, Aug. 14 1994.

6 See Carl Bridge and H V Brasted, "Explaining the Transfer of Power in India: An Historiographical Post-mortem," *Occasional Papers*, Neheru Memorial Museum and Library, New Delhi, 2nd Ser. 64 (1992).

7 Asim Roy, "The High Politics of India's Partition: a Revisionist Perspective," *India's Partition: Process, Strategy and Mobilisation*, ed. Mushirul Hasan (New Delhi: Oxford UP, 1994).

8 Gyanendra Pandey, "Prose of Otherness," *Subaltern Studies*, eds. David Arnold and David Hardiman, vol. 8 (New Delhi: Oxford UP, 1994). See also Gyanendra Pandey's "In Defence of the Fragment: Writing of the Hindu-Muslim Riots Today," *Economic and Politcal Weekly of India*, 26.11 (1991): 559-70.

9 See Gyanendra Pandey, "The Prose of Otherness," *Subaltern Studies*, eds. David Arnold and David Hardiman, vol. 8 (New Delhi: Oxford UP, 1994). For a critique of the dominant historiographical understanding of "nationalism" and "communalism" as two distinct tropes, see his *Construction of Communalism in Colonial North India* (New Delhi: Oxford UP, 1990).

10 Ashis Nandy describes this silence "as a joint venture of the victims, the historians and the State [in Pakistan]. It is not the silence of unconscious memories; it is the silence of a secret self." See his "The Invisible Holocaust and the Journey as an Exodus: the Poisoned Village and the Stranger City" in *Postcolonial Studies*, 2.3 (1999): 305-29.

11 See Krishna Kumar, *Learning from Conflict* (New Delhi: Orient Longman, 1996) 11-14.

12 All important magazines defended *Tamas* and gave coverage to the controversy. For a forceful presentation of this viewpoint, see Rajendra Yadav, "Tamas: Andheri Raat Mein Khaufnak Safar," *Hans*, March 1988. Also *India Today*, 29 Feb. 1988: 124-25.

13 See the cover story "Reliving the Holocaust" in *Sunday*, 7 Feb. 1988.

14 See Swapan Dasgupta's column "Right Angle" *Sunday*, 8 Dec. 1991, a review of "In Defence of the Fragment: Writing of the Hindu-Muslim Riots Today," *Economic and Political Weekly*, 26.11 (1991): 559-72. See also Pandey's rejoinder to Dasgupta in *Sunday*, 19 Jan 1992.

15 Vallabhbhai Patel, *Speeches of Patel: For a United India* (Delhi: Publications Division, Old Secretariat, 1950) 135.

16 Vallabhbhai Patel, "Speech on 3 Jan, 1948," *Speeches of Patel: For a United India* (Delhi: Publications Division, Old Secretariat, 1950) 137.

17 Vallabhbhai Patel, *Speeches of Patel: For a United India*. p. 142.

18 Vallabhbhai Patel, "Awaken the Conscience," Broadcast from New Delhi, Feb. 1848." *Speeches of Patel: For a United India*.

19 The abducted women did not face a complete closure of choices. Many of them chose to start life anew, at times even with their erstwhile violators. They resisted the coercive methods of the State to get them back. Thus the State's strong-arm recovery of honour created multiple tragic twists to their tales. See Begum Anees Kidwai, *Azadi Ki Chhaon Mein* (Delhi: National Book Trust,1990). For an analysis, Urvashi Butalia, "Community, State and Gender: On Women's Agency During Partition," *Economic and Political Weekly of India*, 28.17 (1993): 12-24.

20 Vallabhbhai Patel, "Lucknow Address, 6 Jan, 1948" *Speeches of Patel: For a United India*. p. 69.

21 *Collected Works of Mahatma Gandhi*, vol. 90 (Delhi: Publication Division, 1989) 427-28.

22 *Collected Works of Mahatma Gandhi*, vol. 90, footnote 1, p. 428.

23 "Speech at Prayer Meeting, January 13, 1948," *Collected Works of Mahatma Gandhi*, p. 416.

24 See Shani, "Abhi Dilli Door Hai," in *Hans*, Jan 1988: 27-29.

25 See Rajendra Prasad's "Introduction" to U R Rao, ed., *The Way to Communal Harmony* (Ahmedabad: Navjivan, 1992) vi-xi.

26 See Rajendra Prasad's "Introduction" to U R Rao, ed., *The Way to Communal Harmony* (Ahmedabad: Navjivan, 1992) xii.

27 See Ritu Menon and Kamla Bhasin, *Borders and Boundaries: Women in India's Partition* (New Delhi: Kali for Women, 1998); Urvashi Butalia, *The Other Side of Silence: Voices from the Partition of India* (New Delhi: Viking, 1998); Veena Das, *Critical Events: An Anthropological Perspective on Contemporary India* (New Delhi: Oxford UP, 1995); Gyanendra Pandey, *Memory, History and*

the *Question of Violence: Reflections on the Reconstruction of Partition* (Calcutta: Center for Study in Social Sciences, 1999).

28 Krishna Sobti, "Abhi Dilli Door Hai – II" in *Hans*, Oct 1987.

29 For a general survey of riots in post-independence India, see Ashis Banerjee, "Comparative Curfew: Changing Dimensions of Communal Politics in India," in Veena Das, ed., *Mirrors of Violence: Communities, Riots and Survivors in South Asia* (New Delhi: Oxford UP, 1990) 37-67.

30 The point has been made earlier in the article. To give one more example, see Vinod Bharadwaj, "Tamas ki Garm Hawaen," *Dinman,* 5 Feb, 1988.

31 See, for example, the panel discussion amongst Namvar Singh, Shani and others in *Samkaleen Bhartiya Sahitya*, Varsh 11, 14 (1990): 189-98.

32 Akbar S Ahmed, "Bombay Films: The Cinema as a Metaphor for Indian Society and Politics," *Modern Asian Studies*, 26. 2 (1992): 289–320.

33 See "Urdu: A Linguistic Genocide," in *Seminar,* 332, April 1987. Also Mushirul Hasan, "Adjustment and Accomodation: Indian Muslims after Partition" in K M Panikkar, ed., *Communalism in India* (Delhi: Manohar, 1991) 62-99.

34 Azra Razzak, "Growing up Muslim," *Seminar*, 387, Nov. 1991. Also Shahid Amin, "The Musalmaan as the Other: Image, Belief, History," P C Chatterjee, ed., *Self-images, Identity and Nationality* (Simla: IIAS, 1989) 112-23.

THE *VARTMAN* AND PAKISTAN:
THE "DAILY" REALITY OF PARTITION

SAUMYA GUPTA

Nations are necessary exercises in remembrance and "forgetting"; they remember through ritual commemoration and forget through collective amnesia. While commemorating the fiftieth year of their Independence, Indians, however, decided to remember what they had hitherto chosen to suppress or forget. As the "subaltern" became the authorized alternative to elite officialese, quite a few "sacred" binaries were opened up for scrutiny, if not reversed. The Partition, as the effaced annexe to our national history, became the privileged site for such corrective treatment. So half a century after it happened, the Partition and not just Pakistan – which has always been a constant presence for both the Indian State and the people – again finds itself at the centre of both political rhetoric and academic ruminations.

But Pakistan and Partition had always made good copy. Right from its nebulous birth in 1940, through the myriad definitions that were attached to it, till 1947 when its contours first became visible, the Pakistan demand was one sure way for politicians of all hues to get reported on the front page of national and local newspapers. Its unclear and imprecise parameters added to its mystique. The idea of Pakistan travelled the whole gamut of terrain from utopia to dystopia. On the one hand, it was heralded as a panacea for all the problems of Indian Muslims (and of India, by extension), and on the other, it was decried as a Satanic conspiracy aiming to stall indefinitely India's march towards freedom and progress. A thematic developed with Partition and Pakistan at its center. Major national events – Quit India Movement, Cripps and Cabinet Missions, Rajagopalachari Plan, Mountbatten Plan and so on – followed one after another; local incidents continued in their own dynamic. There remained, however, a kind of basic cohesion in the way these happenings were articulated by the contemporary press and digested by public opinion. "News" of various happenings was refracted through the prism of Pakistan: the reader was encouraged to understand these newsworthy happenings through the over-arching categories of nation, culture, religion, history and tradition – all of which were seen as hostage to the notion of Pakistan, or conversely, for the Muslim League sympathizers, to be actualized only through Pakistan itself.[1]

Historians have used newspapers, mostly to corroborate opinions and viewpoints backed by hard archival data. Works on the print media rarely go further than commenting on its links with political parties, or on the "impact" of the national movement on the press. The press is seen as a contemporary commentator, a kind of participant observer of the political scene, and it is this very participatory nature which supposedly makes it unfit to serve as an unbiased and objective historical source. Moreover, the non-fixed nature of the newspaper – in Benedict Anderson's phrase, the "one-day best-seller" – denies it the very "finality" normally associated with printed texts.[2] Conversely, newspapers have also been used as direct pointers to popular consciousness. Rarely are they opened up to historical scrutiny as historical agents involved in the formation of discursive structures that map historical events; the focus has almost exclusively been on newspapers as unshuttered windows to historical reality.[3]

A product of modernity, the newspaper ventures information that is instant and efficient. Efficiency and speed in collection and dispatch are vital for the dissemination of news as print. The mechanics of this rendering of the "event" into "news" is, however, a temporal process that is kept well-hidden from view. What is overlooked, or wilfully forgotten, is that the "daily" gives news that is *delayed*, by at least a day. In the 1940s, perforce, the delay was even greater – about two days before an event (of national importance) was reported by a daily newspaper, and about eight to ten days in the case of weeklies. Yet this late news has a kind of immediacy – for the reader, the event happens only when it flashes as printed news. Moreover, the spatial economy of the newspaper conveys the relative importance and newsworthiness of the event: front page left side (the right side, in case of Urdu newspapers) news in bold typeface solicits attention as an event of signal importance. It remains in this privileged position till another of its ilk shifts it to the inner pages, or even out of the paper, and finally out of the reader's mind. The format of news production then automatically limits news reception. News values and news judgements not only direct our thinking to specific areas, but also direct it away from other, apparently non-important areas, contributing thus to our mental maps of the world. In the realm of politics, "they define – and define away – opposition."[4]

Analyses of news value show that this choosing and prioritizing of information is not random, but involves an implicit understanding of the nature of society, the location of power in it, as also a notion of how this power is or should be exercised. Key categories of newsworthiness – the elite, the government, political parties – all have, according to Stuart Hall, "the routine knowledge of social structures" inscribed within them. To be intelligible to its audience, the press must "infer what is already known, as a present or abstract structure ... but (this structure) is a construction and interpretation about the world."[5]

It is an "interpretation" that parades itself as "truth." This was especially the case with colonial India in the 1940s. The press was then, for many, the only available means of engaging with the wider world. Most contemporary newspapers were openly partisan (of course with an eye on the colonial censor), and partisanship was glorified as service to the national movement. A nation could only be made if "national facts" were known by all. The press, especially the vernacular press, rendered singular service in disseminating the preferred nationalist view of the events as the only correct way of understanding them. Moreover, many a time the truth offered by the press was the only version that reached the individual in a small town or qasba.

This is not to imply that other versions of events were not available. Contestation was the order of the day in the fractured politics of the 1940s. Even a cursory look at *Dawn* and *National Herald* would give diametrically opposed viewpoints for similar events, or even the same event. But not many people would have read both the *Dawn* and the *Herald*. The constituencies of these newspapers, like their truths, were different; but their respective readers passionately believed in their renderings. For each of these newspapers, as also for their audiences, it was the "others" who peddled propaganda, while they, on their part, gave voice to enlightened public opinion and to national sentiments.

By commenting on, and reiterating ad infinitum a subject – say, for example, Pakistan – the press in effect constructs images. These images, like coins of exchange, acquire public acceptability, and can be recalled by the sheer mention of a single word, or by a news clip from the past. Crucially, this image cannot be dismissed as irrational fabrication. Some may question the veracity of the press account, but few people would doubt that the event reported took place in some other way. For people living in "a second hand world ... symbols focus experience (and) meanings organize knowledge, guiding the surface perceptions of an instant no less than the aspirations of a life-time."[6]

The dependence on mediated knowledge about the world was increased manifold in a milieu where the levels of literacy were not very high, but the level of political participation was considerable. Along with pamphlets and posters, newspapers formed the basic source of knowledge about leaders and political parties. The only other means of mass communication remained the grand sabha or public meeting, often organized as a reaction to reports (gathered primarily from newspapers) about events or calamities of national importance. As riots occured frequently in the country between 1946 to 1948, Kanpur was deluged with various "days" or "diwas" being celebrated or observed. There was a Noakhali Diwas to protest against atrocities on Hindus in Noakhali, a Bihar Day (yaum-e-Bihar) for those against Muslims, and a Pakistan Day that was countered by a Punjab Diwas. These were organized after reports of massacres or riots were published by the local newspaper.[7] In turn, these sabhas themselves were news enough to get reported in local papers, often inciting other reports and "events." Beyond such obvious relations between these "aural" gatherings and printed material, orality, freely and crucially, intermixed with printing and literacy. The last and most often, the mass audience of the newspaper was the one that *heard* it – transliterated, moreover, from the shuddha bhasha (pure language) into a variety of regional, local dialects, and "explained" with the help of familiar, and frequently, even familial metaphors and analogies.[8]

It is to open up and interrogate these "realities"– Pakistan and Partition – at a local level that I look towards the *Vartman*, a local but immensely popular newspaper published from Kanpur during the 1940s. In its pages, Partition is enacted at various levels, and Pakistan "established," before it actually came into being. In its own way, the *Vartman* was engaged in outlining and consolidating a realm of knowledge that revolved around Hindustan and Pakistan, nation and community, religion and individuals, the "Hindus" and the "Muslims," as well as the *different* Hindus and Muslims. Though these characterizations were formed over the years, Partition made them more strident and uncompromising. Inasmuch as *Vartman* was involved in the fashioning of this discourse, and as much as it was part of it, it offers insights into the complexities of the movements for and against Pakistan.

By the 1940s, *Vartman* was an influential presence in the journalistic landscape of Kanpur. The first and only daily paper to be consistently published from Kanpur for about two decades, *Vartman* positioned itself as the plebeian counterpart to the *Pratap*, the better-known weekly printed from Kanpur. From the very beginning, Ramashankar Awasthi, its proprietor and editor, very consciously located the paper within a "Kanpuriya" idiom. Almost all its pages were steeped in local colour. National news was of course important, but its local ramifications mattered more to *Vartman*. Interestingly, the process through which the "news" of a national event got translated into local jargon was quite transparent in *Vartman*. The paper framed its "report" in three stages. The

first was when an event made it to the front page as "news."[9] Catchy
headlines laid out the paper's – and presumably its readers' – reaction
to the news. Stage two appeared two days later: a long editorial on what
presumably was judged as the most important news item worth commenting
on. This editorial delineated the relative importance or non-importance
of the "news," and placed it in its historical context. It broadcast for its
audience the "actual" meaning and the correct way of understanding the
event/news. Stage three commenced – again approximately after two
days – when the daily satirical column "Manoranjan" unscrambled that
editorial for popular entertainment. Through a dialogic tone and
impudent lampooning, the event/news was given a local inflexion, placing
it firmly within the realm of the prevalent common sense.[10]

Vartman addressed its own, largely Hindu audience in Kanpur. This
predominantly upper caste (though not always upper class) readership
was divided politically between the Congress – and its two factions in
Kanpur – and the local Hindu Sabha. *Vartman*, in deference to this
division, was constantly engaged in a delicate balancing act. Inspite of
the paper's latent leanings towards the Hindu Sabha, the national
stature of leaders like Nehru and Gandhi almost always tipped the scale
towards the Congress. Most of the time, however, *Vartman* tried to walk
the tightrope – rooting for the Congress while fraternizing with the
local Hindu Sabha. As such, it offered a perfect platform for the
Congress right wing, which by 1945, had come to author and
hegemonize the public discourse in Kanpur.

From around the time C Rajagopalachari put forward his
argument for a "rational" consideration of the Pakistan demand (July
1944), and convinced Gandhi to hold talks with Jinnah, the paper's
rhetoric became crowded with the motif of Pakistan.[11] Notwithstanding
the still ambivalent nature of Jinnah's Pakistan, *Vartman's* "Pakistan" was
understood as an all-encompassing catastrophe about to befall India:
"a death-wish from the unparalleled horrors of which even a thousand
Gandhis (sic) would not be able to save India, its history and culture."[12]
Gandhi's consent to meet Jinnah at the latter's house in Bombay was
portrayed as his acquiescing in the demand for Pakistan.[13] Further,
"Gandhi's love for Muslims" and his "mastery of the art of surrender"

was a pointer that a "shudh," unalloyed Pakistan would inevitably result out of such meetings.[14] Jinnah's rebuffs to Gandhi's offer were insults added to injury, and the breakdown of the talks was something to be welcomed. "Sab achcha hi hua" (all's well that ends well!) was the paper's verdict on the episode.[15]

For *Vartman*, Pakistan was not just synonymous with Muslim communalism, though it was primarily that. The "nationalism versus communalism" dichotomy of the nationalist discourse, when rewritten as "nation" versus "Pakistan," grounded notionally at least, a homogeneous nation (which is Hindu) in opposition to Pakistan (which is Muslim). The discomfiture with Pakistan – at such an early date when its contours had hardly taken shape – was that it questioned, centrally, the totalizing narrative of Indian nationalism. *Vartman* showed Pakistan as miasmic: it totally destabilized the category of nationalism, making it open and accessible to all other groups within the political spectrum. As the paper remarked early on, "giving in to the Pakistan demand would only lead to endless partitions ... We will not be able to sit peacefully ... All minorities would ask for the right to self-determination. How would we then stop them? Even women ... would one day demand a separate Jananistan."[16]

To counter the Muslim League's two-nation theory, *Vartman* (almost) posited India as a "multi-national" entity, led into modernity and progress under the aegis of the Congress party. The Congress' seminal work of infusing the spirit of nationalism into an eternal but fragmented India, was what legitimized its (attempted) monopoly of the national political space. Since Pakistan had opened a Pandora's box by contesting this monopoly, a radical restructuring of the nationalist discourse was required. Either the discursive limits of the nation were to be modified and extended beyond the ideal represented by the Congress, or conversely, various contesting groups/nations be disciplined and appropriated within a "hierarchized" (rather than homogenized) nationalism. *Vartman's* advice was to go for the second option; it even provided a blueprint for it. Trying to make essentialist arguments in a rationalist vein, it managed to create a rather neat classification. Thus, if the Congress represented the modern, constructed version of Indian nationalism, the Hindu Mahasabha represented the "natural" nationalism inherent in the Hindu community. As against the svadhintapriya (freedom-loving) Congressmen and the svabhavik rashtravadi (naturally nationalist) members of the Hindu Mahasabha,[17] the Ambedkar-ites, Dalits and other such groups were argued to be plain "selfish nationalists" – swarthvadi – with their concerns limited to their own "rights." The Muslim League, at the nadir of this scheme, represented "aberrant nationalism" – indeed, "communalism" – based on fraudulent principles, without any legacy of participation in the freedom struggle, or of any kind of sacrifice to the nation.[18]

It can be seen that this hierarchical layout took care of both the past and the future, while neatly delineating the present. The svadhintapriya could agree to Partition – Pakistan – but certainly not the rashtravadi or nationalist for whom the territorial unity of the country was as sacred, if not more, than a territorially compromised freedom. Since both freedom and integrity were desirable, the present political impasse could only be overcome if these two categories of nationalism borrowed from each other rather than remain separate – and opposed – political entities. Only then – by the sheer weight of majority – would "true nationalism" be able to realize "complete liberation" and block any kind of Pakistan, Achhootistan or (god forbid!) Jananistan. *Vartman* was prophetic in asking for this convergence.[19] Its pages soon recorded Veer Savarkar's entreaty to Congressmen to join the Hindu Mahasabha, followed, a mere twenty days later, by Sardar Patel's invitation to the Mahasabha members to join the Congress "in their fight for the unity and integrity of India."[20]

Since Pakistan at this point existed more in the pronouncements of the leaders, *Vartman* too framed its argument through them. Gandhi and Jinnah formed two levers against which the narrative of the paper was positioned. Till about 1944, Jinnah was viewed more as a strong and powerful leader, well able to extract his "blank cheque" from Gandhi and the Congress.[21] With the fragmented Muslim politics of the United Provinces acknowledging his supremacy, the Hindi press was not far behind in lionizing him as such.[22] It is interesting that though he was projected as leading a paper organization rife with internal squabbles (all of which was reported with much glee), Jinnah's leadership over the

Muslim masses was never questioned.[23] Rather, a messianic appeal was attributed to him – "Mr Jinnah is as popular among Muslims as Gandhiji is among Congressmen." However, unlike Gandhi, Jinnah commanded a "community of chauvinistic, aggressive believers." United by religion and passionate about it, they were "compelled by the force of their belief to wipe out the kafirs."[24] This fanatical zeal, when coupled with the "backwardness" of the Muslims, made them incapable of nationalist thought. With Jinnah obstinately clinging on to the Pakistan demand, his image, however, increasingly began to take on negative overtones. Throughout the period between 1944 to 1947, *Vartman* portrayed Jinnah as an irrational and overbearing madman. Even his inconsequential interviews and speeches were reported on the front page, and always with reference to Pakistan.[25] By the mid-1940s, Jinnah had no other identity left, save that of the satanic progenitor of the idea of "Pakistan." In a curious reversal, Jinnah was "imaged" through Pakistan as "the child becoming the father of the man."

Gandhi, on the other hand, largely led the Hindus, who, according to *Vartman*, were a community of disinterested, inert nationalists – a people whose "political behaviour is marked by cowardice, religious enthusiasm by lethargy and who are hopelessly fragmented socially."[26] In short, a people who had made a virtue of passivity by calling it toleration.[27] Though earlier the paper was as deferential to Gandhi as any other nationalist organ of the 1940s, the centre-staging of Jinnah gradually took some shine off the stature of the Mahatma. The preferred and oft-repeated analogy for Gandhi and Jinnah became that of Chamberlain and Hitler – Gandhi, like Chamberlain, bending backwards to appease the firebrand, aggressive Hitleresque Jinnah.[28] Mere willingness to negotiate with Jinnah was construed as his approval of Jinnah's designs, for "his love for Muslims is well-known" and "he is adept in the art of surrender."[29] His personal authority was still powerful enough to carry the nation along, to force his decision on the Congress. However, nothing would stop "Pakistan" from becoming a reality once Gandhi endorsed it.[30] Hence the need to contain Gandhi, to make him weak: he was reminded of his old age and ill health, and repeatedly advised to spend the rest of his days in peace. His vow that

183

Pakistan would be made over his dead body was constantly thrown at him.[31]

Gandhi became problematic for *Vartman*, because he encapsulated within himself the "greatness" of Hinduism (so often parroted by *Vartman* and like-minded sympathizers) as also the present lacunae within it. Gandhi was the focal point from where the image of the "tolerant" Hindu emanated; it was he who gave the most powerful meaning to the notion of passive and secular Hindus. However, the perceived need of the hour was not toleration and passivity, but aggression and retaliation. Gandhi became the locus of the "historical" and the "politically correct" Hindu, as also the point where "correctness" had gone awry. All the present political and communal ills of the country were laid at Gandhi's door, and all these "in effect" stemmed from his advocacy (and practice) of the appeasement of Muslims. This was another pre-history of "Partition" which was being written not with the "fanatical Muslim," but with Gandhian politics at the centre.[32]

Vartman's fascinating dialogue with "Pakistan" did not limit itself to major leaders. It layered its discourse progressively, encountering "Partition/Pakistan" strategically at the national, provincial and local level politics. *Vartman* gave pride of place to those Muslim groups which were publicly opposed to the idea of Pakistan. These groups in the United Provinces consisted mainly of Muslim divines connected to the Jamait-ul-Ulema, or to groups like the Momins, the Ahrars and the Khaksars. Accordingly, all the paraphernalia of "news" was provided: bold typeset, approving editorials, op-ed articles and Manoranjan's applauding endorsement – "ek Musalman yeh hain, ek aap hain ..."(look at these Muslims, and look at you [the leaguers]).[33] News values, however, cannot be just attached, howsoever good the intentions. It soon became clear, especially after the Shimla Conference, that these were but marginal voices against the rallying cries of support for the Qaid and his dreamland. As it became clear that their affirmation of faith in the Indian nation and the Congress was not enough reason for the British to "veto" the League, the paper lost even the rudiment of interest in their politics. Devoid of official "weightage" as well as popular support, these "other" Muslim voices were not "news" anymore.

The non-League Muslims who remained much longer in news were the Nationalist Muslims.[34] Seen as the last vestige of sanity left in the Muslim community, Nationalist Muslims showcased the "secular" credentials of the Congress. Jeered by the Muslim League and its sympathizers, they were handled with kid-gloves by the Hindi press. These were the "others" who had overcome their "otherness": what better example of the syncretic nature of Indian nationalism than to have "members of the other nation" speaking "our" language. Azad, Humayun Kabir, Rafi Ahmed Kidwai, Hamid Khan and Abdul Qayum were given prominence in the pages of *Vartman*. Scuffles, brickbats among Leaguers and Nationalist Muslims during provincial elections in Kanpur, were of course, "prime" news material.[35] The arguments of Nationalist Muslims against Pakistan were given prominence, as if they emanated from some inborn knowledge, from an area of an authentic "Muslim-ness" to which they had privileged natural access.[36]

Inevitably, "Pakistan" managed to spoil even this idyllic relationship. As the paper adopted an increasingly strident tone, and as it manufactured the Muslim "others" suited to this tone, these "Kangressi" Muslims seemed too utopian – and hence unreliable. The construction of a rhetoric against the Muslim nation required the presence of that nation, of a unified Muslim community, for, if the Hindus had to fight Pakistan effectively, they had to realize that Pakistan could exist almost anywhere. Indeed, that Pakistan was synonymous with being Muslim; that Muslims cannot be internally differentiated; that all Muslims – even the friendly neighbour, the ulema or the Momin, and the Nationalist Muslim – were primarily Muslims. Protestations to the contrary, their political identity would always remain conditioned by their "natural" religious identity. Collapsing "nationalist Muslim" with "Muslim nationalists" of the League variety, the paper projected a much more homogenized Muslim community than even the League could have hoped for. Those very Muslims who had been stalwarts of the Congress nationalism, were now termed closet Leaguers.[37] As Pakistan inched forward, it transformed all Muslims into "Pakistanis," divinely ordained, as it were, to sympathize with the Islamic homeland.

The realization of Pakistan, expectedly made matters worse for

185

Nationalist Muslims. The ever curious prefix "nationalist" before their names was as if erased overnight.[38] These, along with countless other Muslims — unconcerned with nomenclature, but consistent in their opposition to Pakistan — who opted to stay in India, were converted into the residual category of "three crore Muslims left in India" and who were to be held as "hostages." Their loyalty to the Indian state was suspect as "that would be going against their conscience and nature."[39] If they insisted upon professing this loyalty, they were required to provide "proof" – by going and fighting (read killing) "their Pakistani brethren in Punjab."[40] The "discovery of arms for Pakistan" in Muslim bastis in Kanpur in September 1947 stepped up this intonation – from "hostages" they were transformed into "spies" and "fifth columnists."[41] "Naturally" and "historically" inclined towards massacres and violence, they were to be denied citizenship rights and banished from India. Within a span of five years, Muslims — who had been Nationalists, Leaguers, Momins, Ahrars, Khaksars, landlords, peasants, workers, neighbours, men, women, children, "hostage" — became solely, "outsiders," "Pakistanis," and "enemies of the nation" for *Vartman*.[42]

At the local level, this increasingly virulent Hindu discourse received reinforcement through the riots that ravaged the nation around this time. The death toll, predictably, did not differentiate between "nations" and peoples, though competing discourses certainly did.[43] The *Vartman* pontificated, "It is not necessary, now, to point out the community which starts the riots ...."[44] History too was made the battlefield and "events," along with men and women, were made eminently mortal: "hindsight" strangely killed or resurrected "happenings" or, if they did not serve the purpose, fabricated them. The language was replete with demagogic rhetoric and combative populism, and *Vartman* became a platform for airing "Hindu" grievances against both the "neighbourhood Muslims," as also the Muslim dominated administration and police in Kanpur. In this strident avatar it proved extremely useful to the now regenerated local Hindu Sabha, which took the Congress government in Uttar Pradesh to task for its "soft" stand on the Muslims.[45] A largely defensive local Congress now broadcast its rightist stance by "congratulating the Hindus for their patience and willpower."[46] The editorials expounded on "civil security" and "political riots," and about the pathological "addiction of one community towards violence."[47]

The Kanpur news page (*Kanpur ki Diary*) offered local, "neighbourly" examples to this theorization. Though "disturbances" took place only in November 1946 and in April 1947, the city atmosphere was generally rife with tension. There was a perceptible increase in mutual suspicion between the two communities. Witness these "news" reports and letters to the editor in *Kanpur ki Diary* – "Chief ki zyadati: Hindu gharon mein gana-bajana band" (Highhandedness of the Chief: Ban on music in Hindu houses) when a police inspector, Usman Ali, intervened in a noisy birthday party going on outside a local masjid, during the time of namaz.[48] "Miyanji ki paintare-bazi: roz roz naye shagufe ho rahe hain" (The antics of Miyanji: new mischiefs are being invented daily) was reported about a Muslim priest who challenged an old woman throwing garbage in the masjid premises.[49] Again, it was "not *right* that the Hindus of the ward Patkapur have to cross three Muslim bastis in order to reach the ration shop and are greatly inconvenienced."[50] (emphasis added).

These were small incidents (if that) causing disproportionate alarm. The shop in Patkapur was not a recent one. It was the perception of inconvenience and the problem with the maulavi that were recent. These exaggerated and amplified responses to perceived threats were magnified by press coverage. The phobic unease of people living next door was fuelled by widespread rumours, and *Vartman's* relationship with them is clear. Rumours increasingly found their way in print, thereby gaining credibility and legitimacy.[51] The Pakistan-in-every-mohalla that *Vartman* was cautioning against was largely a product of such rumour mongering, concerned with just about anything. Rumours about the Bihar, Noakhali, and Punjab riots circulated with astonishing regularity and effectiveness. Cheaply produced pamphlets and wall writing augmented their word-of-mouth renditions. "Noakhali ka hatya-kand" (the carnage at Noakhali) and "Bihar ka katl-e-aam" (the massacres in Bihar) jostled for space on the crowded walls of the city.[52] Rumour was regarded such a legitimate means of communication, that a mere shout of "chal gayi" (it has started) was enough to provoke another riot.

Fear and panic remained by far *the* dominant motifs around which the

187

discourse of *Vartman* was woven. In Kanpur, fear was not a novelty associated with the current Partition atmosphere. Rather, it was grounded in the memory and experience of the 1931 riot.[53] Even from the vantage point of the "nation," 1931 was an event which made Kanpur memorable, if notoriously so. Much had changed between 1931 and 1946-47. In the charged pre-Partition days, even the 1931 riot was framed within the all-pervasive trope of "Pakistan." Nineteen thirty one was now used to make vivid the phantom of Pakistan and this "Pakistan" – that was known, yet was unfathomed – became the source of almost unlimited apprehension. The city had witnessed riots before, but earlier riots had taken their toll in people and property: they had not threatened the very existence of the city, the mohalla and the family. The "national" question of Pakistan had, however, devolved to touch the very interstices of people's lives, the consequence of which was an almost paranoid reaction to otherwise "normal" events.

Vartman's relationship with the "Pakistan" rumours was contingent upon its changing relationship with the idea of Pakistan itself. In the early forties (up till 1945), *Vartman* strove to counter rumours circulating in the city. In fact, all the time it believed Pakistan to be a "shagoofa" (a baseless mischief), it dismissed rumours as the brainchild of "goons" out to make a quick profit by disrupting trade and commerce, and the general well-being of the city.[54] Even after the Noakhali and Bihar riots, the Manoranjan column implored Kanpur-walas to steer clear of "gigantic rumours which are being manufactured *within* the city."[55] *Vartman* kept a sarcastic distance from all kinds of rumours – to the extent that it treated Pakistan as a giant rumour believed in only by the credulous, gullible and illiterate Muslim masses.

But as Pakistan became comprehensible and tangible, *Vartman* abandoned this sense of distance and restraint. Far from asking people to pay no heed to hearsay and gossip, the paper took to printing unauthenticated "reports" purporting to illumine Pakistani, i.e. Muslim actions and ambitions. Generally published as small pieces in the *Kanpur ki Diary*, or as "articles" (usually uncredited) following the editorial, these patterned the Muslims of Kanpur – as of "anywhere else" – as recalcitrant and fanatical. Each of their action – whether it be the largely harmless pranks by children or the panic buying of gold by big Muslim businessmen – was indicative of their Pakistani, i.e. anti-India and anti-Hindu proclivities and beliefs.[56]

With the recovery of some arms in the Muslim dominated areas in Kanpur, this paranoid abuse reached a new high. Any and every Muslim was feared to be a stockpiler of deadly war-weaponry, field rifles, mortar guns, tommy guns. Machine guns were allegedly recovered from Muslim houses, along with gardening tools and kitchen knives. Many more deadly weapons would have been discovered, reasoned *Vartman*, but for the fact that the criminals – Muslims – were obviously shielded by the Muslim police officers.[57] Rumour was patently news now, and was authenticated by being printed as news. Also, beyond a point, it did not matter whether what *Vartman* was printing was true or not. For even if these reports were true, their news-value was only through their association with that omnibus bogey of Pakistan. What was news and what merited reporting had now become exclusively "reports" about Muslim complicity in the riots and their unstinted, total support for Pakistan. Rather than a deliberate manipulation of the news, a process of *orchestration* seems to be at work here.[58] In conveying the sense of "panic" and by placing it within the fluid political situation, *Vartman* was voicing and feeding into the concerns of its audience, along with exploiting existing ways of thinking, to perfect and season its own discourse about Partition.

For the people of Kanpur, Pakistan was not located somewhere out there, in Punjab or Bengal, or even in Aligarh and Lucknow. Rather it was perilously close and proximate. There was no time, or indeed rationale, for "maintaining a sarcastic distance," of calling Pakistan a "shagoofa," or deriding the very idea of Pakistan as unstable. The local idiom in which *Vartman* outlined Pakistan, as well as the arguments and metaphors through which it countered Partition, made Pakistan a dangerous reality within the United Provinces. Indeed for many people in the city, especially those who "believed" in *Vartman's* projections, Punjab and Bengal were just pre-empting instances of the drama that was to unfold in the heart of the United Provinces, in Kanpur itself.

There can be little doubt that *Vartman* contributed in making Partition "present" as an immediate and unmitigated disaster about to engulf Kanpur and its residents. *Vartman* was just one of the many doomsday diviners in the city. It was one for whom, however, the question of Partition and Pakistan overwhelmed all others. In little over two years (from 1945 to 1947), Vartman changed its heroes, its agenda and of course, its language. It charted the whole territory from being anti-Pakistan to being anti-Muslim. In this, it reflected the changing character of the city of Kanpur and its changed political orientations. A constant motif in the *Vartman* from about 1944, Pakistan appears curiously local in flavour, deployed to spice up just about any news. It acquired varied meanings and myriad hues, all of which could scarcely be contained within its larger and more national "reality." In *Vartman's* discourse, Pakistan was both circumscribed and extended; its presence was made immediate even as its meaning was made malleable to include both a social and a political community.

Notes

1   This analysis of newspapers' construction of the past and the present has benefited from some of the ideas in Patrick Wright, "A Blue Plaque for the Labour Movement?: Some Political Meanings of the 'National Past'," in *Formations of Nation and People*, (London: Routledge, 1984) 42-65.

2   Benedict Anderson, *Imagined Communities: Reflections on the Origins and Spread of Nationalism*, rev. ed. (London: Verso, 1991) 33.

3   Shahid Amin's brilliant article, "Gandhi as Mahatma: Gorakhpur District, Eastern UP, 1921-2" in Ranajit Guha ed., *Subaltern Studies*, vol. 3 (New Delhi: Oxford UP, 1984) 1-61, was one of the pioneering efforts that used the newspapers imaginatively to historicise the mystique of the Mahatama.

4   T Gitlin, *The Whole World Is Watching* (U of California P, 1980) 2.

5   Stuart Hall, "The Determination of the News Photograph," in S Cohen and J Young, ed., *The Manufacture Of News*, (London: Constable, 1973) 183.

6   C Wright Mills quoted in Edward Said, *Covering Islam* (New York: Pantheon, 1981) 43.

7   "Kanpur Mein Noakhali Divas," *Vartman* (Kanpur), 31 Oct. 1946: 1; "Bihar Divas Par Sabha," *Vartman*, 26 Nov. 1946: 4; "Kanpur Mein Teen Baar Firing," *Vartman*, 1 April 1947: 1.

8   Partition, for example, was frequently explained in contemporary newspapers like "when a family divides," and Hindus and Muslims were quite often referred to as "two brothers." These naturalized descriptions are still standard in accounts of the

Partition, as is evident from their almost ubiquitous presence in the recent journalistic endeavours commemorating the fifty years of India's Independence and the Partition.

9   Thus, while the speeches of Mahatma Gandhi and Jawaharlal Nehru were reported as their "bhashan," "vichaar" and/or "udgaar" (speeches, ideas, statements), those of Mohammad Ali Jinnah and other League leaders were almost always captioned as their "pralaap," "behak" and/or "dhamki" (outcry, blabber, threat): "Leagueon ki Uchhalkood," *Vartman*, 24 Nov. 1945: 6; "Mister Jinnah ka Pralaap," *Vartman*, 11 March 1946: 2.

10.   "Mister Jinnah ke Naam Khuli Chitthi," *Vartman*, 8 Aug. 1944: 4; "Bahaar-e-Pakistan," *Vartman*, 2 Nov. 1946: 4.

11   "Rajaji ki Behak," editorial, *Vartman*, 15 July1944: 2; "Rajaji se Prashn," editorial, *Vartman*, 21 July 1944: 2; "Raja Yojana se Haani," *Vartman*, 8 Aug. 1944: 2.

12   "Dr. Mukherjee ki Chetavani," editorial, *Vartman*, 12 Aug. 1944: 2.

13   "Gandhiji ne Pakistan Maan Liya?," *Vartman*, 7 Aug. 1944: 1.

14   "Gandhi-Jinnah Milan," editorial, *Vartman*, 4 Aug. 1944: 2.

15   "Rajaji ki Behak," editorial, *Vartman*, 15 July 1944: 2.

16   "Bharat Hamari Bhoomi Hai," editorial, *Vartman*, 30 Nov. 1942: 2. Jananistan literally means, "country of women."

17   "Kanpur ke Hindu Navyuvko se Appeal," *Vartman*, 12 Dec. 1942: 4.

18   Pandit Gangaprasad Mishra, "Hindu-Muslim Samasya ko Hal Karne ka Ek Upaaya!" *Vartman*, 8 May 1945: 4.

19   Bhudev Vidyalankar, "Congress se Ek Nivedan," *Vartman*, 11 Oct. 1945: 2. Achhootistan literally means, "country of untouchables."

20   "Hindu Congress ko Chhod Dein – Agar Ve Bharat ko Swatantra Dekhana Chahate Hain," *Vartman*, 1 Nov.1945: 1, and "Mahasabha ke Netaon se Nivedan," editorial, *Vartman*, 20 Nov. 1945: 2.

21   "Pakistan Yojana par Ek Mat," *Vartman*, 11 Aug. 1944: 2.

22   "Yeh Chillapon Kyon?," editorial, *Vartman*, 8 July1945: 2.

23   "Muslim League ka Netritva Kaun Karega?," *Vartman*, 7 July 1944: 1.

24   "Samjhaute ke Liye," editorial, *Vartman*, 24 June 1943: 2.

25   "Mr. Jinnah ka Pralap," *Vartman*, 19 Jan. 1946: 1; "Mr. Jinnah Phir Behake!" *Vartman*, 11 March 1946: 2.

26   "Hindu Mahasabha!" Manoranjan, *Vartman*, 17 Dec. 1942: 4.

27   "Samjhaute ke Liye," editorial, *Vartman*, 24 June 1943: 2.

28   "Gandhi-Jinnah Milan," editorial, *Vartman*, 4 Aug. 1944: 2.

29   "Gandhi-Jinnah Milan," *Vartman*, 4 Aug. 1944: 2; "Rajaji ki Behak," Vartman, 4 Aug. 1944: 2.

30   Bhudev Vidyalankar, "Hindu Hiton Par Kutharaghat," *Vartman*, 6 July 1945: 4.

31   "Bhari Haani," editorial, *Vartman*, 16 July 1944: 2.

32   "Congress ne Bahut Badi Bhool ki," *Vartman*, 19 July 1945: 3; "Sab Achcha Hi Hua," editorial, *Vartman*, 20 July 1945: 2.

33   "Sampradayikta," editorial, *Vartman*, 26 March 1944: 2.

34   See Mushirul Hasan, *Legacy of a Divided Nation* (New Delhi: Oxford UP, 1998).

35   "Leagueon ki Uchhalkood," *Vartman*, 24 Nov. 1945: 6; "Leagueon ne Eint-Patthar

Phenke," *Vartman*, 29 Nov. 1945: 6; "Ek Nayi Aawaz," editorial, *Vartman*, 30 Nov. 1945; "Leagueon ne Eint-Patthar Barsaye: Pandrah Nationalist Muslim Ghayal," *Vartman*, 12 March 1946: 1

36 "Rastriya Musalmano ne Pakistan Thukraya," *Vartman*, 18 April 1946: 1; Humayun Kabir, "Musalman aur Pakistan," Sahityik Parishisht, *Vartman*, 23 April 1946: 3.

37 See Mushirul Hasan, *Legacy of a Divided Nation* (New Delhi: Oxford UP, 1998).

38 "Hindustan aur Musalman," editorial, *Vartman*, 19 June 1947: 2.

39 "Do Samasyayen," editorial, *Vartman*, 9 Sept. 1947: 2.

40 "Hindustani Musalman," editorial, *Vartman*, 18 Sept. 1947: 2; "Maanneeya Pantji ki Pakki Baat," editorial, *Vartman*, 21 Sept. 1947: 2.

41 "Masjid Mein League ka Magazine," *Vartman*, 2 Oct. 1947: 4; "Hamare Prant ki Topen," editorial, *Vartman*, 16 Dec. 1947: 2.

42 "Chargesheet," editorial, *Vartman*, 2 Oct. 1947: 2. This extremely virulent piece appeared on the Mahatma's birthday, an occasion usually reserved for accolades for him. Nothing can exemplify more the "helplessness" of Gandhi in the hostile climate of the time. However the "chaupai," penned by one "Avadhesh," and titled "Rashtra ki Niti," that appeared on the front page (set in bold type-face and encased in a box), does come close: "Jo kapti ya kritaghn usey, apne kabhi gupt vichar na dijiye; jo nirmohi mille "Avadhesh" usey, apna pyar kabhi na dijiye; mitra banana kisi ko pade yadi, to usko adhikar na dijiye." (Do not reveal your secrets to the treacherous and ungrateful one; Do not give your love to the unloving one; Even if you have to perforce make him your friend, do not give him any rights [trans. mine]).

43 The findings of the Mridula Sarabhai Committee of the Garhmukteshwar riots were published in *Vartman* as "Rashtriya Naaron ke Sath Hamla: Congress ko Badnam Karne ka Shadayantra," on 16 Nov. 1946. However, no further news, report or reference to these findings appear again in the paper.

44 "Griha-yudh ka Prarambh?" editorial, *Vartman*, 23 Aug. 1946: 2.

45 "Hinduon Nirbhay Bano!" editorial, *Vartman*, 4 Nov. 1946: 2.

46 "Shahar ki Halat par Kangress ki Vigyapti," *Vartman*, 17 Nov. 1946: 6; "Parade ke Hinduon par Hone Wale Jurmane ka Virodh: Kangress Kameti ke Sabhapati ka Vaktavya," *Vartman*, 12 April 1947: 4.

47 "Dango ki Pragati!" editorial, *Vartman*, 12 Nov 1946: 2.

48 *Vartman*, 25 April 1946: 6.

49 *Vartman*, 1 May 1946: 4.

50 "Yeh Uchit Nahi Hai," *Vartman*, 24 May 1946: 6.

51 Georges Lefebvre, *The Great Fear of 1789: Rural Panic in Revolutionary France* (London: New Left Books, 1973).

52 "'Bihar ka badla le lenge' nara khadiya vah koyale se Hindi aur Urdu se sadako par likha hua dekha gaya ..." (The slogan "We will avenge Bihar," written with chalk and charcoal in Hindi and Urdu was seen

all over the streets), "Bihar Divas Par Sabha," *Vartman*, 26 Nov. 1946: 4. "Hindu-Musalmano se Appeal," *Vartman*, 10 Nov. 1946: 2.

53   In 1931, the city witnessed one of its most violent riots ever, surpassed only by the Ayodhya disturbances of 1989. In 1931, the Hindu-Muslim riot broke out because some Congress activists were forcing shops to shut down to protest the hanging of Bhagat Singh. Since just a few days ago Hindu shopkeepers had not closed down after the death of Mohammad Ali, some Muslim shops remained open this time. The result was a large-scale riot that killed many, most notably Ganesh Shankar Vidyarthi, Kanpur's leading journalist, Congressman and a crusader of Hindu-Muslim unity.

54   "Nagrik Suraksha," editorial, *Vartman*, 8 April 1946: 2.

55   "... Yeh shahar to afvahon ka centre hai. Akhbarvale bhala kya likh-pad sakate hain. Public ke dimag mein aisi-aisi afvahen paidayash pati hain ki bade-bade dimag chakkar mein pad kar bhounchakke reh jate hain," (This city is a den of rumours. What can the journalists write? Such rumours germinate in the heads of the people here that even the most rational minds are bewildered), "Kampu Sharief," Manoranjan, *Vartman*, "Nagrik Suraksha," editorial, *Vartman*, 8 April 1946: 2.

56   *Vartman*, 18 Sept. 1947: 3.

57   "*Namra Nivedan*," editorial, *Vartman*, 14 July 1947: 2.

58   P Golding and S Middleton, *Images of Welfare*, quoted in Ralph Negrine, *Politics and the Mass Media in Britain* (London: Routledge, 1994) 129.

THE WOMAN PROTAGONIST IN PARTITION LITERATURE

BODH PRAKASH

The partition of the Indian subcontinent in 1947 is probably the most horrifying and cataclysmic event in our recent past. The resultant displacement of millions, the mayhem that accompanied cross-border migrations, and the impetus it gave to communal ideology have been examined and analyzed by historians, social scientists and more recently, by feminists and cultural anthropologists. Initial writings focused on the political factors that made the Partition inevitable even as we achieved Independence. The role of ordinary people or the impact the Partition had on their lives was restricted to statistical details.[1] Later historians have looked at the Partition from a holistic perspective.[2] Studies in the nineties have largely focused on the "subaltern."[3] Recent writings have highlighted the silence of the subaltern in the historiography of the Partition, and have argued for the inclusion of oral testimonies and the subaltern perspective in the writing of history. In particular, women victims have become important subjects in most feminist and culture discourses. Women have always borne the brunt of most catastrophes in the history of the human race, be it civil wars, displacement, or poverty. In this, the experience of the Partition was no different. Physically and emotionally brutalized, forced to leave their homes, and totally at the mercy of rapacious males from both communities, they were also often rejected by their own families after being rescued. With their deeply ingrained notions of sexual purity and honour, many of them opted for death. But many also survived the carnage:

> ... thousands of women on both sides of the newly formed borders ... were abducted, raped, forced to convert, forced into marriage, forced back into what the two states defined as "their proper homes," torn apart from their families once during the Partition by those who abducted them, and again, after the Partition, by the state which tried to 'recover' and 'rehabilitate' them."[4]

In our view, creative writing about the Partition constitutes an important source for an understanding and appreciation of the terrible catastrophe that befell women. These works are significant for their exploration of the complex dynamic of this event and even though (or perhaps because) they are fictional, they provide glimpses into the subjectivity of victims and aggressors alike. Moreover, the artist's unique sensitivity enables her/him to explore uncharted areas of human consciousness, something not necessarily available to a social scientist.

This paper proposes to trace the ambivalent, hesitant, stumbling trajectory of women groping towards selfhood in the following three short stories and two novels in Hindi and Urdu – "Banished" by Jamila Hashmi, Rajinder Singh Bedi's "Lajwanti," "Mozel" by Sa'adat Hasan Manto, Bhisham Sahni's *Tamas* and *Jhoota Sach* by Yashpal. Some of the questions that are raised, pertain to the author's and character's perception of women, both from the victim and the aggressor communities. Are they primarily perceived as victims of a violent patriarchal order in which they exercise no volition, that is, are they completely denied any agency? Or, can one perceive them as quietly asserting humanitarian values in the inhuman environment, accepting the burden of womanhood from a new and perhaps enlightened consciousness, and emerging from the traumatic experience with a greater degree of self-awareness?

Representation of women in Hindi and Urdu fiction underwent a change from the late nineteenth century onwards. In many of the early prose works in these languages, women were idealized as makers of homes and nurturers of children. They symbolized the values of love and compassion. Prescriptive texts laid out the duties and responsibilities of a woman's role as a daughter-in-law, a wife and a mother. The sati-savitri figure was normally a minor and static adjunct to the dynamic and public figure of the male protagonist. In this and in many other aspects, Nazir Ahmad's *Mirat-ul-Arus* (1869), Gauri Dutt's *Devrani Jethani ki Kahani* (1870), and Kishorelal Goswami's *Hriday Harni* (1890) broadly reflected the restricted roles that society had ascribed to women.[5]

The second half of the nineteenth century witnessed an impassioned public debate on the issue of women's education, as "English" education exposed the local intelligentsia to the idea of female emancipation. While many considered this a desirable ideal, there were considerable differences in opinion among social reformers and the emerging nationalists as to how this was to be achieved. The debate was not restricted to Indians alone. Sections of the Indian intelligentsia questioned the legitimacy of the colonial state's intervention in banning practices such as sati and child marriage. Colonial domination meant that any "Western" idea could not find easy and immediate acceptability among the nationalists. However, as the national movement with its propagation of the ideas of equality gathered momentum in the twenties and thirties among the Indian masses, women from different classes began to participate in the movement directly and indirectly. The freedom struggle was a cause, which became a rallying point for women without inviting the outright opprobrium of conservative sections. The task of social reform, the improvement of the condition of women and their education became inextricably linked to the goal of national independence.

All these developments found subtle reflections in the direction that Hindi and Urdu fiction took in the first half of the twentieth century. Realism emerged as the dominant mode, and in its initial phase attempted to reconcile the competing claims of individual choice and a hierarchical restrictive society, especially in the context of women and romantic love.[6] With the arrival of Premchand, socially realistic fiction achieved a higher level of concretion and sophistication as it moved away from the didactic and the supernatural.[7] While his women characters still played out domestic roles in novels like *Sevasadan* and *Karambhumi*, some of them were conscious of the inequality in their relationships with men and their exploitation by them. Writers like Jainendra Kumar, Ismat Chughtai and Agyeya, who experimented with psychological realism in the 1930s and 40s, attempted to represent the repressed self of the woman in a conservative, patriarchal[8] society.

The event of the Partition found an almost immediate and direct reflection in the works of contemporary progressive writers. Short stories by Krishna Chander, Manto, Krishna Sobti, Ahmad Nadeem Qasimi and many other Hindi and Urdu writers described horrific scenes of inhumanity. Apart from the murders, looting and mass migrations, women were an important focus in these narratives. Given the onus that society placed on their chastity and honour, their physical mutilation and rape became some of the major ways in which fanatics from one community recorded their bizarre victory over the other. The victimized women characters in such narratives evoke the strongest revulsion for the perpetrators of such inhuman acts. Vulnerable and dependent on male protection, more so in those insecure times, women have little or no agency in most of the early narratives. Condemned to a life of both social and familial humiliation, many of them prefer to commit suicide. But not all representations of victims end on such bleak note. Some of them also trace the subjectivity of the victimized women, as they attempt to renegotiate their relationship with a society that condemns them for an act to which they were forcibly subjected.

Rape figures prominently in many narratives of the Partition. From a "feminist" perspective it is important to look at how literary conventions, patriarchy, inter- and intra-gender relations influence and shape the representation of rape. Rajeshwari Sunder Rajan has argued that, unlike texts that make rape the central event and focus on its motives and rationale, "feminist" or women centered texts concentrate on the aftermath of rape from the perspective of the victim. The actual event of rape is positioned at the beginning and pre-empts expectation of its later occurrence. It serves a purely functional purpose, and interest is centered on what follows as a consequence.[9] In the Partition narratives one observes at least two kinds of representations. First, those in which rape is a part of large scale rioting, arson, loot and abduction, as in "Peshawar Express," "Khol Do," et cetera. Here the victims are generally, not individually, identified; the gory and horrifying details follow a naturalist tradition, and the dehumanization of people is represented with a view to both shock and sensitize the reader. And second, those in which rape is an event of the past and the focus is on what happens to the victim subsequently. Both Lajwanti, in Rajinder Singh Bedi's "Lajwanti," and the narrator of Hashmi's "Banished" are victims of abduction and rape, and the latter event is assumed rather than overtly stated. By shifting the focus away from the "materiality" of the event to the consciousness of the victim, such stories move away from issues such as the reasons that led to these events, that is, they move away from the area of historical/scientific explanations of the cause to an examination of their impact on the inner selves and the consciousness of individuals.

Jamila Hashmi's "Banished"[10] is an unusual Partition story, as it is narrated from the point of view of a woman who is also the protagonist. The story uses the image of a permanently exiled Sita who stays with Ravana, her abductor, with no hope of Ram (here, represented by her brother?) coming to rescue her.[11] The contrast between the "pure" Sita of yore who is rescued by Ram and the present day Sita who is "defiled" and lives in a permanent state of exile, provides the narrator with a more comprehensive awareness of her situation as a woman. The story contains two strands: the past, that is, the narrator's childhood, in which she yearningly remembers her family, especially her brother who left for England and never returned to rescue her, and the present, where she has become the unwed bahu of Gurpal, the mother of his three children, and a domestic servant, to be cursed and beaten by Gurpal's mother. Both these strands come together in the narrator's consciousness, and while the past is clearly more desirable than the present, there is also an acute consciousness that it is irrecoverable. Her "despoiled" state, the absence of her brother and the death of her parents have shattered that world. Her children, especially Munni, whom she is particularly fond of, ameliorate her sense of entrapment. "The pear tree has blossomed every year since Munni was born. When the season changes, its branches become filled with flowers, the tree bends over heavy with fruit, deepening its bond with the earth. Its roots burrow deeper into the soil. No one can rupture that bond" (88). While she uses the image of a barren tree to describe herself, the narrator nevertheless makes explicit the relationship between herself and her "rooted" daughter. "Munni stands in my way. She is the great distance that separates me from my own family" (95).

The dichotomy between her public and private self is a significant aspect of her character. Inwardly, she does not lack agency. She is aware and conscious of her status and identity, and occasionally protests against its erasure. When referring to the murder of her parents and her abduction, Gurpal says, "Can't you ever bring yourself to forget that incident?" she quietly resists, "That was a different time. How can I make him understand that time never changes. Man suffers because Man cannot forget. That time lives on in my memory just as it was ..." (99). Outwardly, her status in Gurpal's home has undergone a change over the years. When he first brought her home he had told his reluctant mother, "You don't have to put up with the airs of the mahris and kaharis anymore. Here, I've brought you a bahu. She is your maid. She will do whatever you tell her to do – grind grain, fetch water, anything you want ..." (89). Over the years she has managed to impress Gurpal's mother with her submissive, uncomplaining nature. "With time Bari Ma grew fond of me. Our bonds became stronger and deeper as I severed my last remaining links with my past. I am her prized daughter-in-law now, her Lakshmi. She shows off the yarn spun by me to everyone she meets. When other women complain about their daughter-in-law, she praises me to high heaven just to rub it in" (104). However, inwardly she still feels that "bahu" is a term of abuse, since she was abducted and kept without any legal, religious or social sanction.

It is an act of resistance that makes Hashmi's narrator record her life story. The social compulsions that make Gurpal and his mother attempt to efface her "real" identity (of an abducted, raped and kept woman) and substitute a "false" identity (of a bahu) in its place, are resisted by the narrator in her consciousness, by her act of recalling, remembering and recording the past.[12]

Her self-consciousness as a victim pervades the narrative. But unlike other women characters in Partition stories, she does exercise a choice in favour of her commitment to her children. Of course, the other alternative of a return is perhaps bleaker. But her awareness of her predicament and her deliberate choice sets her apart from others, whose stories end with rape and murder.

The question of how or where their agency is to be located is an important one. R Sunder Rajan has argued in the context of "Prison," Ramanan's short story, "Clearly, the exercise of choice cannot be sufficient condition of a woman's freedom when her choices are both limited and severely determined."[13] What can be argued in the context of "Banished" is that an incipient feminist gesture can be perceived in the *consciousness* of the abducted woman, in the way she evaluates and perceives herself, her victimhood, and the unjust patriarchal order, without necessarily bringing about a radical change through protest. As Sunder Rajan says, "When a woman's consciousness of individualistic identity is forced into existence through social isolation brought on by the stigma of sexual impropriety ... it stands in contrast to the politics of feminism."[14] Ramanan's Bhagirathi, like Hashmi's narrator, has to chalk out strategies of survival after her rape. As destitute women, both need protectors. Yet, as Sunder Rajan argued, (and her thesis is tenable for Hashmi's narrator too), "... a tenuous individualism shapes the female subject's resistance. Ideally, this selfhood constitutes for the female subject existential freedom, space for growth and change, a full inner life, and some access to power, even if it ends as a costly or self defeating venture ..."[15]

If the identity and self of Hashmi's narrator is constituted to a very large extent in relation to her abductor, Bedi's short story "Lajwanti" traces the subtle and imperceptible impact that abduction and rape leave on the relationship of a couple from a victimized community. Lajo, the non-heroic protagonist, an average, male dominated wife, is forcibly abducted, but rescued and returned to her home. Her apprehension that she may not be accepted in her home dissolves as Sunderlal, her husband, who is on the committee for the rehabilitation of abducted women, apparently practices what he preaches. However, while Sunderlal publicly argues for the acceptance of abducted women, he does not have the capacity to cope when faced with the same situation in his own life. Elevating her to the status of a devi or goddess, he distances himself from her emotionally. Used to a conventional dominating husband, Lajwanti is confronted with a worshipping one on her return. The twin experiences of abduction and rehabilitation undermine – in a subtle and radical manner – the very basis of her relationship with her husband, which constitutes her entire world. Lajwanti wants to revert to her earlier relationship with Sunderlal and become Lajo again. But in order to accept her, Sunderlal has to distance himself by transforming her from Lajo to a "devi." The victim wishes to come to terms with her abduction and rape by talking about it to her husband, but her "benefactor" refuses to acknowledge her past. For Lajwanti, his refusal is a constant and humiliating reminder of her altered status. From her perspective, the term "devi" symbolizes an emotionally alienated, impure womanhood. Paradoxically, the same humiliating experience that breaks up her relationship with her husband, also enables her to recognize its weakness. Bedi leaves his heroine at a point from which she can, and probably will, realize her own lack of agency. This, perhaps by itself, marks the beginning of the process of empowerment, as we have noted in the story "Banished."

While for some women victims in Partition fiction, an incipient feminist consciousness was combined with a sense of entrapment in their situations, others waged a slow, relentless and unnoticed struggle in order to create a space for themselves in the post-Partition period. As Menon and Bhasin have pointed out:

> Very large numbers of women who had never before stepped out of their homes joined the workforce after the Partition. Force of circumstances, economic necessity, and the urgency to rebuild homes and fortunes pushed many women of all classes into earning and supporting family incomes. There were thousands who rehabilitated themselves, so to speak, enabled to do so by the breakdown of traditional constraints on their mobility.[16]

In Yashpal's "Jhoota Sach," the breakdown of her home and her displacement bring about a radical, progressive transformation in the life of Tara, one of the central characters. An educated, middle class girl from a conservative family in Lahore, she is forced to marry Somraj, a disreputable character, as a result of her father's uneasiness with the prospect of a young, unmarried daughter in a fast deteriorating communal situation. Violated sexually, and subsequently rejected by her family, she is successful in renegotiating her relationship with a patriarchal order in the post-Partition scenario.

Tara's physical and moral humiliation on her wedding night is preceded by the "emotional" violence of her family (who emotionally blackmail her into marrying Somraj), and merges with the sexual violation that follows when she runs away from her in-law's house when the Muslim mob attacks. By juxtaposing Somraj's inhuman treatment of Tara with her abduction and rape, Yashpal blurs the distinction between socially "sanctioned" violence and the "illegitimate" communal violence directed against women. Both aggressors see Tara as "property," Somraj wants to "domesticate" her, and Nabbu, her abductor, wants to "spoil" her sexual purity and then sell her off.

The violence of Partition ironically provides Tara with a clean slate to begin life anew. Deserted by her family (all conveniently presume her to be dead) and stripped of any identity, humiliated (but not destroyed) with her self-respect and dignity still intact, Tara successfully carves out a career for herself. Two aspects of her evolution to selfhood need to be emphasized. One, her alienation from her family (as a result of her abduction) provides her an opportunity to realize herself. Tara is freed from the taboos of a restrictive, dominating family. Second, one must emphasize that Tara's karambhumi, the society in which she realizes her potential, is no less patriarchal than pre-Partition Lahore. In fact, the rejection of Banto, an abducted refugee woman by her family, and her subsequent suicide, harden Tara's resolve to never return to her own family.

The trajectory of Tara's growth to womanhood has two significant markers. First, she becomes financially independent. A senior position in the bureaucracy confers status and respect in a hierarchical society. Then, Tara relates to her work not merely as a job, but in a larger sense, as a vocation. As a victim of the Partition herself, she empathizes with other victims. She goes out of her way to assist and resettle widows, young abducted women, and even unites a couple by assisting the woman to walk out of a loveless "arranged" marriage of the pre-Partition days.

However, Tara's social and economic emancipation is not matched by a corresponding intellectual and emotional maturity in her personal relationships with men. Her acceptance of the proposal of marriage from Pran Nath – her benefactor, both in Lahore and Delhi – brings back an adolescent Tara who dreamt of eloping with Assad, and then expectantly waited for Somraj on her wedding night. Although her relationship with Pran Nath is based on mutual trust, faith and concern, the image of Tara washing his clothes and cleaning his house, which precedes the proposal of marriage, suggests that her perception of the role of a wife does not transcend traditional stereotypes.

Representations of women from the aggressor communities, like those from the victimized communities, do not conform to a single type. Their attitude to the other community, and in particular its women victims, varies considerably. None of them indulges in any physical violence, but this does not make them immune to patriarchal or communal ideology. "Feminist convictions are not given or inherent in women, after all."[17] Gurpal's mother in Hashmi's story easily acquiesces in the abduction of the Muslim girl. Even the women in Hafiz's family in "Jhoota Sach" who are so loving and caring towards Tara, after she is freed from the clutches of Nabbu, her abductor and rapist, merely see in her an opportunity for converting an infidel. They lose all interest in her as soon as it becomes clear to them that Tara will not be pressurized into conversion. Further, where abducted women are rejected by their husbands, other women are party to such decisions. Banto, an abducted peasant woman in Yashpal's novel, goes through a harrowing ordeal before being rescued by an official rescue team. With Tara's help she is finally able to locate her family in Delhi after a long and exhausting search. But both her husband and mother-in-law refuse to accept her, ostensibly because of her "impurity." Frustrated in her desire to be reunited with her son and husband, Banto breaks her head on the portico of her family's new house and dies, even as the entire mohalla of women look on, and her family keeps the door barred to her.

While Bhisham Sahni's *Tamas* unveils a vast canvas of situations and characters, all consumed by the raging fire of communal feeling and violence, most of the women characters exhibit an amazing capacity to retain their basic human values in spite of the upheaval around them. Their own experience of suffering predisposes them towards a natural empathy for the victim, even when it involves resistance towards males in their own family. Rajo, the Muslim woman, who insists on giving shelter to Harnam Singh and his wife against her daughter-in-law's more practical advice, carries within her the humanitarian values that her son has almost completely abandoned in his frenzied state. Her natural and instinctive sympathy for the old and defenceless couple, her acute embarrassment at her daughter-in-law's greed, and her severe reaction to her son's murderous intent, mark her out as an independent, self-motivated, "feminine" woman. Her rustic background and apparent domesticity do not equip her for any independent action, and yet, an urgent, totally new and risk-fraught situation brings out reserves of resistance within her, which perhaps even she has not dreamt of. The situation cries out for a saviour, and she finds herself pitchforked into the role. While it must be conceded that circumstances do work in her favour (her husband is an old acquaintance of Harnam Singh, and her son recognizes Harnam Singh just when he is about to strike the fatal blow), her independent initiative in the matter cannot be denied.

The patriarchal system – of which she is clearly a part – has not completely desensitized and devitalized her. Her moral responsibility for the defenceless couple who implore her for shelter is in sharp contrast to her daughter-in-law's indifference and fear of the males in her family. Rajo is an outstanding example of a woman who retains and exercises her humanitarian agency against tremendous odds.

Both Nathu's wife and Liza, the wife of the Deputy Commissioner, Richard, share a common concern for the victims of communal violence. Neither belongs to any warring community, Hindu or Muslim, nor are they affected directly by the violence. Yet both feel a deep sense of responsibility. In the case of Nathu's wife, her guilt is attributable to her husband's killing of the pig, which when thrown in front of the mosque, triggers off a riot. Though she tries to justify her husband's action by insisting that he was ignorant about the consequences of his action, she cannot bring herself to touch the money he gets for killing the pig. Lady Macbeth-like, she starts sweeping her house to drive out the evil spirit that has entered it. Chamars by caste, Nathu and his wife are neither Hindu nor Muslim; their identity resides on the margins of a respectable society, and yet they embody human values clearly absent elsewhere.

Liza, the Deputy Commissioner's wife, also acts as a significant contrast to her husband Richard, with his bureaucratic and theoretical attitude towards the violence and loss of lives. Richard represents the male centered and imperialist point of view. A typical colonial administrator, he carries out his duties with unswerving loyalty to his mother country, with little regard for the people he governs. His interest in Indian civilization, the ruins of Takshila, his awareness of a common racial identity amongst Indians, are merely paraded to impress his wife or win acclaim as an "orientalist" author; they never serve as useful inputs in his governance. It is Liza, his bored, restless, frustrated wife, who refuses to occupy the "inner" space of the "Anglo-Indian" wife, and brings out the contradiction in Richard's life. Caught in the trap that Forster's Adela ran away from, Liza nevertheless rebels against her marginalization in Anglo-India. Her desire to establish and live out a meaningful relationship with Richard is constantly thwarted, since he persists in segregating his public and private life. For him the Hindu-Muslim conflict is a source of assurance of colonial power, ("... when people fight between themselves, what need the ruler fear?" he says),[18] but for her it represents a denial of human values. When she innocently suggests that he should intervene in the Hindu-Muslim conflict, ("You must also tell them that you belong to the same race, you should not fight between yourselves ..."[47]), he laughs away her suggestion. Liza is the victim of a larger patriarchal, imperialist framework that sees self-interest as its prime objective, compartmentalizes the spheres of life, and sanctions violence if it is not directed towards oneself. Liza, as a "woman" outside the circle of Hindu-Muslim conflict, cannot sleep since she constantly hears the clanging of the alarm bell signalling the beginning of the riot. Her instinctive sympathy for the victims of violence brings to the fore the total incompatibility in her relationship with Richard. For

Richard, as she tells him, is a strange man since he can hear the lark singing in the midst of such bloodshed and violence. "What sort of a creature are you Richard that you can see new birds and hear the lark even in such places (of death, bloodshed and destruction)?" (233).

Liza's perspective is holistic and sympathetic. Though she is not directly involved in the communal riot, she voices a concern that grows out of, but goes beyond her personal predicament. Restricted and marginalized in her role as an "Anglo-Indian" wife, she nevertheless vainly attempts to make Richard less egocentric and insensitive in his public life.

Like Liza, Mozel, the protagonist of Manto's short story of the same name, is a woman character from a community not directly involved in the Hindu-Muslim riots. As a Westernized, bohemian Jew, living in Bombay at the time of the Partition, she is critically distanced from the conflict. She ridicules Tirlochan's rather hypocritical respect for Sikh religious markers, especially in the face of impending danger, when they attempt to rescue his trapped fiancée from a Muslim mohalla. A strong independent woman, Mozel refuses to be dominated by any man, and all her relationships are short-lived, precisely because she refuses to be slotted in any "womanly" role, that is, as wife, mother or sister. Impulsive and totally guided by her instincts, she sympathizes with the defenceless victims of communal violence and dies saving Tirlochan's fiancée.

The preceding examination of a broadly representative range of women characters in Partition narratives suggests that their representation is extremely varied and complex. However, the critical point that needs to be emphasized is that the victimization of women pushes them into situations, which at one end of the spectrum can raise disturbing questions in their own consciousness regarding their identities as women, and at the other end, can significantly alter the balance of their relationships with men. Strategies of resistance to patriarchal exploitation vary, depending upon individual contexts. And not all women put up resistance. However, those who do, begin a journey towards a self-definition that attempts to shed generations of patriarchal orientation. They become aware of their own selves as women and as victims. The exercise of their agency results in the creation of a new female self.

The representation of women in the Partition narratives highlights numerous issues that are extremely diverse in their implications for womanhood. While an understanding of the patriarchal system enriches sensitive feminist critiques of these texts, in the absence of an informed consideration of the historical, social and cultural specificity of the subject, some recent writings in this genre dwindles into axiomatic, self-evident truth. In sharp contradistinction, the concern informing this exploration into literary representations of the predicament of the Indian woman at a crucial moment in our recent history, springs from a political engagement with the fashioning of a post-independent society and culture.

Notes

1   A good example of this is G D Khosla's *Stern Reckoning: A Survey of the Events Leading up to and Following the Partition of India* (New Delhi: Oxford UP, 1989).

2   The characterization of the national movement as a mass movement underscores this idea. Among others, Bipan Chandra, Sumit Sarkar, Barun De have seen the national movement, the growth of communalism, and the Partition as the expression of the mass and popular will of the Indian people, which was given direction and form by the political leadership.

3.   Feminist critics, together with cultural anthropologists, continue the legacy of left wing and radical historians by their anti-Indian National Congress stance. While the latter have described the organization as "bourgeois" and "power-hungry," the former attempt to establish its "communal," "patriarchal" and "statist" credentials. See Urvashi Butalia, "Community, State and Gender: On Women's Agency during Partition," in *Economic and Political Weekly of India,* 28.17 (1993), and Mushirul Hasan, *Inventing Boundaries: Gender, Politics, and the Partition of India* (New Delhi: Oxford UP, 2000).

4   See Urvashi Butalia, "Community, State and Gender: On Women's Agency during Partition," *Economic and Political Weekly of India,* p.14.

5   Meenakshi Mukherjee has argued that with the advent of realism in India (which was closely linked to individualism in its European context), romantic love "could only be illicit, involving either a widow or a courtesan ..." Both lived outside structured society, in which "not only were conventions of marriage restrictive, even social intercourse between the sexes was not common in the upper classes." *Realism and Reality: The Novel and Society in India* (New Delhi: Oxford UP, 1994) 70.

6   "Individualism had been emerging as a human ideal in the West for a couple of centuries, and even though in actual fact a woman's life lacked the relative autonomy of a man's, the possibility did exist as an idea. In India even though exposure to the West was beginning to make an alternate ideal available in the nineteenth century,

such individualism was alien to traditional thinking" (Mukherjee 99). Women protagonists of late nineteenth century novels like Ruswa's *Umrao Jan Ada* or O Chandu Menon's *Indulekha* reveal this inner tension.

7   The didactic or prescriptive element in literature was never completely jettisoned. Premchand's *adarshonmukh yatharthwad* (idealistically inclined realism) and the socialist inclinations of the progressive writers indicate this.

8   The term "patriarchal" describes both a mind-set and a social order in which the woman's life is virtually scripted from birth to death by the male. Locked in a grossly unequal relationship with the male, defined totally in relation to the family males, and denied any freedom both inside or outside the home, the woman in a patriarchal society is a slave to the wishes of first her father, then husband, and finally her son.

9   "In both Alice Walker's *The Color Purple* and Maya Angelou's *I Know why the Caged Bird Sings*, the development of the female subject "self" begins after the rape and occupies the entire length of the narrative," writes Rajeswari Sunder Rajan in *Real and Imagined Women: Gender, Culture and Post-colonialism* (London: Routledge, 1993) 73.

10   All references to "Banished" by Jamila Hashmi are from Muhammad Umar Memon ed. and trans. from the Urdu, in *An Epic Unwritten: The Penguin Book of Partition Stories from Urdu* (New Delhi: Penguin, 1998).

11   The use of the Sita myth in an altered context by a Muslim writer shows how mythic consciousness transcends religious creed. It also underlies the point that both Indian and Pakistani writers formed a part of a broader consensual framework for many years after the Partition.

12   In the context of totalitarian regimes, Milan Kundera makes a similar comment on the importance of memory: "It is 1971, and Mirek says that the struggle of man against power is the struggle of memory against forgetting." Milan Kundera, *The Book of Laughter and Forgetting* (Calcutta: Rupa, 1992) 3.

13   Rajeswari Sunder Rajan, *Real and Imagined Women*. Ramanan's Tamil Story "Prison" is the story of Bhagirathi, a Brahmin priest's wife, who is raped by a Christian landlord. Ostracized by her husband and society, she confronts her rapist, and lives in his house without any intercourse with him, insisting on her caste purity. Over the years, he begins to feel guilty, and leaves her a substantial portion of his property when he dies. On his death, however, Bhagirathi mourns for him as his widow.

14   Rajeswari Sunder Rajan, *Real and Imagined Women,* p. 73.

15   Rajeswari Sunder Rajan, *Real and Imagined Women,* p.71.

16   Little, however, is known about such women. They fought their lone battles, fighting discrimination by using their wits and gradually establishing some measure of economic independence. These unheroic women find little space in the grand sagas of victimization. Menon and Bhasin's *Borders and Boundaries* is a pioneering work as it devotes some space to survivors who were able to free themselves from patriarchal domination to some extent. The authors concede, though with qualifications, "the liberatory potential of the

disruption caused by Partition." Based on their interviews with women survivors, they argue that "survival and strategies for survival can also be instrumental in women finding their feet ..." Ritu Menon and Kamla Bhasin, *Borders and Boundaries: Women in India's Partition* (New Delhi: Kali for Women, 1998) 222.

17   T Sarkar and U Butalia eds., *Women and the Hindu Right: A Collection of Essays* (New Delhi: Kali for Women, 1985) 4.

18   Bhisham Sahni, *Tamas* (New Delhi: Rajkamal, 1984) 47.

TIMELINE

1837   Hindustani written in Persio-Arabic script introduced as court language in Bihar, the North West Frontier Provinces, and parts of the Central Provinces.

1871   Publication of W W Hunter's *The Indian Musalmans: Are they Bound in Conscience to Rebel Against the Queen?*

1875   Publication of Dayanand Saraswati's *Satyarth Prakash*

May
1875   On the initiative of Sir Syed Ahmed Khan, Muhammadan Anglo-Oriental college begins as a primary school. In 1877, the foundation-stone is formally laid; in 1878, intermediate and in 1881, BA classes are started.

1885   Formation of Indian National Congress, Bombay, 28 December, 1885.

1900   Anthony MacDonnell permits use of Hindi written in Devnagari script in court in the United Provinces.

1905   Partition of Bengal.

1906   Simla deputation petitions the Viceroy for separate Muslim electorates and weightage in representation.

1947

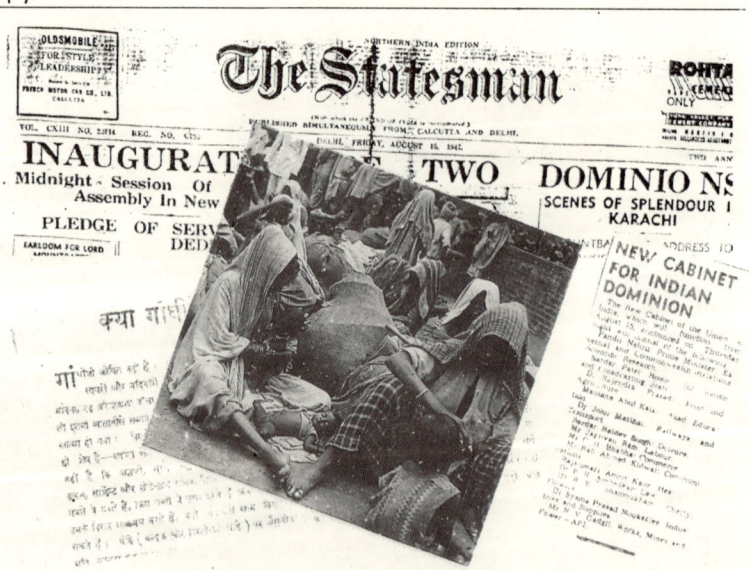

212

1906   Foundation of All India Muslim League at Dhaka.

1909   Indian Councils Act. Morley-Minto reforms to the legislative councils introduce elections at the centre and separate electorates for Muslims in all councils.

1915   Hindu Mahasabha started at Kumbh Mela, Haridwar.

1916   Congress and the Muslim League conclude the Lucknow Pact, a joint constitutional scheme for India, on the basis of dominion status.

1919   Indian Councils Act. Montague-Chelmsford reforms extend the Morley-Minto logic of separate electorates for Muslims to the enlarged provincial and central legislatures.

Growth of communal antagonism at the level of High Politics, as well as mass politics (1920's witnessed a series of riots in the United Provinces).

1921-   Khilafat-Non-Cooperation Mass Movement under the
22   leadership of Gandhi. Withdrawal and frustration, after Chauri Chaura incident.

Mopla Rebellion, conversions and counter-conversions through *Shuddhi* and *Sangathan*, and later through *tabligh* and *tanzim*.

: 1947

213

1925   Foundation of Rashtriya Swayamsevak Sangh, at Nagpur.

1928   Nehru Report proposes a Constitution in which India would attain dominion status with a fully responsible government at the Centre and in the provinces, and which in character is more unitary than federal. It recommends the abolition of separate electorates for Muslims, but an increase in the number of Muslim majority provinces from two to four.

1930   Muhammad Iqbal, in his address to the Muslim League, suggests the formation of a Muslim State within the Indian Federation.

1930-32   Communal Award grants separate electorates to Muslims, Sikhs and Untouchables. Gandhi fasts in protest; Poona pact replaces separate electorate for Untouchables with some reserved seats. Round Table conference boycotted by Congress, but attended by the Muslim League, Hindu Mahasabha and some Liberals.

1933   Chaudhary Rahmat Ali, a law student at Cambridge, in a pamphlet, *Now or Never*, puts forward a scheme for a fully independent territorial Muslim State consisting of the Punjab, the Frontier province, Kashmir and Baluchistan.

: 1 9 4 7

1935   Government of India Act gives almost complete autonomy to
        the provinces. It establishes "The Federation of India"
        comprising both provinces and princely states, with a federal
        Central government and Legislature for the management of
        Central subjects. The principle of diarchy is abolished in the
        provinces and transferred to the Centre.

1937   First general elections under 1935 Act. Congress wins 711
        out of 1585 provinces, adding an eighth in 1938.
        Congress launches its mass contact campaign among Muslims
        without much success. It is abandoned by 1939.

: 1947

1939	Congress governments resign because Government of India declares war without consulting Indians.
	Celebrated as "day of deliverance" by Jinnah and Ambedkar.
1940	Muslim League adopts Pakistan as its goal at Lahore.
1942	The Cripps Mission comes to India, but fails to reach a settlement with Congress.
	Quit India mass movement.
1945	Simla Conference of all political groups fails to agree over the composition of the Executive Council.
1945-46	Second general elections under 1935 Act. The Muslim League wins over 90 percent of reserved Muslim seats.
1946	Cabinet Mission fails to win agreement from Congress and Muslim League over India's constitutional future.
	Indian National Army Trials, Royal Indian Navy Mutiny.
	Direct Action Day and the beginning of Partition violence in Calcutta, followed by Bombay, Noakhali, Bihar and Garhmukteshwar (Uttar Pradesh).

1947

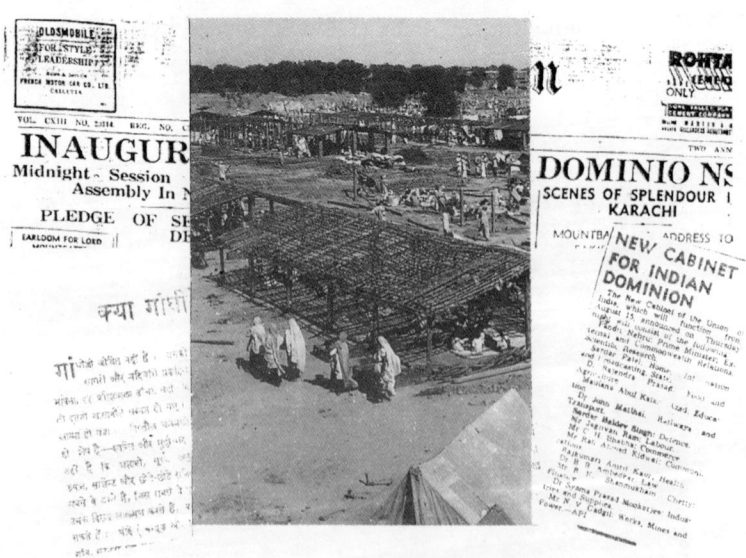

"Gandhi's Finest Hour" – his fast brings the violence in Noakhali to a temporary halt. Gandhi continues his campaign against violence, away from Transfer of Power parleys and negotiations.

1947   14th August: Pakistan attains independence.

15th August: India becomes independent.

1948   Gandhi assassinated by Nathuram Godse, a Hindu extremist, at a Prayer meeting on 30th January, at Birla House, New Delhi. Violence gradually abates.

.1947

We would like to thank the photo division, Government of India & *The Hindustan Times* for giving us the permission to use the Partition photographs.

217

We would like to thank *The Statesman* for providing us the photocopies of newspages.

The Statesman

NORTHERN INDIA EDITION
PUBLISHED SIMULTANEOUSLY FROM CALCUTTA AND DELHI.
VOL. CXIII NO. 33114.   REG. NO. C133—   DELHI, FRIDAY, AUGUST 15, 1947.   TWO ANN

INAUGURATION OF TWO DOMINIONS

Midnight Session Of Constituent Assembly In New Delhi

SCENES OF SPLENDOUR I KARACHI

PLEDGE OF SERVICE AND DEDICATION

MOUNTBATTEN'S ADDRESS TO

NEW CABINET FOR INDIAN DOMINION

The New Cabinet of the Union of India, which will function from August 15, announced on Thursday night will consist of the following:

Pandit Nehru: Prime Minister; External and Commonwealth Relations, Scientific Research.

Sardar Patel: Home, Information and Broadcasting, State.

Dr Rajendra Prasad: Food and Agriculture

Maulana Abul Kalam Azad: Education

Dr John Matthai: Railways and Transport.

Sardar Baldev Singh: Defence.

Mr Jagjivan Ram: Labour.

Mr C H Bhabha: Commerce

Mr Rafi Ahmed Kidwai: Communications.

Rajkumari Amrit Kaur: Health.

Dr B R Ambedkar: Law.

Mr R K Shanmukham Chetty: Finance

Dr Syama Prasad Mookerjee: Industries and Supplies.

Mr N V Gadgil: Works, Mines and Power.—API.

TO-DAY'S PROGRAMME IN DELHI

8-30 a.m. Swearing in of Governor-General and Ministers at Government House.

9-40 a.m. Procession of Ministers to Constituent Assembly.

9-50 a.m. State Drive to Constituent Assembly.

9-55 a.m. Royal Salute to Governor-General.

10-30 a.m. Hoisting of National Flag at Constituent Assembly.

10-35 a.m. State Drive to Government House.

6-9 p.m. Flag ceremony at India Gate.

7-8 p.m. Illuminations.

7-45 p.m. Fireworks display at Great Place.

8-45 p.m. Official dinner at Government House.

10-15 p.m. Reception at Government House.

TOMORROW EVENING.

8-30 a.m. Flag hoisting over Red Fort.

7-30 p.m. Reception at Queen's Gardens.

7-40 p.m. Illuminations.

8-30 p.m. Fireworks display opposite Red Fort.

RIOT DESTRUCTION

क्या गांधीके बधिकको मार देना चाहिए ?

पछे बक्त

गांधीजी बीलित नहीं है । इनको नस्स तास्पूर्ण भारतके
सागरों और नदियोंमें प्रसिद्ध कर दी गई है । अतेत
मोंस, एक परीख्याका डंचा, बड़ो आपु, इस आदर्श-बानी
तो हतनो भारतवोंसे समाप्त दी गए । एक क्षणमें दो मक्का
थाल्या दो गया । किंतील चकनेको खकाज और निर्मल शान्ति
दो गेय है—शान्ति और सुतोंभार भाग । यह कोई अधर्ष
नहीं है कि महानो, मूरो, अतुराम आक्मिक्षारक, बरल,
कजल, सांगेन्द और छोटे-छोटे सेनिक दिगाजे प्रेमी हैं । जिस
सच्चे ने बरते हैं, किन तपणें से एणा करते दें और ने राम जो
उसके लिएर समान्या बरते हैं, वही ज्ञानाओंके कम किए ज
सच्चे हैं । पांछे (बन्दुक और किलीतके गोंछे) पर ओखुलीको
शान्ति, बरला …

सरल होता दे । लोग उतकमों और भारतखठलोंने उनके बड़े
दें, कोंगिंद ने बरल सकड़े भवकोल दें ; पर सत्य परिक्षणीय
नहीं दे । यह फिर भी बरल दे । बह बाम बांधुधे अपेश
अधिक बुनिद्धा दे ।

यस अकल दिल्लुश खरात कीजिए, जो आज आरामामें
बेछ छुवा दे । उनकी हतनी अधिक देव-रत दर्शाइए दे,
कोंगिंद उसमें गांधीजी बप किया दे । मगा जो मतथ दे या
बौलित रखना दे । यदि इस गांधोजोंदी मदाया बधिक कभों
समारो, अर्थात् जो बे कड़ते थे, उनोको हम मारें, और मेरा
खलान दे कि उनका तादस्ये वही था कि आप रनको कड़ें बात
को उसी-बान्ती तपी के सकथा-म …

SELECT ANNOTATED BIBLIOGRAPHY: SECONDARY READINGS

1   **Colonialism, Reforms and Identity:** Nineteenth century was important in terms of preparing the ideological background to Indian nationalism. The colonial discourses laid out the administrative context in which various socio-religious reform movements tried to imagine India anew. Bolstered by the emergent print culture, new identities articulated themselves through language, religion and caste. The subject has been addressed by numerous macro and micro level studies. Kenneth W Jones, *Arya Dharm: Hindu Consciousness in 19th Century Punjab* (Berkeley: U of California P, 1976), and *Socio-religious Reform Movements in British India* (Cambridge: Cambridge UP, 1987) are good introductions to start with.

On the logic of the transition from fuzzy to enumerated communities Sudipta Kaviraj, "The Imaginary Institution of India" in *Subaltern Studies,* eds. Partha Chatterjee and Gyanendra Pandey, vol. 8 (New Delhi: Oxford UP, 1992) is incisive. For a general account of Muslim identity and politics Peter Hardy, *The Muslims of British India* (Cambridge: Cambridge UP, 1972) may be used as a point of departure.

The specific themes of the emergence of Sir Sayyid Ahmad Khan's Aligarh as an important centre of Muslim reforms and politics has been investigated by David Lelyveld, *Aligarh's First Generation: Muslim Solidarity in British India* (New Delhi: Oxford UP, 1978), Rafiuddin Ahmed, *The Bengal Muslims, 1871-1906: A Quest for Identity* (New Delhi: Oxford UP, 1981) remains a classic on early Muslim identity in Bengal. Francis Robinson, *Separatism among Indian Muslims: The Politics of the United Provinces' Muslims, 1860-1923,* (New Delhi: Oxford UP, 1993) is another useful account.

2   **Issues in Contention:** Some issues acquired a privileged status in the North Indian public sphere as the Hindu/Muslim identities increasingly defined and positioned themselves in opposition to each other. Language was one crucial issue. Paul Brass, *Language, Religion and Politics* (Cambridge: Cambridge UP, 1974) provides a good overview. Amrit Rai, *A House Divided. The Origin and Development of Hindi/Hindavi* (New Delhi: Oxford UP, 1984) traces the origins of modern Hindi as well as the process by which a distance appeared between the Persianized Urdu and Sanskritized Hindi. Christopher R. King has written extensively on the Hindi-Urdu Controversy. His *One Language, Two Scripts: The Hindi Movement in Nineteenth century North India* (New Delhi: Oxford UP, 1994) is a useful reference. Sudhir Chandra analyses the ambivalent stance of the early makers of Hindi with regard to the question of language, history, community and nation in *The Oppressive Present: Literature and Social Consciousness in Colonial India* (New Delhi: Oxford UP, 1992). Vasudha Dalmia, *The Nationalization of Hindu Traditions. Bharatendu Harishchandra and Nineteenth Century Banaras* (New Delhi: Oxford UP, 1997) is a brilliant intellectual history of Hindi based on a study of the life and works of the "father of Modern Hindi." What is significant is that this search for a "pure" Hindi not only created a rift between Hindus and Muslims, but managed to alienate itself from an even wider social base constituted by the so-called bolis or dialects. The process has been strengthened in the post-independence period with Hindi acquiring the official

status of the National Language. Ram Vilas Sharma, Krishna Kumar, Francesca Orisini and others have commented extensively on the subject. Alok Rai, *Hindi Nationalism,* Tracts for the Times Ser. 13, (New Delhi: Orient Longman, 2000) is a brilliant account of this politics of language.

Cow-protection was a contentious issue around which some late 19th and early 20th century Hindu-Muslim riots took place. Anand Yang, "Sacred Symbol and Sacred Space in Rural India: Community Mobilization in the 'Anti-cow killing' Riot of 1893"and Sandria B Frietag, "Sacred Symbol as Mobilising Ideology: the North Indian Search for a 'Hindu' Community" in *Comparative Studies in Society and History*, 22. 4 (1980) along with C A Bayly, "The Prehistory of 'Communalism?' Religious Conflict in India, *1770-1860*" *Modern Asian Studies*, 19.2 (1985) and J R McLane, *Indian Nationalism and the early Congress* (Princeton, NJ: Princeton UP, 1977) study the genealogies of some of these mobilisations and riots. Gyanendra Pandey's study of Shahabad riots of 1917, "Rallying Round the Cow: Sectarian Strife in the Bhojpuri Region," in *Subaltern Studies,* ed. Ranajit Guha, vol. 2 (New Delhi: Oxford UP, 1983) reviews some of this material. Suranjan Das, *Communal Riots in Bengal: 1905-47* (New Delhi: Oxford UP, 1991) contains a rich archive on sectarian conflict. Also, Sandria Frietag, *Collective Action and Community: Public Arenas and the Emergence of Communalism in North India* (Berkeley: U of California P) 1989.

3   **Nationalism/Communalism:** For a general account of the freedom movement and communalism, readers may consult Sumit Sarkar, *Modern India: 1885-1947* (Delhi: MacMillan, 1983). Communalism is central to any history of the Partition. It should be useful for the students to go through some of the theoretical discussions on a vast subject on either side of the 1947 temporal divide. Readers will notice that by and large the nationalist history writing equates Communalism with Muslim Identity politics. Similarly, Bipan Chandra portrays Communalism as a distortion

of the real, as a kind of "false consciousness" in his *Communalism in Modern India* (New Delhi: Oxford UP, 1984). The position has been found increasingly untenable. For a critique, Gyanendra Pandey, *The Construction of Communalism in Colonial North India* (New Delhi: Oxford UP, 1990). Pandey also questions the binary opposition between Nationalism and Communalism in the traditional historiography.

The late 80s and 90s have produced a large number of historical and sociological reflections. Veena Das, ed., *Mirrors of Violence: Communities, Riots, Survivors in South Asia* (New Delhi: Oxford UP, 1990), has valuable contributions by Ashis Nandy, Dipesh Chakrabarti, Sudhir Kakkar, Ashish Banerjee and others. David Ludden, *Making India Hindu: Religion, Community, and the Politics of Democracy in India* (New Delhi: Oxford UP, 1996) carries reflections dealing with the period following the demolition of the Babri Masjid. From a historical standpoint, essays by Peter Manuel, William Pinch, Tanika Sarkar, Sandria Frietag, and Sumit Sarkar are significant. Christophe Jaffrelot, *The Hindu Nationalist Movement and Indian Politics, 1925 to the 1990s* (New Delhi: Oxford UP, 1999) is the most comprehensive account of its kind. All the books listed here have good bibliographies.

4   **High Politics of Partition:** As many contributors in the volume have argued, there exists a huge body of works on the Partition, particularly around the theme of causation and the Transfer of Power. From Penderel Moon to David Page, and Maulana Azad, Ram Manohar Lohia to H M Seervai, from Larry Collins and Dominique Lapiere to Patrick French – the list is too long to be redrawn here. Mushirul Hasan, ed., *India's Partition: Process, Strategy and Mobilization*, (New Delhi: Oxford UP, 1993) has a range of documents, articles and memoirs as well as an excellent annotated bibliography. Of particular interest to the students should be the Introduction and articles by Farzana Shaikh, Asim Roy – which is a good summary of the recent debates among historians of the

high politics – Mushirul Hasan's essay on the failure of the Muslim Mass Contact Campaign, Partha Chatterjee on the Bengal Politics, Ian Talbot on the growth of the Muslim League in Punjab, Lance Brennan on Uttar Pradesh, the memoirs of Mohammad Mujeeb and the Raja of Mahmudabad. Readers interested in exploring the theme may consult Anita Inder Singh, *The Origins of the Partition of India, 1936-47* (New Delhi: Oxford UP, 1987), Ayesha Jalal, *The Sole Spokesman: Jinnah, the Muslim League and the Demand for Pakistan* (Cambridge: Cambridge UP, 1985), and David Gilmartin, *Empire and Islam: Punjab and the making of Pakistan* (London: Oxford UP, 1988).

5   **Paradigm Shift:** Recent works mark a departure from causation and elite politics and the history of blame. Rejuvenated by a surge in the 90s, the Partition Studies is now a truly inter-disciplinary domain. Violence, trauma, and the struggle for rehabilitation is the concern of scholars using unorthodox sources such as fiction, memoirs, interviews, films, etc. to reconstruct alternative accounts of the Partition. The subjects of these narratives are naturally, ordinary men and women of the divided nations. The scholars are also crossing physical and administrative boundaries to come to terms with a common difficult past. (The history of non-statist accounts is perhaps as old as the Partition itself. It is instructive to remember that the social science's interest in Manto's oeuvre might be relatively new, but the writer himself did not live beyond the first quarter of 1955. Similarly, G D Khosla's *Stern Reckoning: A Survey of the Events Leading up to and Following the Partition of India* (New Delhi: Oxford UP, 1989). Alok Rai interrogated the literature produced in the immediate aftermath of the Partition in "The Trauma of Independence: Some aspects of Progressive Hindi Literature" in *Journal of Arts and Ideas*, 6 (1984). Veena Das and Ashis Nandy too demonstrated an early interest in Manto in an article: "Violence, Victimhood and the Language of Silence" in *The Word and the World: Fantasy, Symbol and Record*, Veena Das ed., (New Delhi: Sage Publications, 1986).

Veena Das followed it up with reflections on the culture of violence in her *Critical Events: An Anthropological Perspective on Contemporary India* (New Delhi: Oxford UP, 1995). Urvashi Butalia wrote on women's memories of the patriarchal violence during the Partition in the special issue of *Oxford Literary Review*, "On India: Writing History, Culture, Post-Coloniality," 16.1-2, eds. Ania Loomba and Suvir Kaul. The issue had important contributions from Susie Tharu on Partition literary narratives, Ravi Vasudevan on the 1950s cinematic imagination, and Dilip Simeon on contemporary culture of terror during the *Tamas* telecast and the secular responses, among others. Gyanendra Pandey extended his line of enquiry into Communalism to the Partition by questioning the dominant historiography in "The Prose of Otherness" in David Arnold and David Hardiman, eds., *Subaltern Studies,* vol. 8 (New Delhi: Oxford UP, 1994), and *Memory, History and the Question of Violence: Reflections on the Reconstruction of Partition*, (S G Deuskar Lecture, CSSS, Calcutta, 1995).Urvashi Butalia wrote about memories of the survivors of the Partition on both sides of the border in *The Other Side of Silence: Voices from the Partition of India* (New Delhi: Viking, 1998). Ritu Menon and Kamla Bhasin, *Borders and Boundaries: Women in India's Partition* (New Delhi: Kali for Women, 1998) was another scathing critique of the dominant patriarchal discourses on the Partition. Mushirul Hasan continued with his journey into the Partition and beyond in his *Legacy of a Divided Nation* (New Delhi: Oxford UP 1997) and *India Partitioned: The Other Face of Freedom,* 2 vols., (New Delhi: Roli Books) 1995.

6   **Partition, Present-Continuous:** The 90s also witnessed the appearance of a series of anthologies of short stories translated into English. Alok Bhalla compiled and edited a huge collection of stories as *Stories about the Partition of India* (New Delhi: Indus, 1994), and a collection of essays on *The Life and Works of Saadat Hasan Manto* (Simla: IIAS, 1997). M U Memon came out with a more professionally produced translation of Urdu stories called *An Epic Unwritten: the Penguin Book of Partition Stories* (New Delhi:

Penguin India,1998). The special issue of *Seminar* 420 (1994) was dedicated to memories of the Partition. Likewise, the issue of *Outlook,* New Delhi, May 28, 1997, devoted itself to the Partition. Ashis Nandy's essay "The Invisible Holocaust and the Journey as an Exodus" in *Postcolonial Studies*, 2. 3 (1999) and works by Gyanendra Pandey, Veena Das, Shail Mayaram, Suvir Kaul are indicative of the fact that silence about the Partition has indeed been broken and there is more to come. This sudden spurt of Partition Studies has also raised questions with regard to the ethics of remembering what many wanted to forget. See for example, "Remembering Partition," a dialogue between Javeed Alam and Suresh Sharma, *Seminar*, 461 (1998).

Novels: English

Baldwin, Shauna Singh. *What the Body Remembers*. New Delhi: HarperCollins, 1999.

Desai, Anita. *Clear Light of Day*. 1980. Rpt. London, Vintage, 2001

Ghosh, Amitav. *The Shadow Lines*. 1988. Rpt. Delhi: Ravi Dayal, 1995.

Hosain, Attia. *Sunlight on a Broken Column*. 1961. Rpt. New Delhi: Penguin, 1994.

Malgonkar, Manohar. *A Bend in the Ganges*. London: Hamish Hamilton, 1964.

Rajan, Balachandra. *The Dark Dancer*. London: Heinemann, 1959.

Rushdie, Salman. *Midnight's Children*. London: Picador, 1982.

Shah Nawaz Mumtaz. *The Heart Divided*. 1957. Rpt. Lahore: ASR Publications, 1990.

Sidhwa, Bapsi. *Ice Candy Man*. 1988. Rpt. London: Penguin, 1989.

Singh, Khushwant. *Train to Pakistan*. 1956. Rpt. New Delhi: Ravi Dayal, 1986.

Novels: Hindi/Urdu

Baano, Jeelani. *Aiwan-e Ghazal*. Trans. Surajit. New Delhi: Rajkamal, 1999.

Ehtesham, Manzoor. *Sookha Bargad*. New Delhi: Rajkamal, 1983.

Hyder, Qurratulain. *River of Fire*. Trans. by author. New Delhi: Kali for Women, 1998. Trans. of *Aag ka Dariya*. Delhi: Educational Publishing House, 1959.

Husain Intizar. *Basti*. 1979. Trans. Frances W Pritchett. New Delhi: HarperCollins, 1995.

Hussein, Abdullah. *The Weary Generations*. Trans. by Author. New Delhi: HarperCollins, 1999. Trans. of *Udas Naslein*. Allahabad: Kitabmahal, 1963.

Kamleshwar. *Kitne Pakistan*. Delhi: Rajpal, 2000.

—. *Subah ... Dopahar ... Shaam*. Delhi: Rajpal, 1985.

—. *Registan*. Delhi: Rajpal, 2000

Kohli, Dronveer. *Wah Camp*. Delhi: Kitabghar Prakashan, 1998.

Paul, Joginder. *Sleepwalkers*. Trans. Sunil Trivedi and S P Kumar. New Delhi: Katha, 1998. Trans. of *Khwabrau*. New Delhi: Educational Publishing House, 1990.

Raza, Rahi Masoom. *The Feuding Families of Village Gangauli*. Trans. G Wright. New Delhi: Penguin, 1994. Trans. of *Adha Gaon*. Delhi: Rajkamal, 1966.

—. *Os Ki Boond*. Delhi: Rajkamal, 1970.

—. *Topi Shukla*. Delhi: Rajkamal, 1977.

Sahni, Bhisham. *Tamas*. Trans. Jai Ratan. New Delhi: Penguin, 1988. Trans. of *Tamas*. Delhi: Rajkamal, 1974.

Vaid, Krishna Baldev. *Steps in Darkness*. Trans. by author. New Delhi: Penguin, 1995.

—. *Guzra Hua Zamaana*. Delhi: Radha Krishna Prakashan, 1981. Trans. Charles Sparrows and the author as *The Broken Mirror*. New Delhi: Penguin, 1994.

Yashpal. *Jhootha Sach*. 2 Vols. Lucknow: Neelabh, 1967.

Memoirs:

Malihabadi, Josh. *Yaadon ki Barat*. Trans. Hansraj Rahbar. Delhi: Rajpal, n.d.

Qidwai, Begum Anees. *Azaadi ki Chhaon Mein*. New Delhi: National Book Trust, 1990.

Sahni, Bhisham. *Apni Baat*. Delhi: Vaani Prakashan, 1980.

Stories: English

Anand, Mulk Raj. "The Parrot in a Cage." *Orphans of the Storm: Stories on the Partition of India*. S Cowasjee and K S Duggal eds. New Delhi: UBS, 1995.

Hosain, Attia. "After the Storm" and "Phoenix Fled" in *Phoenix Fled*. 1953. Rpt. Delhi: Rupa, 1993.

Sidhwa, Bapsi. "Defend Yourself Against Me." *Orphans of the Storm: Stories on the Partition of India*. S Cowasjee and K S Duggal eds. New Delhi: UBS, 1995.

Collections of Hindi/Urdu Stories:

Cowasjee, S, and K S Duggal, eds. *Orphans of the Storm: Stories on the Partition of India*. New Delhi: UBS, 1995.

Bhalla, A, ed. *Stories About the Partition of India*. 3 Vols. Delhi: HarperCollins, 1994.

Hasan, Khalid, ed. *Kingdom's End and Other Stories*. New Delhi: Penguin, 1989.

Hasan, Mushirul, ed. *India Partitioned: The Other Face of Freedom*. 2 Vols. New Delhi: Roli Books, 1997.

Leslie, Fleming, ed. *Another Lonely Voice: The Life and Works of Sa'adat Hasan Manto*. Trans. Tahira Naqvi. Lahore: Vanguard, 1985.

Menra, Balraj, and Sharad Dutt, eds. *Sa'adat Hasan Manto: Dastavez*. 5 Vols. New Delhi: Rajkamal, 1993.

Rizvi, Zubair, ed. *Fasadat ke Afsane*. Delhi: Zehn-e-Jadeed, 1995.

Sahni, Bhisham, ed. *Kitne Toba Tek Singh*. Delhi: People's Publishing House, 1987.

USER'S GUIDE TO NOTES AND
BIBLIOGRAPHIC REFERENCES

Here are a few points about the style that has been followed in
documenting sources in notes and bibliographies.

Documenting volume and issue number in journals.
Volume number precedes issue number. For example, Volume 8, issue
7 is documented as, 8.7.

Note on the use of abbreviations.
University presses are documented as UP. Thus Oxford University
Press is Oxford UP. University of California Press is U of California P.
If a book is part of a series, it is indicated by the abbreviation Ser. For
example,
Alok Rai, *Hindi Nationalism*, Tracts for the Times Ser 13 (New Delhi:
Orient Longman, 2001).
rev. ed for "revised edition."
rpt. for "reprint."
n.d for "not dated."

BIOGRAPHICAL NOTES

Anisur Rahman, Professor of English at Jamia Millia Islamia University, New Delhi, works in the areas of post-colonial literature and translation. He translates both from Urdu to English and English to Urdu. Amongst his publications are two monographs, *Nissim Ezekiel* and *Kamala Das*, published by Abhinav Publications, 1981, *New Literatures in English*, published by Creative Books, 1995, and *Anthology of Modern Urdu Poetry in English Translation*, published by Rupa, 1996.

Anuradha Marwah Roy teaches English Literature at Zakir Hussain College, New Delhi. She is a novelist and critic; her most recent novel *Idol Love,* was published by Ravi Dayal in 1999.

Atanu Bhattacharya has been associated with Katha's translation work. His translations have appeared in previous Katha Volumes.

Attia Hosain (1913-1998) was born in Lucknow. She obtained a degree from the Isabella Thorburn College in Lucknow. After Partition she moved to Britain, where she began her career as a writer. She was associated with radio broadcasting for a while. *Phoenix Fled and other Stories* (1953) and *Sunlight on a Broken Column* (1963) are her major works, reflecting her distinctive sensibility.

Arjun Mahey has an MA in English from Cambridge, and an MA in South Asian Languages with emphasis on Buddhism from the University of Chicago. He has been teaching English at St Stephen's College since 1986, and is currently on leave to study Modern Indian Literature at Columbia University.

Bhisham Sahni born in Rawalpindi in 1915, migrated with his family to India at the time of Partition. He taught English Literature for some years at Zakir Hussain College in Delhi. *Bhagya Rekha* (Line of Fate), his first collection of short stories in Hindi, was published in 1953. After a stint as a translator in the former Soviet Union (translating from Russian into Hindi) he edited the literary magazine *Nai Kahaniyan* (1965-1967). Amongst his major works, the novel *Tamas*, dealing with the Partition experience, won the Sahitya Akademi Award in 1975.

Bodh Prakash teaches English Literature at Zakir Hussain College. He is currently working on Partition Literature for his Ph D at Jawaharlal Nehru University in Delhi. He has presented papers on his research in India and abroad.

Deeba Zafir teaches at English Literature at Lakshmibai College, Delhi. She has translated Qurratulain Hyder's memoir of Ismat Chughtai.

Gulzar, born in Deena (now in Pakistan) in 1936, migrated to Delhi after the Partition. He began his film career in the 1960s. He has won best director, best lyricist, best dialogue, best storywriter, best feature film, and best documentary awards since then. Films directed by him include *Mausam*, *Namkeen*, *Ijaazat*, *Libaas* and *Maachis*. Gulzar's short stories and poetry include, *Raavi Paar and Short Stories*, published by HarperCollins, 1997, *and Pukhraaj*, published by Rupa, 1994.

Joginder Paul, born in Sialkot Pakistan, migrated to India at the time of the Partition. After a long and active career in the field of education at Kenya and India, he settled in Delhi and concentrated on his writing. He has to his credit three novels, two novellas and many collections of short stories and *short* short stories – a genre enriched markedly by his contribution. His novellas include *Bayanat* (1975) and *Khwabrau* (1990) (translated as *Sleepwalkers* by Katha). His collection of short fiction include *Mitti ka Idrak* (1970) and *Bai Muhavara* (1981). Acknowledged as one of the leading Urdu writers of the subcontinent, his fiction has received much critical acclaim and has been translated into various Indian and foreign languages.

Kamleshwar (born in 1932) has been associated with the Nai Kahani movement in Hindi Literature since its inception. His editorial skills became apparent during his stint at *Sarika*, as he fostered new talent and created the space for generic innovation. He has published a number of collections of short stories, including *Kohra*, published by Rajpal, 1994, as well as a number of novels. His most recent novel is *Kitne Pakistan*, published by Rajpal, 2000. He has authored ten novels, ten short story collections and a number of film scripts. In the seventies he edited the monthly journal *Sarika*, and before that *Nai Kahaniyan*.

M Asaduddin teaches English Literature and Translation Studies in the Department of English at the Jamia Millia Islamia University, New Delhi.. He translates frequently from and to Bangla, Urdu, Hindi and English. His publications include *Image and Representation: Stories of Muslim Lives in India,* co-edited with Mushirul Hasan, and published by Oxford UP, 2000, and *Sa'adat Hasan Manto: Stories and Sketches*, published by Oxford UP, 2001.

Naiyer Masud (born in 1936) taught at Lucknow University as Professor of Persian from 1965 till his retirement. He is renowned as a short story writer in Urdu – his collections *Seemiya*, *Itr-e-Kafoor* and *Taus Chaman ke Maina* have been published to critical acclaim. He received the Presidential Certificate of Honour in 1997 for his "contribution to Persian."

Ravikant works with Sarai, at the Centre for Studies in Developing Societies, Delhi. "Remembering the Past," his translation of "Ateet ki Smriti," an essay by Ramchandra Shukla, appeared in *Hindi: Literature, Discourse, Language*, vol. 1.1 (2000).

Saadat Hasan Manto was born in 1912 in Samrala near Ludhiana,

233

Punjab. He lived at Amritsar, Lahore, Delhi and Bombay, and migrated to Pakistan after the partition of India. Manto started his literary career in the early thirties as translator of the well-known English, Russian, and French classics, but soon made his mark as a short story writer of great distinction. Manto's works include, *Aatish Paray* (Fragments of Fire, 1936) *Baghair Unwan Ke* (Without a Title, 1940) *Teen Auraten* (Three Women, 1942), *Siah Hashie* (The Black Marginalia, 1948) and *Badshahat ka Khatima* (End of a Kingdom, 1951). Many of his stories reflect the gruesome experience of violence, rape and the chaos related to the Partition of the country. Manto died in 1955 in Lahore.

Saumya Gupta is working with Sarai, at the Centre for the Study of Developing Societies. She is currently working on Journalistic Writing and Oral Accounts of the Partition in Kanpur.

Stuti Khanna teaches English Literature at Hindu College, University of Delhi. She is currently working on her M Phil at Delhi University. Her areas of interest include Translation Studies and Indian Literature.

Surendra Prakash is the pen-name of Surendra Kumar Oberoi, Sahitya Akademi Award Winner for Urdu in 1989. Following the Partition he migrated to Delhi from Lahore and made his living as hawker, rickshaw-puller, flower-seller, and travelling salesman. His works include *Doosre Aadmi Ka Drawing Room* (1968) *Barf Par Makalma* (1980) and the award winning anthology, *Baz Goyi* (1988). He now lives in Bombay and writes scripts for films and television plays.

Tarun K Saint teaches English Literature at Hindu College, University of Delhi. His poetry has been published by *Wasafiri* (University of London). *Bruised Memories: Communal Violence and the Writer*, an anthology of writing edited by him is forthcoming by Seagull Books, 2002.

INDEX

Abbas, K A, "A Debt to Pay," 144-45, 155

Accountability, evasion of, xxii

Agyeya, S H V, xix, xxxn35; "Asylum," xx; "Badla," 144, 155; "Muslim-Muslim Bhai-Bhai," -142-44, 155

Ahmed, Ashfaq, "Gadariya," xx, xxxn40

Akhtar, Salim, 147, 157

Aligarh School, Muslim intelligentsia, xxviiin4

Allegory, 94, 158

Asaduddin, M, 120-28

Babri Masjid, 116

Badiuzzaman, "Antim Iccha," xxi, xxxn43

Bedi, Rajinder Singh, xx, xxxn41; "Lajwanti" 133, 134, 195, 200-201

Betrayal, 144, 149, 154; of promise of past, 148; tragic division, 148

Bhalla, Alok, xxv, 160

Bharatriharinama, 15, 16, 17, 21, 22, 24; apbhranshization as reworked cultural signifier, 109, 110

Border(s), 1-10, 63-71, 96, 94-103, 112; crossing of linguistic and geographical, 32, 33, 48, 83, 126; hardening of, 115; Indo-Pak, 145; exchange at, 69-70

Boundaries; mindless identification of language and community, 71, 101; logic of, 97, 107

Butalia, Urvashi, 119; *The Other Side of Silence. Voices From the Partition of India*, 119, 173n19

Communal; amity and hostility, xx, 123; ideology, xxii; ills and Gandhi, 184; inter-connectedness, 126; 29-52,112-119; interests and religion, 113; riots, xxi, 132, 186-7, 11-28, 194-111; unity, 167; violence, literary representation of, xxii, 162

Communalism, 112-19, 132; disabling potential of, 107, 110, 112; devaluation of religious totems and, 108; ghettoization of culture, xxi; Muslim League, 167; in Punjab, xxviiin3;

persistent, xxvii, 116; today, 112-19

Community, consolidated, 115; fissures in, xxii, 101

Congress, xii, 167, 180; monopoly of political space, 181; nationalist Muslims and secular credentials, 185; culture; all encompassing, 110; composite (India), xii, xviii,122; Punjabi, 97, 99-100; of remembrance, 121; rupture in transmission of, 121

Cyril Radcliffe (cartographer), Partition, xii, xxviii*n*8, 90

Das, Veena, xv, xxix

Devnagari, transcription, 10, 91, 99; Partition Literature in, 10, 91, 99

Dinkar, Ramdhari Singh, 159, 160, 172

"Dream Images," see Surendra Prakash, 53-61, 120-28; continuity and disjunction in, 58, 61, 125; fusion of reality and imagination in, 58, 125; as imaginative recreation of composite community life, 56, 122

English, Partition writers in, xxv, 73-9, 116, 127; Partition Literature in, 73-77, 116, 127; translation of Hindi text, 109

Exile, xviii, xxi, 21; literary narrative of, 122, 11-28, 198-209

Faiz, Ahmed Faiz, 160, 172

Families, truncated, 36, 54, 124, 133, 29-52,

Fear, 77, as dominant motif, 187; as "oppressive present," 163

Fragmentation, xviii, 11-28, 107; of Indian State, 165

Gandhi, 139, 190, 192n42; appeasement of Muslims, 180, 183, 184; assasination of, xiii, xvii, 166; art of surrender, 183; and Patel, 166; and Rajendra Prasad 166-68

Gupta, Saumya, xxiv, 175-93

Hamid, Shahid, *Disastrous Twilight*, 155

Hashmi, Jamila, "Banished," xx, xxx*n*42, 195, 198-209

Heer Ranjha, 3, 4; Waris Shah's version of, 96-7, 99-100

Hindi writing; emotionality inherent in, 109; on Partition, xi, 28, 52, 116

Hindu Mahasabha, 90, 180; as svabhavik rashtravadi, 181;

Hindu-Muslim antagonism, 47, 51, 54; and riots, 145, 162, 172n14, 186, 192n52, 206; as Partition Literature theme, 153; relations, 167

Historiography, colonial, 161; communalism and nationalism in dominant discourse, 172n9; ordering of past, 121; of riots, 163

History; treatment of Partition, 137-41, 155, 161-62; State's voice, 164-68; truth of, 121

Holocaust; 121, 138

Home; loss of, 23, 31, 82, 83, 122, 137, 133, 138

Hosain, Attia, "Phoenix Fled," xix, xxv, 73-78

Husain, Intizar, xiv

Hussein, Abdullah, xvii, xxix*n*29; *Udas Naslein*, xxix

Hyder, Qurratulain, 98, 105; *Housing Society*, 133

Identity, 150; ambivalence in, xvi, 105, 146; fixing of, 59, 97, 143-4, 146; formation, 123; Hindu-Muslim as markers of 54, 123, 146, 185; language, xxiii; loss by betrayal, 144; past and retrieval of, 199; personal, xiii

Independence, disillusionment post, xiii, 160; (fiftieth year) and Partition coverage, 160, 172, 175; discourse of Muslims after, 168

Indo-Pak conflict, xxvii, 54, 94, 162
Islam, conversion to, 114;
Islamic State; Hindus as kafirs in, 131, 134

Jinnah, xii, 65, 95, 190, 191; and Pakistan demand, 65, 180; and narrative of Vartman, 182
Josh Malihabadi, 98, 105

Kamleshwar'(s), "Apne Desh Mein" 105; "How Many Pakistans?" xxii, xxvii, 11-28, 104; Kitne Pakistan, xxxn50; Kohra, 104; Nai Kahani tradition, 105, 108
Kanpur, xxiv, 187; of presence in Vartman, 179, 180, 186-90
Kargil conflict, 96
Kashmir, 88, 95; Pakistan occupied, 96
Khilafat, 167
Khanna, Stuti, 104-111
Kidwai, Begum Anees, xx, xxxn38, 173n 19; Azadi ki Chaaon Mein xx

Language(s), brutalization of, xv; and communication of emotional complexity, 103; of historical narratives, 141; politics of, xii, xxii, (and identity) 101, 103, 150, 13;
Loyalties, conflicting pulls of, 98, 168; to Indian State, 186; unambiguous, 98

Mahey, Arjun, 135-58
Manto, Sa'adat Hasan, xvi, xiv, xxiv, 90-91, 98, 100, 137; naturalism of, xvi, xxix, 147; Urdu short story trends, (Progressives and Realists) 146-48, 156; writings of; "Aakhri Salute" xvii, 95; "Gurmukh Singh ki Vasiyat" xiv, "Khol Do" xv, xvi, xxix, 144; "Khuda ki Kasam," xxvi; "Mozel," 195, 206; "Pandit Manto's First Letter to Pandit Nehru," 87-91, 98; "Shah Dauley ke Chuhe," 128; "Siyah Hashiye," xv, xxix; "Tetwal ka Kutta," xvii, 1-10, 145; "Thanda Gosht," xv, xxix; "Toba Tek

Singh," xvi, xxix, 63-72, 133-137, 148-52, 157
Marwah Roy, Anuradha, 112-119
Masud, Naiyer, xxix, 130-134
Mountbatten, 139
Muslims, in India (growing up) 171; and non-Muslims in Pakistan, 131, 168; post-Partition categories of, 130-131; nationalist anti-Pakistan, 184, (as synonymous with), 185
Muslim League, xii, 65, 139, 167, 176, (as aberrant nationalism), 182

Nandy, Ashis, 159, 172
Narrative of Partition; history and fiction, 138-39; cause-effect-in, 139-40; focus on individual consciousness in, 105; recovery of self in, 106; genre icon, 140; moral inflection in, 140; statistics, 140; of Indian nationalism, 181; literary, 142-46; novels, short story, 142; literature as resistance to elite nationalist discourse, 170;
Nationalist discourse, nationalism versus communalism, 181; Hindu nationalism, 103, 139
Nehru, J L, 88-91, 139, 160, 190; mock celebration addressed to, 169-70
Nihalani, Govind; Tamas, 115, 119

Pakistan, 5, 30, 54, 64, 106, 107, 123, 175, 176, 188; creation of, 18, 65, 167-68, 179, 180; Indian Muslims and 171, 176, 185-86; nation versus, 181, 188; demand and endless partitions, 181; as metaphor of separation, 12, 13, 18, 28
"Pali," 29-52; humanism/religious falsity in, 115; loss in translation, 116, 118; pessimistic determinism in, 114
Pandey, Gyanendranath, xxvii, xxviiin3, 172n 8, 9

Partition, ban on reference to, xxi, 162; causes of, 123, 139; communal riots post, 132, 169, 174n29; and closure of choices, 98; dominant discourse's silence on, xi, xxvii, 137, 139, 160, 162, 172n10; effects on women's consciousness, xxiv, 194; on language, 136-37, on ordinary people, 110-11, 115, 194; historiography, xxvii, xxiv, 154-55; subaltern perspectives in, 194; in contemporary newspapers, 175-93; ideology, xxi, 165; irrationality in, xvii, 150, 162; lack of documentation on, 160; as metaphor, xxi, xxvii, 82, 162, 170; negotiating trauma of, xxvi, 11-28, 83-84, 95, 136, 161; (silence in) 20, 138; and Pakistan as thematic in newspapers, 175-93; political absurdity of, 149; present day reverberations of, xviii, xxi, xxvi, 44, 54, 106, 136, 163, 171; reorganization post-, 94, 164; as watershed, xiii, xxi

Patel, Sardar, 160, 182; patriarchal attitude towards abducted women, 165

Paul, Joginder, "Dariyaon Pyas," xx, *Khwabrau*, xix, xxxn36, 124; "Thirst of Rivers," 79-86

Political divisions, ·152

Populance, exchange of, 134

Pluralism, 114

Prakash, Bodh, xxiv, 194-208

Prakash, Surendra, "Dream Images," xxii-xxiii, 53-62, 120-28; stories, "Jamghorah," "Ulfram," "Bazgoi," "Tadposaiyas," 121

Prasad, Dr Rajendra, 166-68, views on Gandhi; communalism and partition, 162

Punjabi, 71, 117; cultural background, 96, 101; Gurmukhi/Urdu (Shahmukhi) script, 102

Qasimi, Ahmad Nadeem, xxv

Rakesh Mohan, xix, xxxn34; "Malbe ka Malik," xix, 144

Rajagopalachari, C. 180

Rai, Alok, xv, xxixn21

Rai, Amrit, xv, xxixn20

Rape and narration, 197-198, 208n 9; rape and survival in Partition Literature, 198-201

Ravikant, xi-xxx, 1-10, 93-103, 160-74

Refugees, xiii,xx, xxviii, 30, 49, 97, 101; and fractured way of life, xxi, 160; rehabilitation of, xxvi;

Religion/ous critiques of, 113, 123; and politics, 123; hostility dismantled, 43, 145; identities, 37, 54; (creation of), 38, 102, 103; (hardening of) xii, xxvii, 185

Riots, xiii, xxi, 16, 19, 24, 132, 162, 163, 178, 186, 192n53, 206; post independence, 169, 173n29; sociology/motivation for, xxiii, victims of, xx, xxiii

Rumours, 187-88, 193n55

Sarkar, Sumit, xiii, xxviii

Sahni, Bhisham, xiv, xxix; *Kitne Toba Tek Singh*, xviii, xxix; "Pali," xix-xx, 29-52, 112-19, 145-46; *Tamas*, xvii, xxix, xx, xxx, 105, 115, 142, 153, 162-63, 195

Saint, Tarun K, xi-xxx, 1-10, 93-103

Sathyu, M S, *Garam Hawa*, xxi, 163

Sheikh Ayaz, "Neighbour," 145

Singh, Khushwant, xix, xxixn18

Singh, Maheep, "Pani aur Pul," 144, 155

Sobti, Krishna, 105, 169-70

Sunder Rajan, Rajeswari, 200

The Dog of Tetwal, 94-103; and Hindu-Muslim antagonism, 145

Toba Tek Singh, viii, ix, xvi, 63-71, 137, 148-52, 157; death as statement in, 150, as a fable, 146-52; narrative skills of metaphor and metonymy in, 149-50 transfer of population, 139; of power, xii, 94, 172n6

Translation, accuracy in, xxiv, 109, culture specific responses and, xxv, 99-100, 109, 116, 127; difficulties in process of, 108-9, 116; English, 127-28; flattening of cultural idiom in, 101, 117, 127; objectives/ attributes of, 118-19; readership and, 119; two nation theory, xii, 168, 181

Unionist Party, xii, xxviii
Unity, Independence and project of, 168
Urdu, 109, 157; and Islamic identity, 102; marginalization of, xxiii, xxx, 90, 102, 171 short story, 130-38, 146; age of progressives in, 146, 147, 156; and Partition specific themes, 133-34; tradition of realism in, 147; writings on Partition, xi, xxiv, 53-61, 63-71, 79-86, 99, 127, 195

Victimization, choice and self-consciousness of, 199, 200; non-sectarian being and, 146;
Violence, bureaucratic attitude to, 205; communal, 132; and psychic disfigurement, physical mutilation, xxii, 169; subalterns as victims/perpetrators of, xxiii; see riots

War, dehumanization, 98
Waris Shah, 96, 101
Women, abducted, xiii, xxviii, xx, 41; and State, 173n.19; education, social reform of, 196; experience of Partition, 194-208; Hindu/Urdu fiction and representation of, 195-207; freedom and limitation of choice, 200; Premchand's women and patriarchy, 196-67; Sati-savitri restrictive role, 196; strategies of

resistance, 195, 206-7, 208n16, violation of, xv, xix, 76, 195, 202; violence against, 115, 119

Yashpal, *Jhoota Sach,* 195, 201-203

239

ABOUT KATHA

A nonprofit organization, Katha endeavours to spread the joy of reading, knowing, and living amongst adults and children, the common reader and the neo-literate. Katha's main objective is **to enhance the pleasures of reading for children and adults**, for experienced readers as well as for those who are just beginning to read. And, inter alia, to —

- Stimulate an interest in lifelong learning that will help the child grow into a confident, self-reliant, responsible and responsive adult.
- Help break down gender, cultural and social stereotypes.
- Encourage, foster excellence, and applaud quality literature and translations in and between the various Indian languages.

A QUICK LOOK AT KATHA'S WORK

KALPAVRIKSHAM: The Centre for Sustainable Learning
- **Kalpana**: Nonformal Education Resource Centre (Tamasha!; Teacher training; T/L materials development)
- **KATHA KHAZANA: A learning centre for one of Delhi's largest slum clusters in Govindpuri** The components in this programme are:
- **The Katha School of Entrepreneurship**: (1300 children, 0 – 17 years of age)
- **Shakti Khazana**: the women's empowerment & income-generation programme
- **Saat Sahelia:** Post literacy material development & publishing programme

KATHA VILASAM: The Story & Translation Research & Resource Centre was begun in 1989 and has seen steady growth and development in terms of ideas and vision. It consists of —
- **Katha Books**: Publishing of Quality Translations under various series
- **Academic Publishing Programme:** Books for teaching of translation and Indian fiction
- **Applauding Excellence**: The Katha Awards for fiction, translation, editing
- **Kathakaar**: The Centre for Children's Literature
- **Katha Barani**: The Translation Resource Centre
- **Katha Sethu**: Building bridges between India and the outside world
  - **The Katha Translation Exchange Programme**
  - **Translation Contests**

KATHA SCHOOL OF TRANSLATION AND INNOVATIVE EDUCATION was started in 1994 with the Vak Initiative for enhancing the pool of translators between the various bhashas.
- **Katha Academic Centres**. In various universities across the country
- **The Faculty Enhancement programme**. Workshops, seminars, discussions
- **Sishya:** Katha Clubs in colleges; workshops, certificate courses, events and contests
- **The Katha Internship programme** for students from outside India
- **The Friends of Katha Network** with its more than 3,000 volunteers.

Be a Friend of Katha!

If you feel strongly about Indian literature, you belong with us! KathaNet, an invaluable network of our friends, is the mainstay of all our translation-related activities. We are happy to invite you to join this ever-widening circle of translation activists. Katha, with limited financial resources, is propped up by the unqualified enthusiasm and the indispensable support of nearly 5000 dedicated women and men.

We are constantly on the lookout for people who can spare the time to find stories for us, and to translate them. Katha has been able to access mainly the literature of the major Indian languages. Our efforts to locate resource people who could make the lesser-known literatures available to us have not yielded satisfactory results. We are specially eager to find Friends who could introduce us to Bhojpuri, Dogri, Kashmiri, Maithili, Manipuri, Nepali, Rajasthani and Sindhi fiction.

Do write to us with details about yourself, your language skills, the ways in which you can help us, and any material that you already have and feel might be publishable under a Katha programme. All this would be a labour of love, of course! But we do offer a discount of 20% on all our publications to Friends of Katha.

Write to us at —
Katha
A-3 Sarvodaya Enclave
Sri Aurobindo Marg
New Delhi   110 017   Or call us at: 652-4511, 652-4350